Key Concepts in
Youth Studies

Recent volumes include:

Key Concepts in Tourism and Research
David Botterill and Vincent Platenkamp

Fifty Key Concepts in Gender Studies
Jane Pilcher and Imelda Whelehan

Key Concepts in Sport and Exercise Research Methods
Michael Atkinson

Key Concepts in Medical Sociology
Jonathan Gabe, Mike Bury and Mary Ann Elston

Key Concepts in Media and Communications
Paul Jones and David Holmes

Key Concepts in Leisure Studies
David Harris

Key Concepts in Sport Psychology
John M. D. Kremer, Aidan Moran, Graham Walker and Cathy Craig

Key Concepts in Urban Studies
Mark Gottdiener and Leslie Budd

The SAGE Key Concepts series provides students with accessible and authoritative knowledge of the essential topics in a variety of disciplines. Cross-referenced throughout, the format encourages critical evaluation through understanding. Written by experienced and respected academics, the books are indispensable study aids and guides to comprehension.

Key Concepts in
Youth Studies

MARK CIESLIK AND DONALD SIMPSON

Los Angeles | London | New Delhi
Singapore | Washington DC

KH

Los Angeles | London | New Delhi
Singapore | Washington DC

SAGE Publications Ltd
1 Oliver's Yard
55 City Road
London EC1Y 1SP

SAGE Publications Inc.
2455 Teller Road
Thousand Oaks, California 91320

SAGE Publications India Pvt Ltd
B 1/I 1 Mohan Cooperative Industrial Area
Mathura Road
New Delhi 110 044

SAGE Publications Asia-Pacific Pte Ltd
3 Church Street
#10-04 Samsung Hub
Singapore 049483

Editor: Chris Rojek
Editorial assistant: Martine Jonsrud
Production editor: Katherine Haw
Copyeditor: Gemma Marren
Proofreader: Camille Bramall
Marketing manager: Michael Ainsley
Cover design: Wendy Scott
Typeset by: C&M Digitals (P) Ltd, Chennai, India
Printed by: CPI Group (UK) Ltd, Croydon, CR0 4YY

© Mark Cieslik and Donald Simpson 2013

First published 2013

Library of Congress Control Number: 2012941361

British Library Cataloguing in Publication data

A catalogue record for this book is available from the British Library

MIX
Paper from
responsible sources
FSC
www.fsc.org   FSC® C013604

ISBN 978-1-84860-984-6
ISBN 978-1-84860-985-3 (pbk)

10/6/14

contents

about the authors

Mark Cieslik is a Senior Lecturer in Sociology at Northumbria University. He has taught youth studies for many years and has conducted several research projects into young people's lives. His work has explored the structuring of marginal transitions into adulthood as well as young people's experiences of schooling and education. He has been the convenor of the British Sociological Association's (BSA) Youth Study Group and has published many research papers and a number of edited volumes on youth research. He is currently convenor of the BSA Happiness Study Group and is researching the area of well-being and young people.

Donald Simpson is currently a Senior Lecturer in Education at Teesside University where he works on several undergraduate and postgraduate programmes in the areas of childhood, education and youth studies. He previously worked as a school teacher before becoming a contract researcher. Donald has several research interests and these include a focus on youth. He has worked upon youth research projects sponsored by organisations such as the Joseph Rowntree Foundation and the Economic and Social Research Council. Donald has authored and co-authored many publications and these include contributions reporting youth research for Policy Press, *Journal of Youth Studies, Young: Nordic Journal of Youth Research and Sociology.*

acknowledgements

We would like to thank Robin Haggart for all his work chasing up material for this book. We also would like to thank Northumbria University and the University of Teesside for research support that allowed us time to complete the book. We also thank the editorial team at Sage for their patience and advice during the writing process. Our thanks also go to our respective families for their support and understanding over the past few years when we have been busy working on this project.

key concepts in
youth studies

introduction: making sense of young people today?

This book offers an introduction to the key concepts in youth studies in a way we hope is accessible to both tutors and students. Many textbooks in the social sciences are structured around lengthy chapters whereas the short entries in this text will give you the essence of some of the major debates and issues in youth studies. Our entries begin with foundational concepts and debates, which we feel represent some of the most significant areas of discussion in youth research, which are then followed by entries that reflect some of the other major research areas in youth studies. Such short entries cannot possibly hope to cover all of the developments in research but they provide a way into a particular topic and give guidance for further reading and investigation.

This introduction sets out to contextualise the different entries in the book, offering ways to link different areas of youth research that may at first glance seem unconnected. We do also make efforts throughout the text to highlight connections between entries, so where these occur we employ bold text to illustrate how, for example, the issue of **crime** is also linked to entries of **gender** or **class.** Although this book is written so that one can dip in and out of different entries as one might access online material, a more nuanced understanding of entries might be had if you spend a few minutes reading the next few pages. Here we give you an overview of some of the main themes in youth research that will help you 'situate' your own particular focus of interest.

YOUTH RESEARCH: SOME KEY THEMES AND ISSUES

Our approach to studying young people, reflected in this book, is to understand youth in relation to their social identities and cultural practices as well as the life course transitions they make towards adulthood. These are analytical distinctions researchers make to ease their investigations – in other words youth cultures/identities and transitions are models or shorthand forms that are used to represent a more complex empirical world. The notions of transition or identity then do not in themselves accurately depict young people's lives – young people, for example, do not make simple linear transitions from childhood to adulthood. Such analytical concepts used in youth studies have evolved over many years distilled from countless projects and come to guide the thinking of researchers and students.

In writing this book we asked ourselves a range of questions that helped us focus on the most important issues in youth research. For example, how might we define 'youth'? Are young people those at that developmental stage between childhood and adulthood?[1] We are also concerned with the distinctive everyday experiences that young people have in the different spheres of their lives such as education, training, leisure, work and families. How do the relationships that young people have in these settings influence how they see themselves and how others see them – their social identities? With time as they age how do young people's roles in these settings evolve, as we see with the movement from school to university or from living at home with parents to sharing a flat with friends? We are also interested in the power relationships that enmesh young people – how do other actors (both individuals and more complex processes) condition (constrain and enable) young people who then create and reflect patterns of divisions and inequalities within and between the generations? For example, how do the policies and practices of state organisations influence young people's identities and transition routes? Who are the winners and losers when governments raise the school leaving age or cut welfare benefits? What sort of agency do young people exercise so they can pursue their own interests and contest, challenge or subvert the agendas of other actors such as these governments? Do some young people enjoy more autonomy in their lives than others because of the economic or cultural resources they can access, as their parents can fund their education and housing costs?

As sociologists we are also interested in the 'social construction' of youth – how young people see their own lives in contrast to how adults often view the young (Mannheim, 1952). By this we mean that the very category of youth itself – and how we discuss the idea of young people and their lives – reflects distinctive cultural and political practices that vary from one society to another and through history. In particular we explore how the mass media and new social media shape popular notions of 'youth' and how this may have positive or negative consequences for young people themselves. How, for example, are young people's social identities affected if the popular press is sexist and homophobic? How have technological changes affected young people's work and leisure experiences and do these changes impact on young people in different ways around the world?

A further set of overarching questions that inform our entries are those concerned with the ways that youth researchers undertake their work (see Heath et al., 2009; Heath and Walker, 2012). Our entries are interested in the theories and methods researchers employ and how these impart a distinctive character to their research. One can develop a critical, evaluative approach to youth research by teasing out the methodological influences on particular studies. Do researchers rely too heavily on secondary sources or qualitative or quantitative approaches? If, for example, feminist or postmodern concepts are employed what biases and interpretations might these encourage and what might therefore have been overlooked in the research?

A further key area of debate in youth studies has been between cultural studies researchers and those more interested in youth policy and transitions (Furlong et al., 2011). Hence some research is driven by an interest in the differential material resources of young people and how life course transitions and social inequalities emerge from such disadvantages (MacDonald, 2011). Whereas other researchers are more interested in questions about the cultural lives of young people and their interest in music, shopping and fashion (Deutsch and Theodorou, 2010). These different research questions create distinctive emphases in the research process that in turn shape the sorts of theory and methods used and the findings generated by these projects. The result being that some research (around youth cultures) can create the impression of young people as creative actors shaping their identities and cultural lives, while other researchers (who focus on policy or transitions) can generate the image of young people more heavily constrained by economic and political forces. A criticism that often applies to both these schools of youth research is their preoccupation with only a minority of young people – those who are marginalised economically (in the case of transitions research) or those leading spectacular cultural lives (in subcultural or post-subcultural research). This interest in the unusual, the pathological or the oppressed can mean the overwhelming majority of ordinary young people are neglected by youth researchers. There is a risk that youth research itself contributes to a distortion or misrepresentation of young people's lives (Cieslik, 2001).

One common theoretical position for youth researchers, following the work of C. Wright Mills (1959) is to situate young people's lives in their wider social and historical contexts. We ask ourselves, therefore, how do changes to the wider economy or welfare policies ripple out across the lives of the young setting up new patterns of division and disadvantage? The issues of global warming and sustainability, the expansion of the Internet and economic and political crises are all having profound influences on young people around the world (White, 2011). We can promote the importance of youth research by documenting how the changing experiences of youth also have in turn significant implications for other parts of society. For young people are often at the forefront of political protest around the world, they make up most migrants and are often the first to adopt new forms of technology. Youth therefore are very often agents of social change and transformation as we have been witnessing in Europe and the Middle East in recent years.

YOUTH RESEARCH: SOME RECENT DEVELOPMENTS

Globalisation

Over the past twenty years youth studies has been concerned with several key developments such as globalisation, the extension of the youth phase and shifting conceptions of identities. These stem from social change such as the increasing mobility of people, commodities and ideas, and also new theoretical formulations such as the 'risk society' thesis (Beck, 1992) and postmodern theories (Bauman, 1991). The spectre of globalisation is the backdrop to many entries in this book. The industrial rise of countries such as South Korea, Taiwan, China and India helps explain the painful de-industrialisation of Western societies since the 1970s and its impact on the life chances of young people in both East and West. The collapse of traditional manufacturing employment in the West heralded a shift away from relatively short transitions from school into employment to more protracted, circuitous routes through training, welfare dependency and waged work (Cieslik and Pollock, 2002; Dillabough and Kennelly, 2010). The shift in production from the West opened up new employment opportunities and consumerist lifestyles for young people in the East and the Global South. Yet during this period we have still witnessed the continuing poverty of young people in developing societies despite countless economic initiatives from domestic policy-makers and organisations such as the World Bank and International Monetary Fund (ILO, 2006). The global mobility of information also raises questions about the emergence of a 'global youth' as Internet technology allows young people, despite their differing traditions and languages, to produce and share culture (Furlong, 2012). The ease with which one can record events on a mobile phone and post these online to be accessed by millions of viewers in just a few hours has transformed our lives. Fashion, music, film, as well as political issues around global warming, poverty and citizenship are all ideas that move rapidly around the globe transforming the perspectives, ambitions and behaviours of young people.

Extended Transitions, Inequality and Social Unrest

A major focus in youth studies has been how adult statuses such as marriage, secure employment and childrearing that once would have occurred in the West during the teenage years now occur ten or more years later when young people are in their twenties and thirties. A confluence of social changes – rising costs of housing, scarcity of well-paid work and rising aspirations – have all contributed to this extension of the youth phase. However, some commentators are critical of these arguments contending instead that youth ends in the mid-twenties and the notion of 'emerging adulthood' more accurately reflects the phase until the early thirties when adult independence is achieved (Arnett, 2004).

As we discuss in various entries in this book the lengthening of transitions, though offering time for experimentation and exploration, also raises questions about how young people are increasingly dependent on their families, the state and charities for their wellbeing. Being denied opportunities to work, to establish their own homes and participate in leisure activities has become a feature of many young people's lives in so-called 'rich societies'. Longitudinal research since the 1980s (Bynner et al., 1997) has illustrated the divisions between affluent and disadvantaged young people, and this in turn has shaped the wider social inequalities and decline in social mobility in Western societies (Wilkinson and Pickett, 2009). More recently these concerns over extended transitions have focused on the growing inequalities between the generations and how the middle aged (the so-called baby boomers born in the 1950s and 1960s) have benefited at the expense of today's youth (Howker and Malik, 2010; Willetts, 2010). Recent economic crises have focused attention on the significance of these long-term demographic changes and the associated costs of welfare provision at a time when rich nations are struggling to compete economically with emerging economies of the East and South. The now ageing population of baby-boomers is monopolising welfare yet a shrinking taxpayer base

introduction

(because of a falling birth rate) has led governments to cut the education, health and social security benefits that were enjoyed by earlier generations. Young people today are therefore having to pay more tax, work longer and receive much less welfare provision than their parents and at a time of insecure employment and global warming. The ambitions that many young people had of a comfortable consumerist life have been dashed, replaced by a new era of insecurity (Wierenga, 2011). Accordingly many young people feel a sense of injustice and disillusionment in the economic, social and political processes of Western capitalism. The result in many societies around the developed world has been student unrest and social disorder – young people are increasingly challenging the austerity policies of European governments that disproportionately impact on their lives rather than the ones responsible for the crises in global capitalism. Just as we saw in previous decades – the civil rights movement in the 1960s and the fall of communism in the 1980s – young people it seems are at the forefront of political protest and are agents of social change. As we write it is difficult to see how such protest will play out and shape the societies in which we live.

At the same time many young people in other societies around the world are marching on the streets, protesting at the erosion of opportunities and personal freedoms. At the time of writing young people have been at the forefront of protest and social change in many Arab states – the so-called 'Arab Spring' – young people in Muslim states taking to the streets to protest against the lack of freedoms in these authoritarian regimes. In Tunisia, Egypt, Syria, Libya and many other countries the young have called for a free press, free elections and economic policies that will provide opportunities for them to lead more prosperous and secure lives as they see in other countries around the world.

Young People in Late Modernity: Theories Old and New

Youth researchers have drawn on theories old and new to understand the changing lives of young people. The classical writings of Marx, Weber and Durkheim can still help us make sense of young people's lives even today. For struggles over economic resources profoundly shape the character of societies and the differential access to waged work is a key driver of young people's life chances and cultural identities. Bourdieu's reworking of these thinkers and his concepts of habitus, field and capitals (Bourdieu, 1977; 1986) have been used extensively to unpack how social divisions are reproduced and experienced by young people (Henderson et al., 2007; Thornton, 1995). Despite the social justice agenda of welfare policies Bourdieu's work can show us how inequities are built into education, health and social security systems marginalising countless millions of young people in the process. Youth studies also draws on feminist and anti-racist ideas to interrogate the structured disadvantages experienced by women and minorities and how gendered/racialised divisions are reproduced through adolescence (Thomson, 2011). What all societies around the world seem to share are gendered and racialised inequalities, with young women and minorities experiencing prejudice and discrimination in all walks of life – through schooling, training, employment, health and social security.

Over the last twenty years youth researchers have also drawn on theories of late modernity such as Beck's (1992) and Giddens' (1991) work on risk and reflexivity or on postmodern theories that have emphasised new ways of researching cultural identities. Risk theories can be used to illustrate how institutional restructuring (such as changing families, labour markets and welfare systems) creates uncertain transition routes and identities. Though economic and cultural divisions remain in risk societies the traditional language of class and gender has given way to more individualised, subjective constructions of everyday life. In late modernity young people in the West are compelled to become more self-conscious and reflexive about their lives – to develop so-called 'choice biographies' where they are personally responsible for their identity work and navigations to adulthood. Drawing on Beck (1992) and Elias (2000), Furlong and Cartmel (1997) apply the notion of 'epistemological fallacy' to describe how structural features in modernity become subjectivised:

> Individuals are forced to negotiate a set of risks which impinge on all aspects of their daily lives, yet the intensification of individualism means that crises are perceived as individual shortcomings rather than the outcome of processes which are largely outside the control of individuals... Blind to the existence of powerful chains of interdependency, young people frequently attempt to resolve collective problems through individual action and hold themselves responsible for their inevitable failure. (Furlong and Cartmel, 1997: 114)

Though in everyday life we use a language of individual agency and choice, most academic commentators recognise how young people's lives are still heavily conditioned by differential access to opportunities and resources – so-called 'structured individualization' (Roberts, 2003). Youth research into transition routes and cultural lives has therefore been concerned to reveal the relative contributions of structural conditioning and choices/agency rather than emphasising one process at the expense of the other (Cieslik, 2001; Threadgold, 2010).

Recently we have seen the influence of postmodern theories on youth research notably through discussion of 'post-subcultures' (Muggleton, 2000). Proponents argue that class processes in particular have become less important to an understanding of young people's cultures and identities (Bennett, 1999). The increasing significance of social media through the Internet and diverse patterns of consumerism have all encouraged a more fluid, creative and autonomous youth which throws up patterns of cultural identification and sociability that defy easy class-based classification. Some argue that concepts such as lifestyles (Miles, 2000), scenes (Redhead, 1993) and neo-tribes (Bennett, 1999) are better placed to describe young people's cultural lives than concepts such as subcultures. Though as some have suggested (Cieslik, 2001; Griffin, 2010) we might argue that subcultural studies and recent post-subcultural research have been pursuing different research agendas that may account for some of the disputes between these two camps. The former wish to make explicit the ways the lives of young people are framed by economic, political and cultural forces in society. Whereas the latter tend to emphasise the irreducibility of young people's experiences through leisure, music and style-based activities.

Young People, Wellbeing and Narcissism

Post-structural theories of the self are also proving influential in youth research, particularly when combined with more traditional ideas around long-term patterns of social change. Unlike the long running disputes between youth cultural and transitions researchers, this emerging focus of study synthesises an interest with complex, stratified ideas of the self with a critical engagement with the impact of consumerism and neo-liberalism on young people. As Jones (2009) has documented we can use Foucault's ideas of 'technologies of the self' (Foucault, 1988) to understand how young people develop ways of working on their bodies and emotions to get on in life. Instead then of young people being dominated and exploited by external others (such as through government policies or by employers) they use self-help manuals and body modification to manufacture, monitor and perfect their own identities.

We witness extreme examples of these processes when they break down, such as in obsessive compulsive behaviour, eating disorders and body dysmorphia (Frost, 2001). But the real force of these arguments is how these 'technologies of the self' are employed by all of us in our daily lives and reveal the extent of our often unknowing subjugation to others or our harmful pursuit of an idealised way of life.

This synthesising of theoretical models of the self and theories of society we argue will prove to be an important area of research for youth studies in the future. The use of psycho-analytical theory by Lacan (2006) and Žižek (2002; 2007) to explore the instability of the self is particularly useful in allowing us to picture our daily struggles trying to flourish and grow. These writers document the internal tensions within ourselves between ego, unconscious and super-ego, and societies' fixation with the presentation of a coherent unified self. The impossibility of achieving a coherent self in a dynamic, consumerist, market-driven world means that young people have to manage such dissonance by recourse to fantasy, consumption, celebrity and online virtual worlds. Where such efforts fail, as Hall et al. (2008) argue, we can often see the growth of problematic behaviour and problems such as youth crime. For youth labour markets offer meagre economic resources for most young people to sustain consumerist identity work leaving young people in an endless cycle of dissatisfaction with the self – consumption – fleeting pleasure – dissatisfaction with the self.

Other writers such as Furedi (2004) have also documented the instability of the modern self and the implications this has for our quality of life. This set of debates we argue will also be influential in youth research in coming years. Drawing on the work of Rose (1989) and Lasch (1996), Furedi argues that late modernity has witnessed a turn inwards into the self so that we have all become increasingly narcissistic – preoccupied with personal growth and the development of an authentic self. We pursue our biographical projects through consumerism in an often quick-fix, instrumental way that prevents us from growing and developing in a rich and deep manner. The growth of the happiness industry that produces countless self-help guides and programmes in emotional literacy is just one manifestation of this rise of a 'therapy culture' (Furedi, 2004). Social policies around the world are also coming to reflect this narcissism, with many governments developing ways of measuring and promoting happiness in schools, work and community at a time of growing economic, social and political divisions. The concern, however, with this focus on subjective wellbeing is that it distracts us from the economic and social divisions that are undermining the life chances of young people. The critics of this narcissism point to how young people are growing up in societies that tend to value the pursuit of a shallow introspective personal fulfilment, at the expense of more outward looking social and political perspectives and activities. The fear is that despite the recent protests led by young people, we may have a generation of youth who not only have a 'one dimensional' way of living but are also ill-equipped to deal with the challenges they face in a world threatened with climate change, conflict and economic uncertainties. Nevertheless we hope that such pessimism will prove to be misplaced and that young people can instead lead the way in challenging the corrosive powers of modernity.

Note

1 Though definitions of the youth phase are contested, see entry on defining youth.

REFERENCES

Arnett, J.J. (2004) *Emerging Adulthood: The Winding Road from the Late Teens through the Twenties*. Oxford: Oxford University Press.

Bauman, Z. (1991) *Intimations of Postmodernity*. London: Routledge.

Beck, U. (1992) *Risk Society: Towards a New Modernity*. London: Sage.

Bennett, A. (1999) 'Subcultures or neo-tribes? Rethinking the relationship between youth, style and musical taste', *Sociology*, 33 (3): 599–617.

Bourdieu, P. (1977) *Outline of a Theory of Practice*. Cambridge: Cambridge University Press.

Bourdieu, P. (1986) 'The forms of capital', in J. E. Richardson (ed.), *Handbook of Theory of Research for the Sociology of Education*. New York: Greenwood Press, pp. 241–58.

Bynner, J., Ferri, E. and Sheppard, P. (1997) *Twenty Something in the 1990s: Getting on, Getting By and Getting Nowhere*. Aldershot: Ashgate Press.

Cieslik, M. (2001) 'Researching youth cultures: some problems with the cultural turn in British Youth Studies', *Scottish Youth Issues Journal*, 2: 27–48.

Cieslik, M. and Pollock, G. (eds) (2002) *Young People in Risk Society: The Restructuring of Youth Identities and Transitions in Late Modernity*. Aldershot: Ashgate Press.

Deutsch, N.L. and Theodorou, E. (2010) 'Aspiring, consuming, becoming: youth identity in a culture of consumption', *Youth and Society*, 42 (2): 229–54.

Dillabough, J. and Kennelly, J. (eds) (2010) *Lost Youth in the Global City: Class, Culture and the Urban Imaginary*. London: Routledge.

Elias, N. (2000) *The Civilizing Process*. Oxford: Wiley-Blackwell.

Foucault, M. (1988) 'Technologies of the self', in M.L. Gutman and H. Hutton (eds), *Technologies of the Self*. London: Tavistock, pp. 16–49.

Frost, L. (2001) *Young Women and the Body: A Feminist Sociology*. London: Palgrave.

Furedi, F. (2004) *Therapy Culture: Cultivating Vulnerability in an Uncertain Age*. London: Routledge.

Furlong, A. (ed.) (2012) *Youth Studies: A Global Introduction*. London: Routledge.

Furlong, A. and Cartmel, F. (1997) *Young People and Social Change: Individualization and Risk in Late Modernity*. Milton Keynes: Open University Press.

Furlong, A., Woodman, D. and Wyn, J. (2011) 'Changing times, changing perspectives: reconciling "transition" and cultural perspectives on youth and young adulthood', *Journal of Sociology*, December, 47: 355–70.

Giddens, A. (1991) *Modernity and Self-Identity: Self and Society in the Late Modern Age*. Cambridge: Polity Press.

Griffin, C. (2010) 'The trouble with class: researching youth, class and culture beyond the Birmingham School', *Journal of Youth Studies*, 14 (3): 245–59.

Hall, S., Winlow, S. and Ancrum, C. (2008) *Criminal Identities and Consumer Culture: Crime Exclusion and the New Culture of Narcissism*. Cullopton: Willan Publishing.

Heath, S., Brooks, R., Cleaver, E. and Ireland, E. (eds) (2009) *Researching Young People's Lives*. London: Sage.

Heath, S. and Walker, C. (eds) (2012) *Innovations in Youth Research*. London: Palgrave.

Henderson, S., Holland, J., McGrellis, S., Sharpe, S. and Thomson, R. (2007) *Inventing Adulthoods: A Biographical Approach to Youth Transitions*. London: Sage.

Howker, E. and Malik, S. (2010) *Jilted Generation: How Britain Has Bankrupted Its Youth*. London: Icon Books.

ILO (International Labour Organization) (2006) *The End of Child Labour: Within Reach, Global Report Under the Follow Up to the ILO Declaration on Fundamental Principles and Rights at Work 2006*. Geneva: ILO.

Jones, G. (2009) *Youth*. Cambridge: Polity Press.

Lacan, J. (2006) *Écrits*. London: Norton.

Lasch, C. (1996) *The Culture of Narcissism: American Life in an Age of Diminishing Expectations*. London: Norton.

Mannheim, K. (1952) 'The problem of generations', in P. Kecskemeti (ed.), *Essays on the Sociology of Knowledge*. London: Routledge and Kegan Paul, pp. 276–320 (1st edn 1927).

MacDonald, R. (2011) 'Youth transitions, unemployment and underemployment: plus ca change, plus c'est la meme chose?' *Journal of Sociology*, December, 47: 427–44.

Miles, S. (2000) *Youth Lifestyles in a Changing World*. Buckingham: Open University Press.

Muggleton, D. (2000) *Inside Subculture: The Postmodern Meaning of Style*. Oxford: Berg.

Redhead, S. (ed.) (1993) *Rave Off: Politics and Deviance in Contemporary Youth Culture*. Aldershot: Ashgate Press.

Roberts, K. (2003) 'Problems and priorities for the sociology of youth', in A. Bennett, M. Cieslik and S. Miles (eds) *Researching Youth*. London: Palgrave. pp.13–28.

Rose, N. (1989) *Governing the Soul: The Shaping of the Private Self*. 2nd edn. New York: Free Association Books.

Thomson, R. (2011) *Unfolding Lives: Youth, Gender and Change*. Bristol: Policy Press.

Thornton, S. (1995) *Club Cultures: Music Media and Subcultural Capital*. Cambridge: Polity Press.

Threadgold, S. (2010) '"Should I pitch my tent in the middle ground"? On "middling tendency", Beck and inequality in youth sociology', *Journal of Youth Studies*, 14 (4): 381–93.

White, R. (2011) 'Climate change, uncertain futures and the sociology of youth', *Youth Studies Australia*, 30 (3): 13–19.

Wilkinson, R. and Pickett, K. (2009) *The Spirit Level: Why Equality Is Better for Everyone*. London: Penguin.

Willetts, D. (2010) *The Pinch: How the Baby Boomers Took Their Children's Future – And Why They Should Give It Back*. London: Atlantic Books.

Wierenga, A. (2011) 'The sociology of youth, the future and the holy grail', *Youth Studies Australia*, 30 (3): 40–6.

Wright Mills, C. (1959) *The Sociological Imagination*. London: Penguin.

Žižek, S. (2002) *Welcome to the Desert of the Real*. London: Verso.

Žižek, S. (2007) *The Universal Exception*. London: Continuum.

Foundational Concepts, Issues and Debates

1
Defining Youth

We need a definition of young people so that we know exactly whom it is that we are researching, working with or developing policy for. Just as we note elsewhere in this book (see **theorising youth**) definitions of youth will reflect the biases of those doing the defining. Sociologists, youth workers and policy-makers will all have their own different notions of what constitutes young people and many of these understandings will be at variance with the ways that young people see themselves (Mannheim, 1952). Similarly writers document how conceptions of the youth phase are historically and culturally specific. In Western societies historical studies show that the category of youth as we understand it today is a relatively recent phenomenon dating from the eighteenth century (Gillis, 1974), though discussion of some notion of youth has been noted as far back as classical Greek society. The idea then of an intermediate stage between childhood and adulthood is commonly associated with the rise of Western modernity. Prior to the 1800s childhood was seen to merge into an early form of adult independence from the ages of eleven to twelve years of age as children took on waged employment and greater duties around the home (Gillis, 1974).

The past two centuries in Western societies have been the history of the gradual emergence and extension of the youth phase as the socio-cultural definitions of dependent childhood and independent adulthood have become more clearly demarcated producing a notion of the youth phase as an interstitial phenomenon – existing 'in between' the dependency of childhood and the autonomy of adulthood. During the late nineteenth century and throughout the twentieth century the development of adult citizenship rights (for example, around the franchise, education, housing and employment (see Marshall and Bottomore, 1997)) helped define the many facets of the transition to adulthood and with it the contours of the career routes and status passages that young people have to travel to achieve adult independence (Coles, 1995; Jones and Wallace, 1992).

In Western societies the late nineteenth century heralded the end of child labour and the separation of employment from the domestic sphere so commentators documented the emergence of common characteristics and experiences of young people. G.S. Hall (1904) and Erickson (1968), for example, discussed the developmental features of the youth phase and the inevitable 'storm and stress' that accompanied this period of identity formation and movement through status passages to adulthood. Key to these early ideas of adolescence was the notion that youth represented a time of flux where individuals had some time to experiment with ideas and identities as well as the actual routes they might take through life. Nevertheless one should be mindful of the fact that most young people during the twentieth century found their lives heavily conditioned by class, race and gender processes that defined much of their early lives and set limits to what they might possibly become through adulthood. Mannheim (1952) and Parsons (1942) were influential in the early twentieth century by noting how many young people came to recognise their common way of life (ideas, culture, life chances) and what they shared with other youth in contrast to adult society, thus setting up the possibility of generational conflict and tensions. As often the different generations had experienced very different forms of socialisation these authors pointed to a certain inevitability of culture wars springing up between the young and the old. Such ideas prefigured later concerns in wider society about the 'youth question' and how young people can be harbingers of disorder, change and conflict (see, for example, Cohen, 1997).

Through the latter part of the twentieth century in affluent societies we have witnessed the youth phase being extended from the teenage years of fourteen and fifteen to the early twenties and beyond as many young people spend longer periods of time in education and training and delay the entry into full-time work, family and household formation. For many, such delays are a result of unemployment, poor quality **work** and social exclusion. Recent commentators talk of a 'boomerang generation' of young people in their twenties and thirties who have tried to secure work and independent homes only to find themselves returning home through unemployment and the high cost of housing (Times Online, 2008). Hence the state has considerable power over the youth phase because of its influence on education and labour markets. Increasingly governments in affluent societies have called for the 'upskilling' of its citizens to help create 'knowledge economies' where all workers acquire higher level educational credentials (Lauder et al., 2007). In fifty years then we have witnessed the significant extension of compulsory **education** from a school leaving age of thirteen to fourteen years of age to one where most young people are in full time education until eighteen years of age and a majority in higher education until twenty-one years of age.

Young people's extended dependence on either their families of origin or on state welfare provision has led commentators to talk of the disempowering or infantilising of young people when they should rightly be enjoying greater independence associated with adult lifestyles. At the same time in many Western societies the commercialisation of childhood, and some suggest the sexualisation of children, has led to the emergence of the 'tweenies' phenomenon – young children whose fashion interests and way of life resembles those of earlier generations of much older teenagers (Hartley-Brewer, 2004). These social changes have consequently led some commentators to express doubts about the usefulness of the concept of youth as the boundaries between childhood and young people and between adulthood and adolescence have become increasingly fuzzy (Cohen and Ainley, 2000). One way of adapting to these social changes in the lives of young people is to understand the youth phase in different ways – for example, some talk of 'emerging adulthood' as a new phase between adolescence and adulthood and which reflects the different characteristics of young people as teenagers and those in their twenties (Arnett, 2004; Tanner and Arnett, 2009; see also Cote and Bynner, 2008). Others simply talk of young adults as a way of depicting the fact that some youth are indeed biologically old yet have lifestyles that lack the usual markers of independence associated with adulthood such as long-term relationships and their own home.

In recent years youth studies professionals have operated with definitions of youth transitions and youth identities that offer us an analytic map of the youth phase. **Transitions** are usually understood as comprising multiple routes into adulthood in relation to key aspects of young people's lives such as education/training and employment; intimate relationships and friendships; housing; and leisure. Some commentators suggest some routes such as education and employment are fundamental and structure the other transitions pathways (Roberts, 2003). In recent years writers in affluent societies have discussed the breakdown of once heavily structured and predictable transitions along classed and gendered lines and hence have moved from using metaphors such as careers and routes (Banks et al., 1992; Roberts, 1968) that denote transitions, to metaphors that convey greater fluidity such as navigations and niches (Evans and Furlong, 1997). The images of youth transitions developed by researchers tend to be socially constructed so they reflect the strong influence of culturally and historically specific events such as deindustrialisation of many European countries in the 1980s and 1990s

(Webster et al., 2004) and the economic growth and cultural transformation of many cities in developing societies during the first decade of the twenty-first century (Farrar, 2002).

Researchers in youth studies have also developed models of young people's social identities that contribute to our ways of defining young people. Prior to the 1970s youth were often understood in relation to quite crude notions of their structural class, race and gender positioning in wider society (Mungham and Pearson, 1976). More recently, however, such constructs have been superseded by concepts of youth identities that define young people as existing through multi-facetted, processual notions of the self where individuals undertake identity work and identity performances creating hybridised identities (Bennett, 1999; 2005). These developments in identity theory have been framed by the growing influence of mediazed interactions (via the web and other digital media) and diasporic, migratory experiences of many young people today. Writers still acknowledge the powerful way that economics, social relationships and cultural formations frame youth identities but many commentators speak of the loosening of conditioning processes so that young people have more space and opportunity to create their identities across what were once rigid and impermeable boundaries (Pysnakova and Miles, 2010). Young people's hybrid selves are also understood in relation to a greater sensitivity to the reflexive processes, so-called internal conversations and self-monitoring, that we all participate in and which make up our daily lives. Young people today then are more conscious of their self-identity than previous generations (compelled because of globalisation and de-traditionalisation and the 'risks' associated with these) and are thus mindful of the ways that one can pursue life projects and seek out self-development (Beck, 1992; Giddens, 1992; Taylor, 1991). Any definition of youth today needs to be sensitive to the effect that these historical processes such as individualisation and de-traditionalisation have had on how young people conceive and live out their lives.

REFERENCES

Arnett, J.J. (2004) *Emerging Adulthood: The Winding Road from the Late Teens through the Twenties*. Oxford: Oxford University Press.

Banks, M., Bates, I., Breakwell, G., Bynner, J., Emler, N., Jamieson, L. and Roberts, K. (1992) *Careers and Identities*. Milton Keynes: Open University Press.

Beck, U. (1992) *Risk Society: Towards a New Modernity*. London: Sage.

Bennett, A. (1999) 'Subcultures or neo-tribes? Rethinking the relationship between youth, style and musical taste', *Sociology*, 33 (3): 599–617.

Bennett, A. (2005) 'In defence of neo-tribes: a response to Blackman and Hesmondhalgh', *Journal of Youth Studies*, 8 (2): 255–9.

Cohen, P. (1997) *Rethinking the Youth Question: Education, Labour and Cultural Studies*. London: Macmillan.

Cohen, P. and Ainley, P. (2000) 'In the country of the blind? Youth studies and cultural studies in Britain', *Journal of Youth Studies*, 3 (1): 79–96.

Coles, B. (1995) *Youth and Social Policy*. London: University College London.

Cote, J. and Bynner, J. (2008) 'Changes in the transition to adulthood in the UK and Canada: the role of structure and agency in emerging adulthood', *Journal of Youth Studies*, 11 (3): 251–68.

Erickson, E. (1968) *Identity: Youth and Crisis*. New York: Norton

Evans, K. and Furlong, A. (1997) 'Metaphors of youth transitions: niches, pathways, trajectories or navigations', in J. Bynner, L. Chisholm and A. Furlong (eds), *Youth, Citizenship and Social Change in a European Context*. Aldershot: Ashgate Press, pp. 17–41.

Farrar, J. (2002) *Opening Up: Youth Sex Culture and Market Reform in Shanghai*. Chicago: University of Chicago Press.

Giddens, A. (1991) *Modernity and Self-Identity: Self and Society in the Late Modern Age*. Cambridge: Polity Press.

Gillis, J. (1974) *Youth and History: Tradition and Change in European Age Relations 1770–Present*. New York: Academic Press.

Hall, G. Stanley (1904) *Adolescence: Its Psychology and Its Relation to Physiology, Anthropology, Sociology, Sex, Crime, Religion and Education*, 2 vols. New York: D. Appleton and Co.

Hartley-Brewer, E. (2004) 'The trouble with tweenies', *The Guardian*, 15 September. www.guardian.co.uk/lifeandstyle/2004/sep/15/familyandrelationships.children (accessed 7 July 2012).

Jones, G. and Wallace, C. (1992) *Youth, Family and Citizenship*. Buckingham: Open University Press.

Lauder, H., Brown, P., Dillabough, J. and Halsey, A.H. (eds) (2007) *Education, Globalisation and Social Change*. Oxford: Oxford University Press.

Mannheim, K. (1952) 'The problem of generations', in P. Kecskemeti (ed.), *Essays on the Sociology of Knowledge*. New York: Routledge and Kegan Paul (1st edn 1927).

Marshall, T.H. and Bottomore, T. (1997) *Citizenship and Social Class*. London: Pluto Press.

Mungham, G. and Pearson, G. (eds) (1976) *Working Class Youth Culture*. London: Routledge and Kegan Paul.

Parsons, T. (1942) 'Age and sex in the social structure of the United States', *American Sociological Review*, 7, October: 604–16.

Pysnakova, M. and Miles, S. (2010) 'The post-revolutionary consumer generation: mainstream youth and the paradox of choice in the Czech Republic', *Journal of Youth Studies*, 13 (5): 533–47.

defining youth

Roberts, K. (1968) 'Entry into employment: an approach to a general theory', *Sociological Review*, 16 (2): 165–84.

Roberts, K. (2003) 'Problems and priorities for the sociology of youth', in A. Bennett, M. Cieslik and S. Miles (eds), *Researching Youth*. Basingstoke: Palgrave Macmillan, pp. 13–28.

Tanner, J.L. and Arnett, J.J. (2009) 'The emergence of "emerging adulthood": the new life stage between adolescence and young adulthood', in A. Furlong (ed.), *Handbook of Youth and Young Adulthood: New Perspectives and Agendas*. London: Routledge, pp. 39–46.

Taylor, C. (1991) *The Malaise of Modernity*. Toronto: House of Anansi Press.

Times Online (2008) 'Return home of "boomerang kids" stretches parents to the limit', 7 February. www.timesonline.co.uk/tol/life_and_style/education/article3321762.ece (accessed 7 July 2012).

Webster, C., Simpson, D., MacDonald, R., Abbas, A., Cieslik, M., Shildrick, T. and Simpson, M. (2004) *Poor Transitions: Social Exclusion and Young Adults*. Bristol: Policy Press.

2
Youth Transitions

Youth transitions remains one of the most prominent and important concepts in the context of youth studies – although a recent challenge to this position will be noted below. In literature focusing on youth transitions made within Western (de)industrialised societies, the concept is used to represent a period for youths of physical and social change that falls between childhood and adulthood in the life course. But there is no consensus in regard to the age at which a youth transition from childhood begins and when it ends with the conferment of adult status. This is because,

> The social markers, which used to define the timing of transitions, have lost their normative force in the course of the last decades of the twentieth century… Today individual biographical timetables do not follow socially expected and culturally transmitted age-norms. The borders between all

phases of the life course have become fuzzy, the timing and duration of transitions between childhood, adolescence, youth, adulthood and old age are less age-dependent and demand a series of individual decisions. (Heinz, 2009: 3)

The youth transition into adulthood is therefore rather contradictorily associated with increased responsibility but also rebellion – especially in the media and by television and movie-makers – and consequently youth has been labelled a 'dangerous age'. Those focusing on the **history of youth** transitions and **representations of youth** demonstrate the on-going nature of such a view. Pearson (1983), for example, documents how transitions have been associated with anti-social behaviour since at least the nineteenth century in the United Kingdom. This is further emphasised by other accounts focusing on the post-war period in the UK and the United States of America (Hebdige, 1982; Osgerby, 1998). Not surprisingly therefore transitions made by young people have always held a fascination for those studying this part of the life course.

A focus on youth transition became the pre-eminent concern of youth studies as a discipline during the twentieth century. As a concept – and despite the ambiguous nature of youth – youth transition was originally conceptualised as being unidirectional and linear. Following childhood a person became a youth and then made the transition into adulthood. Within this process initially there was heavy concentration on what became known as the 'school-to-work transition' made by young people. Across Western societies in much of the post-war period the movement of young people from school into the labour market and **employment** was traditionally seen as unproblematic. However, during the 1960s there were debates about how best to match different sorts of young people (and their associated skills) with different occupations and training opportunities (Roberts, 1968). As Roberts argued, the social background of young people and the structure of opportunities influenced variations in school-work transitions as some young people went straight into paid employment without any period of vocational training, some others completed a short period of vocational training/apprenticeship and some others went on to higher education for a number of years before then entering the labour market. This neat notion of youth transition in the past has been challenged more recently (Goodwin and O'Connor, 2005; Vickerstaff, 2003) but it was and remains a popular view of post-war transitions.

Eventually those studying youth transitions also began to validate the notion that young people experienced not just an extended school-to-work transition but also other additional transitions. Coles (1997) has also made a useful contribution to this debate around multiple transitions. Arguing against the tendency to view transitions purely in terms of young people's involvement in the labour market, Coles suggested that there are three main dimensions to youth transitions: the transition from full-time **education** and **training** to **employment** in the labour market (the school-to-work transition); the transition from family of origin to family of destination (the domestic transition); and the transition from residence with parents, or surrogate parents, to living away from them (the housing transition). For Coles, these three transitions inter-relate, so that the status gained in one may both influence and be influenced by the status that is gained in another. For example, a significant change in a young person's **housing** situation, such as becoming **homeless**, can have dramatic effects in their labour market situation, such as becoming unemployed. An emerging critical approach to studying youth transitions demonstrated how the distribution of young people across these different trajectories was strongly correlated to and influenced (some would say determined) by **social class** background, **gender** and/or **ethnicity** (Roberts, 1997). So, for example, working-class young people left school at sixteen and went straight into relatively low paid employment, while alternatively middle-class youths studied for longer in higher education before taking up posts in relatively higher paid employment. This notion of structural factors influencing a 'youth divide' was to become an enduring sub-theme in debate around youth transitions (Jones, 2002; Webster et al., 2004).

Wider economic and social change has caused some uncertainty about the value of traditional conceptions of youth transition (Miles, 2000; Skelton, 2002), with some querying whether it actually offered 'any theoretical purchase on the experiences of young people in the twenty-first century because of the increasing complexity of the choices required to make the move into adulthood' (Brooks, 2009). As such, the usefulness of the concept of youth transition became 'hotly contested in Anglophone youth studies over the past decade' as the concept:

> Presumes the continuing predominance of linear, obvious, mainstream pathways to adulthood; excludes wider youth questions in focusing narrowly on educational and employment encounters; prioritises normative and policy-focused assumptions and de-prioritises the actual lived

experiences of young people; and is no longer a tenable concept, given the extension of youth phase and the blurring of it and 'adulthood' as distinct life-phases. (Shildrick and MacDonald, 2007: 589)

These criticisms and the context of wider economic and social change from the 1970s onwards have spurred significant rethinking and development around the concept of youth transition. These were framed within wider theoretical developments in the social sciences, which witnessed the emergence of concepts such as 'risk society' (Beck, 1992) and 'structuration' (Giddens, 1991). Simplifying, the theory of risk society suggested a breakdown in traditional 'structurally-determined' transitions as they became more fragmented and less certain. To describe the consequences of these changes, youth scholars 'appended a variety of adjectives to the concept of transition' as they became '"long", "broken", "extended", "protracted", "uneasy" and "fractured"' (Shildrick and MacDonald, 2007: 590). In this new context some youth researchers noted how young people increasingly 'navigated' and 'negotiated' their transitions to adulthood. They moved away from a pre-eminent focus on structural factors such as social class, gender and ethnicity to place greater emphasis on a biographical approach that investigated the role of young people themselves in the process of transition to adulthood across time (Henderson et al., 2007). As such, the issue of biography came to occupy 'an important place in youth studies'. Essentially biographical studies attempt to understand how individuals make sense of their lives within the dynamic processes of transition and change characterising risk societies (Furlong and Cartmel, 2007).

Studies that focused on biographical change over time challenged the notion of a linear youth transition. Rather, reversible transitions were possible with the possibility that young people can move between states of dependence and independence – for example, in the context of finding employment, becoming unemployed and eventually returning to another job. The collapse of the youth labour market in Western societies during the 1980s meant more young people stayed longer in training and education or suffered extended spells of unemployment. Indeed, the notion of an 'extended youth transition' became popular. The emergence of biographical approaches brought into sharper focus a persistent and key theoretical theme in the youth transitions literature. This theme concerns the relative emphasis given to either the constraints on personal choice and decision-making provided by socio-cultural structuring or young people's agency in negotiating and creating individual paths of transition

(Henderson et al., 2007). The debate over structure and agency is at the philosophical (meta-theoretical) and theoretical levels within youth studies and other social sciences. Philosophically it lies in the metaphysical representation of the young person as either 'structured individual' (Roberts, 1997), or 'reflexive individual' (Furlong et al., 2003).

Earlier theoretical models characterised transitions as career trajectories that were largely predetermined by a young person's social position, whereas later ones have seen transitions as becoming increasingly fragmented, individualised and freer from the determining grip of social structure. Most studies of transitions recognise a structural and an agential dimension but the relative emphasis placed on one or the other as a causal influence in youth transitions differs between authors. For example, Furlong and Cartmel (2007) agree that there is increased fragmentation and protraction of youth transitions but they conclude that this does not mean that young people have become free of the influence of social structure. Rather, while individual young people may feel that they have more choice, the pathways that they follow are still strongly influenced by factors such as social class, locality, gender and ethnicity. In contrast, some championing young people's reflexive capabilities are questionable. Contrast this thesis with Spano's suggestion that young people can escape social exclusion and poverty simply by having their 'deficit of reflexivity' resolved (Spano, 2002). The discussion of social class, gender, ethnicity, **place** and **division** within this volume would suggest, however, that Spano may under-emphasise the significance of structural factors in the shaping of youth transitions.

The biographical approach to **researching youth** does appear to have potential in trying to re-think the connection between individual agency and structure in an attempt to understand better the 'holistic and dynamic' character of youth transitions. For example, drawing on late modern theory and in particular the idea of a reflexive project of the self, Henderson et al. (2007) tracked a diverse group of young people over a ten-year period and highlighted the importance of changing policies in the areas of education, employment, drugs, cultures of violence and wellbeing in influencing transitions. But they also considered the significance of things young people attach importance to in influencing their choices such as concerns for mobility, home, belonging, intimacy and social life. Biographical accounts have also placed a stress on the importance of 'critical moments' in youth transitions. Several youth scholars have highlighted the importance of such 'critical moments' within young people's biographies (Thomson et al., 2002).

Indeed, this research has attempted to identify how critical moments are implicated in processes of youth transition, particularly those transitions which feature social exclusion (Webster et al., 2004: 32–3). Such critical moments include parental separation, episodes of ill-health and also bereavements. The significance of such moments was captured by Webster et al. (2004) in their study of 'poor transitions' made within the North East of England; 'While those we researched shared many social and economic experiences in common some had quite different transitions, partly because of the influence of particular critical moments on their lives' (Webster et al., 2004: 32–3). For example, the social and psychological consequences of bereavements 'could play out over a long period and had implications for extended transitions that were not obvious at the time of the event itself'. Indeed, Webster et al. (2004) noted how experiences of bereavement illustrated 'the influence of personal agency' within transitions as responses to such critical moments differed across participants in the research. Thomson et al. (2002: 351) explain such differences in response by observing how the 'descriptive concept of the critical moment provides a way of seeing how social and economic environments frame individual narratives and the personal and cultural resources on which young people are able to draw'. They claim responses to critical moments within youth transitions are 'framed' by circumstances but allow researchers to produce accounts which 'demonstrate the centrality of identity and subjectivity to an understanding of transitions, without reducing the analysis to individual psychology' (Thomson et al. 2002: 351).

There is little doubt the concept of transition has a long history in the discipline of youth studies – although over the last decade there has been an element of uncertainty about its future. However, far from being obsolete, at the time of writing it appears the concept will remain important even though it may evolve further. As this discussion demonstrates, understandings of the concept and its operationalisation within youth studies have already changed over time largely in response to the changing lives of young people but also the critical scrutiny of the concept. But, while the concept has its critics, it certainly has its proponents and the latter are vociferous and passionate in their defence of youth for it is an important heuristic device. As such, it is claimed 'the appeal of a broad holistic, long view of youth transitions is that it offers a privileged vantage point from which to glimpse processes of social structural formation and transformation' (Shildrick and MacDonald, 2007: 601).

REFERENCES

Beck, U. (1992) *Risk Society: Towards a New Modernity*. London: Sage.

Brooks, R. (ed.) (2009) *Transitions from Education to Work: New Perspectives from Europe and Beyond*. Basingstoke: Palgrave Macmillan.

Coles, B. (1997) 'Welfare service for young people', in J. Roche and S. Tucker (eds), *Youth in Society*. London: Sage, pp. 98–106.

Furlong, A. and Cartmel, F. (2007) *Young People and Social Change: New Perspectives*. 2nd edn. Maidenhead: Open University Press.

Furlong, A., Cartmel, F., Biggart, A., Sweeting, H. and West, P. (2003) *Youth Transitions: Patterns of Vulnerability and Processes of Social Inclusion*. Edinburgh: Scottish Executive.

Giddens, A. (1991) *Modernity and Self-Identity: Self and Society in the Late Modern Age*. Cambridge: Polity.

Goodwin, J. and O'Connor, H. (2005) 'Exploring complex transitions: looking back at the "Golden Age" of from school-to-work', *Sociology*, 39 (2): 201–20.

Hebdige, D. (1982) 'Towards a cartography of taste, 1935–1962', in B. Waites, T. Bennett and G. Martin (eds), *Popular Culture: Past and Present*. London: Croom Helm, pp. 194–218.

Heinz, W. (2009) 'Youth transitions in an age of uncertainty', in A. Furlong (ed.), *Handbook of Youth and Young Adulthood: New Perspectives and Agendas*. London: Routledge, pp. 3–13.

Henderson, S., Holland, J., McGrellis, S., Sharpe, S. and Thomson, R. (2007) *Inventing Adulthoods: A Biographical Approach to Youth Transitions*. London: Sage.

Jones, J. (2002) *The Youth Divide: Diverging Paths to Adulthood*. York: Joseph Rowntree Foundation.

Miles, S. (2000) *Youth Lifestyles in a Changing World*. Buckingham: Open University Press.

Osgerby, B. (1998) *Youth in Britain Since 1945*. Oxford: Blackwell.

Pearson, G. (1983) *Hooligan: A History of Respectable Fears*. London: Macmillan.

Roberts, K. (1968) 'Entry into employment: an approach towards a general theory', *Sociological Review*, 16 (2): 168–84.

Roberts, K. (1997) 'Structure and agency: the new youth research agenda', in J. Bynner, L. Chisholm and A. Furlong (eds), *Youth, Citizenship and Social Change in a European Context*. Aldershot: Ashgate Press, pp. 56–65.

Shildrick, T. and MacDonald, R. (2007) 'Biographies of exclusion: poor work and poor transitions', *International Journal of Lifelong Education*, 26 (5): 589–604.

Skelton, T. (2002) 'Research on youth transitions: some critical interventions', in M. Cieslik, and G. Pollock (eds), *Young People in Risk Society: The Restructuring of Youth Identities and Transitions in Late Modernity*. Aldershot: Ashgate Press, pp. 100–16.

Spano, A. (2002) 'Premodernity and postmodernity in Southern Italy', in P. Chamberlayne, M. Rustin and T. Wengraf (eds), *Biography and Social Exclusion in Europe*. Bristol: Policy Press, pp. 61–76.

Thomson, R., Bell, R., Holland, J., Henderson, S., McGrellis, S. and Sharpe, S. (2002) 'Critical moments, choice, chance and opportunity in young people's narratives of transition', *Sociology*, 36 (2): 335–54.

key concepts in youth studies

Vickerstaff, S.A. (2003) 'Apprenticeship in the "Golden Age": were youth transitions really smooth and unproblematic back then?' *Work, Employment and Society*, 17 (2): 269–87.

Webster, C., Simpson, D., MacDonald, R., Abbas, A., Cieslik, M., Shildrick, T. and Simpson, M. (2004) *Poor Transitions: Social Exclusion and Young Adults*. Bristol: Policy Press.

3
Youth Cultures

When discussing the nature of youth culture researchers often employ a wide understanding of the term to mean a 'way of life' that includes ideas as well as the material and social processes individuals and groups employ in their social relationships (see Hall and Jefferson, 1976). In particular we are interested in the ideas, values, attitudes, language and norms that young people use in their daily lives. The concept of subculture is used to denote a distinctive way of life created by young people that is a subset of wider cultural practices derived from, yet often in conflict with, the existing parent or wider culture.

Researchers explore how pre-existing cultures can constrain and regulate young people's lives as they grow up. How young people talk, think, feel, dress, how they see the future and the past are given to them, yet at the same time they have some agency to challenge, synthesise and modify these cultural endowments to create a unique self-identity and with it a unique shared youth culture. Young people establish relationships and it is often in collective ways with peers and friends that they are able to experiment with cultural resources and develop distinctive ways of life that can challenge and rework their cultural heritages. These elements of wider culture, social identity and youth subculture, together with questions about agency and structural conditioning, make up much of the fabric of research into youth cultures (Cieslik, 2001).

Early accounts of a distinctive culture of young people were evident in the portrayal of the poor in eighteenth- and nineteenth-century

youth cultures

15

England. Pearson (1983) writes of how the 'London Apprentices' were poor youths noted for their unruly behaviour, drinking and fighting in the streets. Roberts (1971) writes of similar young men ('the Scuttlers') on the streets of Liverpool and Manchester whose disorderly behaviour was also marked by a distinctive style of dress which included bell bottomed trousers, clogs and thick belts (see Davies, 2008). Several North American studies from the 1920s onwards drew on anthropological techniques to investigate the functioning of youth gangs in the context of changing patterns of inequality and disadvantage in urban communities. Studies such as Thrasher's *The Gang* (1927) and Whyte's *Street Corner Society* (1943) illustrated the structure and organisation of street gangs in disadvantaged districts of Chicago and Boston, respectively. These groups were drawn from specific ethnic groups, marked by a distinctive language and style of dress, conformed to informal codes of conduct and played out particular roles and rituals. Albert Cohen's study of Chicago gangs (1955) popularised the notion of youth subculture and he depicted how gang membership was an important part of the social identities of young people, being seen as a key resource and a way of navigating the journey from childhood dependency to the autonomy of adulthood. Many of these studies examined how this collective exploration of independence allowed for the development of radical and delinquent careers. For Cohen the lack of employment opportunities produced 'status frustration' which was channelled into delinquent activities. Whereas Downes' (1966) study of working-class youth in East London sees disaffection being managed through leisure pursuits but which can in turn produce a drift into criminal activity.

These early studies formed the basis of post-war research that documented the ways that young people's lives were being transformed in response to wider social change. In many Western societies there was economic growth yet continuing poverty; the development of welfare systems; a shrinking working class and growing middle class; growing consumerism; Cold War political tensions; civil rights and concerns for minorities; all of these currents played out across societies and were refracted through the lives of young people (Brake, 1985). Subcultures were seen as collective cultural practices that allowed young people to manage the tensions of growing up in a time of profound social change. Shared interests in **music** and fashion, a common language and similar social position were all resources for coping and surviving in turbulent times.

Phil Cohen's (1972) study of young people in the East End of London during the late 1960s illustrates this notion of youth subcultures emerging as a response to the challenges posed by social change. In the East End the redevelopment of the local community and changes to **employment** opportunities threatened traditional transitions to adulthood and so young people developed their own friendship groups, activities and styles that celebrated their traditions yet also offered spaces to explore new ways of being working class. The Centre for Contemporary Cultural Studies (CCCS) developed this subcultural approach utilising media analysis, ethnography and Gramsci's (1971) concept of hegemony to suggest that young people's cultural practices are important ways in which dominant ideas and cultures are resisted (Hall and Jefferson, 1976). Though such subcultural resistance is important in shaping young people's identities and can frame transitions to adulthood, such practices only tend to offer partial or what the CCCS referred to as 'magical solutions' to the structural problems (such as poor work and training opportunities) that young people face (Clarke et al., 1976: 47–8). This way of interpreting different subcultural groupings in relation to structural characteristics is also seen in the work of Hebdige (1979) and Willis (1978) who wrote of the 'homology' between the cultural and socio-economic backgrounds of young people and the sorts of subcultures they created. Thus we have an interpretation of the Teds as a predominantly English working-class phenomenon combining rock and roll music and drinking with flamboyant upper-class suits and greased hair. This subverting of earlier styles and cultural signifiers through combinations of music, dress, language and demeanour are a common element of much subcultural activity. The Later Mods, though rooted in mainly lower-middle-class communities, combined strident black music with drug use, Italian clothes and scooters. The Skinheads' appearance, seeming to be a caricature of working classness (boots, drainpipes jeans, braces and cropped hair) together with drinking and football hooliganism, also drew on black musical traditions (Clarke, 1976). The Punk movement from the mid-1970s in England was perhaps the classical example of young people's efforts to disrupt traditional ways of life by mixing up stylistic forms to create a rebellious 'outsider' subculture. Shaved and spiked hair, safety pins, ripped clothes, a 'Do It Yourself' approach to music and fanzines, and bands with names such as The Damned, Sex Pistols and The Clash all conveyed a sense of rebelliousness and an estrangement from wider adult society.

Much youth cultures research neglects the lives of women and black and ethnic youth. However, Anne Campbell investigated young women's role in gangs in New York during the 1980s noting how they were often marginalised by the activities of male gang members (Campbell,

1991). Griffin (1985) and McRobbie and Garber (1976) also researched women's cultural lives in the 1970s and 1980s documenting how women's relationships involve wider, more diffuse friendship activities than that seen in subcultural analyses of young men. Working-class women often develop stylised ways (through the use of makeup, clothes and humour) to challenge the expectations that society has of them. Yet paradoxically such resistance, as it involves anti-school behaviour and preoccupation with their femininity and appearance, helped confirm the traditional working-class routes into poor work and motherhood rather than disturb such conventional pathways to adult life (Griffin, 2010). More recently research has documented more diverse cultural lives of young women reflecting the intersection of **class**, **sexuality**, **race** and **gender** and their influence on women's friendship groups, interests and activities (Nayak and Kehily, 2007). Young women can experience distinctive forms of marginalisation because of these structural influences, yet at the same time their classed and racialised backgrounds can offer social/cultural capital to help navigate these forms of domination.

There have been several studies of black youth culture and its influences in the UK (Jones, 1988) and the US (Kitwana, 2003). Hebdige (1979; 1987), for example, discussed Rastafarianism in the 1970s and how black youths drew on the inspiration of Reggae music and its traditions of rebelliousness as a way of countering the economic and racial disadvantages they were experiencing in English cities. In particular Hebdige (1987) noted the ways that black music and friendships groups allowed for a consciousness raising and supported positive black identities in the face of media portrayals (moral panics) of black youth as often threatening, violent and criminal (see also Hall et al., 1978). More recently studies have illustrated the global influence of black or minority street culture such as Hip Hop (Basu and Lemelle, 2006; Bennett, 2000) and also concerns about the growing influence of gang culture on the lives of black and minority youth (Mendoza-Denton, 2007).

Since the 1980s youth cultures research has been influenced by developments in postmodern theorising, the concepts of risk, individualisation and globalisation. All of these wider debates have suggested a reworking of older class-based notions of identity and cultural practice. Researchers have documented the breakdown in homology between social and cultural background and subcultural affiliation, pointing to more fluid patterns of cultural activity among young people (Bennett, 1999; Muggleton, 2000). The increasingly consumerist way of life of young people suggests to some that there exists a 'supermarket of style' (Polhemus, 1997) where one can pick and mix from a variety of subcultural traditions and move in and out of a myriad collection of different cultural forms. The concepts of 'scene' and 'tribe' have been used to denote how young people draw on global cultural flows such as Bhangra or Rave music yet rework such influences to create fluid, fragmentary and ephemeral friendship patterns and cultural affiliations (Bennett, 2000; Bennett and Kahn-Harris, 2004). Others (Miles, 2000) suggest the emergence of individualised forms of leisure and consumption where young people are more involved in personal lifestyle projects than more traditional collective activities. As a counterpoint to such work, some studies have documented the persistence of collective subcultural groupings such as Goth that echo those seen in earlier generations (Hodkinson, 2002). Indeed some suggest the continuing popularity of these older forms of subcultural activity across the life course – appealing to young and not so young adults (Bennett and Hodkinson, 2012). Others have charted the persistence of youth cultural activity as seen with New Age Travellers and new social movements (such as anti-capitalism, anti-globalisation, anti-war and environmentalism), which draw on earlier traditions of the Punks and Hippies that have fused political agitation and bohemian sensibilities to create distinctive counter-cultural youth movements (Hetherington, 2000). Yet others have documented the ways that many young people continue to be marginalised in Western societies, vulnerable to high levels of unemployment, poor education and training, often being blamed by adult society for their own disadvantage (Jones, 2011). The popularity of discourses around a youth underclass or a 'lost generation' and the associated culture of drugs, crime, lone parenthood and anti-social behaviour are a reminder of how young people's lives can become the focus of wider anxieties about the 'state of the nation'.

youth cultures

REFERENCES

Basu, D. and Lemelle, S. (eds) (2006) *The Vinyl Ain't Final: The Globalization of Black Popular Culture*. London: Pluto Press.

Bennett, A. (1999) 'Subcultures or neo-tribes? Rethinking the relationship between youth, style and musical taste', *Sociology*, 33 (3): 599–617.

Bennett, A. (2000) *Popular Music and Youth Culture*. London: Macmillan.

Bennett, A. and Hodkinson, P. (2012) *Aging and Youth Cultures: Music, Style and Subcultures*. London: Berg.

Bennett, A. and Kahn-Harris, K. (2004) 'Introduction', in A. Bennett and K. Kahn-Harris, K. (eds), *After Subculture: Critical Studies in Contemporary Youth Culture*, London: Palgrave, pp. 1–18.

Brake, M. (1985) *Comparative Youth Culture: Youth Culture and Subculture in America, Britain and Canada*. London: Routledge.

Campbell, A. (1991) *Girls in the Gang*. 2nd edn. Cambridge: Blackwell.

Cieslik, M. (2001) 'Researching youth cultures: some problems with the cultural turn in British Youth Studies', *Scottish Youth Issues Journal*, 2: 27–48.

Clarke, J. (1976) 'The skinheads and the magical recovery of community', S. Hall and T. Jefferson (eds), *Resistance Through Rituals: Youth Subcultures in Post-War Britain*. London: Hutchinson, pp. 99–102.

Clarke, J., Hall, S., Jefferson, T. and Roberts, B. (1976) 'Subcultures, cultures and class: a theoretical overview', in S. Hall and T. Jefferson (eds), *Resistance Through Rituals: Youth Subcultures in Post-War Britain*. London: Hutchinson, pp. 9–74.

Cohen, A. (1955) *Delinquent Boys: The Culture of the Gang*. Glencoe, IL: Free Press.

Cohen, P. (1972) 'Subcultural conflict and working class community', *Working Papers in Cultural Studies*, 2: 5–70.

Davies, A. (2008) *The Gangs of Manchester: The 'Scuttlers', Britain's First Youth Culture*. Preston: Milo Books.

Downes, P. (1966) *The Delinquent Solution: A Study in Subcultural Theory*. London: Routledge and Kegan Paul.

Gramsci, A. (1971) *Selections from the Prison Notebooks*, ed. and trans. Q. Hoare and G. Nowell Smith. London: Lawrence and Wishart.

Griffin, C. (1985) *Typical Girls: Young Women from School to the Job Market*. London: Routledge and Kegan Paul.

Griffin, C. (2010) 'The trouble with class: researching youth, class and culture beyond the Birmingham School', *Journal of Youth Studies*, 14 (3): 245–59.

Hall, S., Critcher, C., Jefferson, T., Clarke, J. and Roberts, B. (1978) *Policing the Crisis: Mugging, the State and Law and Order*, London: Macmillan.

Hall, S. and Jefferson, T. (eds) (1976) *Resistance Through Rituals: Youth Subcultures in Post-War Britain*. London: Hutchinson.

Hebdige, D. (1979) *Subculture: The Meaning of Style*. London: Routledge.

Hebdige, D. (1987) *Cut 'n' Mix: Culture, Identity and Caribbean Music*. Old Woking: Comedia/Methuen.

Hetherington, K. (2000) *New Age Travellers: Vanloads of Uproarious Humanity*. London: Continuum.

Hodkinson, P. (2002) *Goth: Identity, Style and Subculture*. Oxford: Berg.

Jones, O. (2011) *Chavs: The Demonization of the Working Class*. London: Verso.

Jones, S. (1988) *Black Culture, White Youth: Reggae Traditions from Jamaica to the UK*. London: Palgrave.

Kitwana, B. (2003) *The Hip Hop Generation: Young Blacks and the Crisis in African-American Culture*. New York: Basic Civitas Books.

McRobbie, A. and Garber, J. (1976) 'Girls and subculture', in S. Hall and T. Jefferson (eds), *Resistance Through Rituals: Youth Subcultures in Post-War Britain*. London: Hutchinson, pp. 209–22.

Mendoza-Denton, N. (2007) *Homegirls: Language and Cultural Practice Among Latina Youth Gangs*. London: Wiley-Blackwell.

Miles, S. (2000) *Youth Lifestyles in a Changing World*. Buckingham: Open University Press.

Muggleton (2000) *Inside Subculture: The Postmodern Meaning of Style*. Oxford: Berg.

Nayak, A. and Kehily, M.J. (2007) *Gender, Youth and Culture: Young Masculinities and Femininities*. London: Palgrave.

Pearson, G. (1983) *Hooligan: A History of Respectable Fears*. London: Macmillan.

Polhemus, T. (1997) 'In the supermarket of style', in S. Redhead, D. Wynne and J. O'Connor (eds), *The Clubcultures Reader: Readings in Popular Cultural Studies*. Oxford: Blackwell Press, pp. 148–51.

Roberts, R. (1971) *The Classic Slum*. Manchester: Manchester University Press.

Thrasher, F. (1927) *The Gang*. Chicago: University of Chicago Press.

Whyte, W. F. (1943) *Street Corner Society: The Social Structure of an Italian Slum*. 4th edn. Chicago: University of Chicago Press.

Willis, P. (1978) *Profane Culture*. London: Routledge and Kegan Paul.

4

Young People and Social Policy

Social policy is ubiquitous, pervasive and connects with young people either directly or indirectly everyday of their lives. But, social policy is another concept within youth studies for which it is difficult to produce a definitive version of its meaning. Both the terms social and policy are difficult to pin down. Meanings of policy usually invoke reference to a guide for taking future action and for making appropriate choices or decisions towards an identified end. But policy can also be defined as a method for outlining solutions to problems – for example, perceived problems involving young people. In this sense, policy offers direction and may indicate choices that are preferable in regard to meeting ends. But several theorists note how despite offering guidance, policies do not normally tell people specifically how to act. Rather, they offer a degree of discretion and options in deciding what to do – these can be narrowed down or changed. A distinction has been made between 'policy as text' and 'policy as discourse'. Policy is actually both. Because policies as texts are not necessarily clear, closed or complete they are usually the product of compromises at various stages in the policy formulation and implementation processes (Ball, 1990). Moreover, the term social also presents difficulties. Social policy is popularly interpreted as policy directed at meeting the social needs of the population, or subgroups within it such as young people. Social needs are considered to be the welfare needs of people. So for young people, social policies concern **education**, care, **housing**, health, **wellbeing** and social security. Law and order, fiscal and labour market (**employment** and **training**) policies are also often considered social policies for young people in the sense that they may involve the preservation of their welfare through protecting them against exploitation or abuse.

Social policy with implications for young people is formulated and implemented at several levels. With increasing **globalisation**, supranational agencies such as the European Union are playing a part in the development of policy, as Ball (2008: 25) writes, 'The nation state is no longer adequate on its own as a space in which to think about policy.' For example, within the field of education Walther and Plug (2006) highlight how common elements of policy discourse have gained currency across several European countries and each has implications for young people. These include ideas about 'employability', 'lifelong (including **informal) learning**' and 'activation' initiatives for employment and training. The Council of the European Union established a framework for European cooperation in the field of youth (known as the Youth Cooperation Framework) in June 2002 and the Bologna process of 1999 set up a European Higher Education Area. The Lisbon Strategy (from 2000 onwards) has resulted in a development plan for the economy of the European Union and this certainly has implications for youth policy across nation states. This is through the support for a European 'information economy'. In 2005 the European Council established the European Youth Pact as it saw a need for young people to benefit from a range of policies. The Youth Pact promotes a spectrum of policies aiming to improve the education, training, mobility, vocational integration and social inclusion of young people across the continent. In 2010, and as part of the Europe 2020 strategy, 'Youth on the Move'

(European Commission, 2011) was launched and is a package of policy initiatives on education and employment for young people in Europe. Consequently, Lawn (2006: 272) talks of a 'European learning space'.

Historically, in many countries across the world there has been the establishment of relatively universal welfare systems through the development of social policies. A common purpose of these welfare systems is to promote social justice and to temper the operation of the market in capitalist societies. A leader in this regard was the social security system set up in Germany during Bismarck's era. Across different countries, the arrangement of the state, non-state sectors (voluntary and private) and individuals within such welfare systems differed and this continues today. Hence scholars such as Esping-Anderson (1990) have attempted to make sense of this complexity identifying three main types of welfare systems which emerged across capitalist countries – the 'liberal', 'corporatist-statist' and 'social democratic'. He later added 'Mediterranean' to depict the welfare systems of Greece, Italy and Spain in which the family **network** continues to play an important part in the provision of welfare. Esping-Anderson's typology highlights that, despite globalisation and movement to standardise welfare policies, there is the continuing influence of the nation state on policy development (see also Pohl and Walther, 2007). But Esping-Anderson's model has been criticised for being over-simplistic because increasingly some welfare systems may feature elements of all of the welfare models of the typology – as we see in the 'third way' philosophy to welfare reform (discussed below), which adopts aspects of social democratic and liberal regimes.

The influence of 'welfare regimes' can be shown in the context of economic and **social change** since the 1970s and the attempts of policy-makers in several European countries to assist young people in making **transitions** to independent adulthood. 'Welfare regimes' in each country are said to inform the different 'transition regimes' that can be found in these countries (Pohl and Walther, 2007), and these strongly influence different experiences of young people across the different countries. The transition regimes shaping policies in countries across Europe are labelled by the author: 1) 'universalistic', 2) 'liberal', 3) 'employment-centred', 4) 'sub-protective' and 5) 'post-communist'. Therefore, policies across countries within Europe and beyond may focus on addressing the same issues such as employability and/or unemployment. But they can differ in the ways in which they do so and this has consequences for the life chances and experiences of young people.

Pohl and Walther suggest a liberal transition regime could be found in the UK. Therefore policies designed to assist youth transitions in the UK emphasise individual rights and responsibilities above collective provision. These policies focus on individuals and the 'facilitation' of their 'employability' so that economic independence can be accomplished as quickly as possible. Young people themselves take primary responsibility for ensuring they take up opportunities to make successful transitions. This contrasts with the 'employment-centred' transition regime of Germany where young people are allocated social positions as part of a socialisation process into adulthood – via the *Sozialstaat*, or 'social state', which assumes this responsibility for allocation. The German 'apprenticeship' programme for young people is highly valued and reflects how social protection of all its citizens – including young people – is a central element of national policy in Germany. For example, unemployment benefit payments are higher than in the UK and yet so are youth employment rates. Charles Murray (1990) and others have blamed relatively generous welfare arrangements for reducing the work ethic and creating dependence and an **underclass** – but the German example seems to cast doubt on this perspective.

Policies that attempt to regulate the welfare environment in which young people grow up in the UK have resulted in age-related rights and responsibilities. Coles (2004; 2006) highlights how over the years some of these policies produced a focus on rights and responsibilities that was 'strangely at odds with changed social and economic circumstances. For instance, care leavers are expected to live independently whilst their contemporaries are dependent on their families for longer' (Coles, 1997: 104). Consequently, recent youth policies do recognise that individual life courses have changed in the last few decades. But, as Jones (2009) claims, a trend in the 1960s and 1970s for social policy 'to treat young people as individuals with welfare rights of their own' was to be 'halted in the neo-liberal 1980s when the balance shifted to responsibilities'. While policies have been developed with an understanding of how transitions have become extended and may include a prolonged period of dependence, these 'policies which have raised the age threshold for entry into independent adulthood have not been matched with legislation explicitly extending parental responsibility until that point' (Jones, 2009: 144). In addition, some key policies which appear to promote citizen rights of young people may actual impinge on them – for example, the UK government's New Deal work activation policy offered young people a limited set of options some of which they may not ideally want to choose. Similarly, the present UK Coalition government's work experience policy for young people has been criticised for withdrawing welfare payments – indeed lawyers are 'mounting a legal challenge' to the work experience scheme known as the 'mandatory work activity' because 'they argue it represents a form of slavery under the Human Rights Act' (*The Guardian*, 2011).

Youth policy in the UK has been influenced by recognition of patterns of inequality experienced by young people making transitions to adulthood. Risks and vulnerability, which can result in 'problematic' or 'marginal' transitions into adulthood and independence are more heavily concentrated among some groups of young people than others. These marginal transitions are more likely among young people aged between sixteen and eighteen that are also not in education, employment or training (NEETs). It is likely that as young people age this unemployment can then influence other transitions (such as housing and relationships) leading to teenage pregnancy, **homelessness** and offending. This notion of problematic transitions and multiple disadvantages came to be described as 'social exclusion' during the 1990s in the UK. Indeed, there was the establishment of a Social Exclusion Unit in the UK charged with developing policy for young people and promoting social inclusion. In developing youth policy therefore, identifying and addressing the risk of problematic transition or social exclusion has become a prime consideration of policy-makers. This is a difficult task because, as Bynner et al. (2004) indicate, the concept of risk itself has changed. For example, some risks to young people's transitions are identified as being either fixed or fluid. Fixed risks include structural socio-economic factors that can contribute to shaping individual life chances – for example, economic and social deprivation in the neighbourhoods where young people live and a lack of opportunities in local labour markets. Fluid – or more 'dynamic' – risks relate more to the personal attributes of an individual – for example, limited learning or a drugs habit. A combination of fixed and fluid risks results in some young people being more vulnerable than others because they have the likelihood of 'multiple risk' factors impacting negatively on their transitions.

The recognition that transitions are more complex and risky has led to the development of more 'holistic' youth policies. A 'holistic approach' to policy development is evident in policies that have attempted to involve inter-department, inter-agency and public/private partnership working. These include policies such as the Teenage Pregnancy Strategy, Connexions and Youth Offending Teams. In addition, policies have tried to respond to multiple risk factors at several levels – national, community, family and individual. Therefore, some policies remain universal for all youths while there has also been a targeting of policies at those with more likelihood of experiencing 'multiple risks' and therefore transitions into long-term disadvantage. Under the New Labour government in the UK (1997–2010) universal policies included tax credits for young mothers and the Education Maintenance Allowances supporting young people in education and training. Under New Labour, targeting was at vulnerable groups such as teenage parents and care leavers and at those youths living in disadvantaged communities through policies such as Education Action Zones (the latter policies are known as Area-Based Initiatives). On their election the Coalition government in the UK embarked on an acceler-ated structural deficit reduction programme which saw them cutting back on public spending and dismantling a great deal of the infrastruc-ture which Labour had put in place to support youth transitions. They faced criticisms for failing to respond quickly enough when unemploy-ment levels rose dramatically among the young and have belatedly estab-lished a Youth Contract similar to Labour's previous September Agreement, with targeted support for 'the most disadvantaged' sixteen to seventeen year olds.

With regard to targeted youth policies, there has been some criticism of both the targeting of 'socially excluded' groups of young people and the targeting of deprived neighbourhoods through social policies. Gill Jones (2002), for example, claims there are dangers in specifically target-ing socially excluded youths with focused youth policy. This is because the nature of the link between facets of disadvantage and social exclusion is not clearly understood – therefore she claims 'we cannot assume that there is a static and homogeneous group of multiply disadvantaged young people who can be targeted for interventions' (2002: 41). Jones also notes how some poor neighbourhoods are not homogenous, a point taken up by Bynner et al. (2004: 13) when they suggest that this means some young people in an area may not need targeted resources while 'some young people outside the area need them a lot'. Reviewing evi-dence concerning the effectiveness of such policies, Bynner et al. (2004: 96) concluded that 'generally speaking, the policies and initiatives reviewed have been effective in working towards their identified targets'. However, they also found 'scope for development' of such policies and 'weak-nesses' within the implementation process. For example, while they claimed recent youth policies were based on an improved understanding of changing youth transitions, those implementing a policy lacked understanding of 'the risk processes the policy is trying to influence' and of what therefore was more likely to work in producing change and why (a 'theory of change'). This indicates how recent policies have been generally well informed and have provided a basis for good practice. But Bynner et al. also suggest that a problem may exist in the practical context with a lack of understanding among those involved in the implementation process.

REFERENCES

Ball, S. (1990) *Politics and Policy Making in Education: Explorations in Policy Sociology*. London: Routledge.

Ball, S. (2008) *The Education Debate*. Bristol: Policy Press.

Bynner, J., Londra, M. and Jones. G. (2004) *The Impact of Government Policy on Social Exclusion Among Young People*. London: The Office of the Deputy Prime Minister.

Coles, B. (1997) 'Welfare services for young people', in J. Roche and S. Tucker (eds), *Youth in Society*. London: Sage, pp. 98–106.

Coles, B. (2004) 'Better connections? Welfare services for young people', in J. Roche, S. Tucker, R. Thomson, and R. Flynn (eds), *Youth in Society*. 2nd edn. London: Sage, pp. 90–101.

Coles. B. (2006) 'Youth policy 1995–2005: from "the best start" to "youth matters"', *Youth and Policy*, 89: 7–19.

Esping-Anderson, G. (1990) *The Three Worlds of Welfare Capitalism*. Cambridge: Polity Press.

European Commission (2011) 'Youth on the move'. View developments at: http://ec.europa.eu/youthonthemove/index_en.htm (accessed 7 July 2012).

The Guardian (2011) 'Young jobseekers told to work without pay or lose unemployment benefits', 16 November. www.guardian.co.uk/society/2011/nov/16/young-jobseekers-work-pay-unemployment (accessed 12 December 2011).

Jones, G. (2002) *The Youth Divide: Diverging Paths to Adulthood*. York: Joseph Rowntree Foundation. http://www.jrf.org.uk/sites/files/jrf/1842630814.pdf (accessed 7 July 2012).

Jones, G. (2009) *Youth*. Cambridge: Polity Press.

Lawn, M. (2006) 'Soft governance and the learning spaces of Europe', *Comparative European Politics*, 4: 272–88.

Murray, C. (1990) *The Emerging British Underclass*. London: Institute of Economic Affairs.

Pohl, A. and Walther, A. (2007) 'Activating the disadvantaged: variations in addressing youth transitions across Europe', *International Journal of Lifelong Learning*, 26 (5): 533–53.

Walther, A. and Plug, W. (2006) 'Transitions from school-to-work in Europe: de-standardization and policy trends', *New Directions for Child and Adolescent Development*, 113: 77–90.

5

Working with Young People

A great number of practitioners work with young people such as teachers, social workers, probation officers, careers advisors and housing specialists. Many of these professionals are employed by national or local state organisations, some may work for charities and some may be volunteers. Youth workers, however, are unique in being professionals who work predominantly with young people and whose traditions unlike state-employed professionals are rooted in voluntary work with their clients.

The origins of organised youth work lie in nineteenth-century industrialisation and the concerns of religious groups, charities and the state about the impact of urbanisation and social inequalities on young people. Church-led youth ministries, community-based youth clubs and organisations such as scouts and guides all emerged out of efforts of these organisations to positively influence the transitions and identities of young people. As Jeffs and Smith (2010) write, youth work has traditionally involved youth-centred activities that aim to enhance the education and welfare of young people and are rooted in building good quality relationships with participants.

Youth work practice does tend to reflect the societies in which it takes place. Youth work can vary according to welfare systems and socio-economic context so that Nordic countries such as Norway have social democratic provision whereas England has a history of liberal youth work while France and German have more conservative traditions (Coussee, 2009). Hence liberal traditions suggest a greater role for voluntary organisations with a greater role of state provision in social democratic and conservative traditions. However, from the Second World War onwards many state organisations in Western societies began to take a greater interest in the nature of youth work provision, encouraging it to support a democratic culture in the face of the challenges presented by communist ideologies and the cultural and political tensions arising from the Cold War. In the UK the *Albermarle Report* (1960) noted how youth work can support democracies by offering young people opportunities for free association, quality training and personal challenge.

Overall the job of youth workers during much of the twentieth century was perhaps more straightforward and less contentious than it is today. With less interventionist government, relatively high rates of youth employment and more secure, predictable transitions to adulthood, youth work faced fewer challenges than those experienced by contemporary practitioners. Today's youth workers have a difficult job as they work in a context of high rates of youth unemployment and social disadvantage, fluid youth identities and **transitions** to adulthood and more instrumental youth **policies** with a narrower focus on employability.

As youth work in the UK relies on voluntary workers and has the welfare and empowerment of young people at its heart, its political and ethical traditions often bring it into conflict with the agendas of the state, the media and business corporations. Commentators have noted (Jeffs and Smith, 2010; Taylor, 2009) how in recent decades youth work has struggled to maintain its traditional critical and independent voice and practice in the face of government and business efforts to influence youth work and the lives of young people in developed societies.

Youth work can take many forms today – some youth workers are based in schools, clubs and sports facilities or they may work in a detached or outreach role in communities where young people live, spending time on the street and public spaces where young people congregate. The support, advice and skills development that youth workers promote has increasingly become organised into formal curricula that inform the sort of activities offered to young people. National organisations such as the National Youth Agency in the UK oversee such curricula and also the training and registration of youth workers. In recent decades, therefore, even though many youth workers remain volunteers, a large regulatory bureaucracy has emerged that monitors and assesses youth work practice just as we see in other state organisations such as teaching and health care. The outcomes of activities, data on progress and attendance, risk assessments and models of best practice are now all key features of a youth worker's life – what some commentators have referred to as a 'new managerialism' shaping youth work in the UK and many developed societies (Taylor, 2009).

A long-standing debate in youth work is how participation in activities might improve the life chances of young people – what sorts of youth work practices can produce positive outcomes for participants. Some recent research points to how support that is too focused on employability (such as that seen in some Connexions provision in the UK) may enhance the relationships and social capital of young people but may not in itself improve the employment prospects of young people. Phillips (2010) suggests that those disadvantaged young people who were successful in finding work also tended to have a range of other personal resources such as self-confidence that aided their job seeking. In some youth work provision, however, these sorts of skills and resources could be enhanced but only through extended participation in youth work activities. The conclusion being that there are no short cuts to social inclusion and employment. These findings echo earlier work of Furlong et al. (1997), Walther (2003) and Halpern et al. (2000) who all documented that youth work provision can have a range of positive benefits such as developing the social relationships and self-esteem of participants. However, these qualities do not always translate into positive outcomes in the labour market, for example, particularly for those young people who have experienced complex forms of disadvantage such as residence in areas of high unemployment, low-level educational qualifications and parental unemployment. Though youth work provision in most developed societies has been expanded in recent decades, there continues to be a long-standing problem across societies of engaging young people from so-called 'hard to reach' backgrounds characterised by multiple disadvantage (Coussee, 2009: 6).

A further area of debate in youth work has been the tension between offering education and welfare support while still providing youth-centred activities that enhance the personal and social development of young people. Since the economic crises of the 1980s governments have focused attention on core youth policies around employability and social inclusion and this instrumentalism has for many commentators such as Taylor (2009) and Batsleer and Davies (2010: 159) threatened the traditional principles of youth work. The authors suggest that government policies have undermined the local, voluntary and independent features of youth work that threaten its critical and creative character (Batsleer and Davis, 2010: 159). In a similar vein, Jeffs and Smith (2008) argue that governments have increasingly developed integrated children's services (as we saw in the development in the UK of the Connexions Service, DfES, 2003; 2005) and a bureaucratic audit culture that is concerned more with economic growth and child safety than the informal, open-ended and creative practice that informs good youth work (Jeffs and Smith, 2010: 11). One aspect of these changes has been the professionalisation of youth work whereby practitioners are required to attain ever higher youth work qualifications and seek waged employment rather than offer voluntary practice.

Many commentators in youth studies argue this growing instrumentalism of youth work risks undermining the ability of good youth work practice to support the overall wellbeing and resilience of young people (Jeffs and Smith, 1994). This is at a time when such personal skills are essential as young people face the uncertainties of what Beck (1990) referred to as a 'risk society' – fluid educational and training opportunities and shifting patterns of employment that throw up myriad choices and routes that young people have to learn to navigate successfully (Batsleer and Davies, 2010: 157). If young people have to develop complex skills needed to reflexively manage their own biographies they need a youth service that offers much more than employment tips and behavioural modification strategies (Van de Walle et al., 2010). They will need sophisticated analytical and interpersonal skills to make sense of the often opaque social relationships they will navigate in their lives. What is needed, suggest writers such as Batsleer and Davies (2010: 159), is a vision of an enlightened education for young people that is outlined in reports such as the Nuffield Review of education for fourteen to nineteen year olds (2009). This sees a youth work provision that helps create critical and resilient young people whose own voice shapes their education to promote a broader human development that defies simple measurement and the narrow concerns with employment and anti-social behaviour.

As we write most youth work provision in Western societies is undergoing reorganisation and significant cuts to funding at a time of growing youth unemployment and wider welfare cuts to education, social security, training and health (Lepper, 2011). The modest growth in provision of recent years has given way to an era of austerity and uncertainty about the sorts of services that will be available to young people and the career opportunities for youth workers.

REFERENCES

Albermarle Report (1960) London: Ministry of Education.

Batsleer, J. and Davies, B. (eds) (2010) *What is Youth Work?* Exeter: Learning Matters Press.

Beck, U. (1990) *Risk Society: Towards a New Modernity*. London: Sage.

Coussee, F. (2009) 'The relevance of youth works history', in C. Verschelden, F. Coussee, T. Van de Walle and H. Williamson (eds), *The History of Youth Work in Europe and its Relevance for Youth Policy Today*. Strasbourg: Council of Europe Publishing, pp. 6–10.

Department for Education and Skills (DfES) (2003) *Every Child Matters*. London: Department for Education and Skills.

Department for Education and Skills (DfES) (2005) *Youth Matters*. London: Department for Education and Skills.

Furlong, A., Cartmel, F., Powney, J. and Hall, S. (1997) *Evaluating Youth Work with Vulnerable Young People*. Glasgow: Scottish Council for Research in Education.

Halpern, R., Barker, G. and Mollard, W. (2000) 'Youth programs as alternative spaces to be: a study of neighbourhood youth programs in Chicago's west town', *Youth and Society*, 31 (4): 469–505.

Jeffs, J. and Smith, M.K. (1994) 'Young people, youth and work and the new authoritarianism', *Youth and Policy* (46): 17–32.

Jeffs, T. and Smith, M.K. (2008) 'Valuing youth work?' *Youth and Policy*, 100: 277–302.

Jeffs, T. and Smith, M.K. (eds) (2010) *Youth Work Practice*. London: Palgrave.

Lepper, J. (2011) 'Local authorities fight to keep integrated youth services universal, research reveals', in *Children and Young People Now*, 6 September. www.cypnow. co.uk (accessed 7 July 2012).

Nuffield Review (2009) *Education for All: The Future of Education and Training for 14–19 Year Olds*. London: Routledge.

Phillips, R. (2010) 'Initiatives to support disadvantaged young people: enhancing social capital and acknowledging personal capital', *Journal of Youth Studies*, 13 (4): 489–504.

Taylor, T. (2009) 'Defending democratic youth work', *Social Work and Society*, 7 (2). www.socwork.net/sws/article/view/79/338 (accessed 7 July 2012).

Van de Walle, T., Coussee, P. and Bouverne-De Bie, M. (2010) 'Social exclusion and youth work: from the surface to the depths of an educational practice', *Journal of Youth Studies*, 14 (2): 219–31.

Walther, A. (2003) 'Empowerment or cooling out? Dilemmas and contradictions of integrated transition policies', in A. Blasco, W. McNeish and A. Walther (eds), *Young People and Contradictions of Inclusion: Towards Integrated Transition Policies in Europe*. Bristol: Policy Press, pp. 183–205.

6
Researching Youth

Although research is a status-laden term, it remains difficult to define. This is because research covers a broad range of activities that can differ in many ways. Research can be used to describe inquiry with the main purpose of contributing to disciplinary knowledge. Equally, research may describe an activity with the main purpose of informing policy-making and practice. Research can involve fieldwork to collect new data (primary data) or it may involve reviewing and appraising data from studies already completed by others (secondary data). Youth research therefore can be undertaken for different purposes and can have different aims. Given these differences youth research is usually described broadly. For example, Alderson and Morrow (2004: 9) define social research with young people as 'broadly, to include any project or process that collects and reports the views and experiences of children and young people'. Youth researchers, like researchers more generally, if they wish to conduct good research, have to be mindful of the relationships between the different aspects of the research design – research question, ethics, theories, methods, data collection, analysis and dissemination. There needs to be a coherent relationship between these elements, and a key part of doing good research is the monitoring of these during the research process.

Youth studies is one of those particular disciplines where the breadth of research purposes and approaches is striking and evident. It can advance understanding of how young people 'develop and live their lives, it can contribute to theoretical debates and its outputs can impact directly and indirectly on the lives of those researched and others in similar situations' (Fraser et al., 2004: 1). For example, within youth studies the discussion of concepts in this book highlights how research with young people has been undertaken by youth researchers to explore **youth transitions** and **youth subcultures**. But research focusing on youth has also been undertaken for all sorts of other reasons and crosses disciplinary boundaries such as **education**, sociology, psychology, health, law and **history**. This research from other disciplines is also often of great interest to youth scholars and sometimes has implications for **social policy** and practices that impact directly and indirectly on young people.

As we discuss elsewhere in this book, youth researchers have developed their work in response to wider social changes to labour markets, welfare policies and attitudes to personal relationships. Hence we see theoretical developments such as 'extended transitions', debates about young people's (in)dependency and ideas of 'young adulthood' (Furlong, 2009: 2) or emerging adulthood (Arnett, 2004). Also other important changes are 'the growth in information and communications technologies together with the influence of the processes of globalisation' (Cieslik, 2003: 2). As we see in the discussion of both **globalisation** and **social networks** within this book these changes 'inevitably have implications for research into youth cultures and identities – more time spent on education and training, greater geographical mobility, the delaying of family formulation, all point to the possibility of a re-shaping of young people's patterns of association and cultural identities' (Cieslik, 2003: 2). Wider developments in social theory attempting to explain these changes have influenced youth research and the methodological approaches they use – for example, the emergence of 'biographical methods' (Cieslik, 2003: 2).

Given the scale of these social and technological changes and their potential influence on young people, it is no coincidence that sponsors of youth research have in the last decade funded many programmes into youth transitions. So, the Fourth, Fifth, Sixth and Seventh Research Framework Programmes of the European Union (i.e. from 1996 to 2013) include a number of youth-related projects – including projects exploring youth transitions (especially from training and education into the labour market), social cohesion and the inclusion of young people, citizenship and participation, and ensuring policy usefulness of key messages from youth research (Feerick, 2009). In the UK from 1996 onwards the Joseph Rowntree Foundation (JRF) (Jones, 2002) sponsored a Young People in Transition Programme and JRF continues to support youth research. At the same time the Economic and Social Research Council (ESRC) also launched a Youth, Citizenship and Social Change Programme. Also, an emphasis on evidence-based policy and practice has added to the need for consultation with young people and this is often undertaken by researchers, for example, in the UK the Green Paper 'Every Child Matters' released in 2003 noted the necessity of involving young people and listening to their views if service improvements were to be attained.

However, while young people have become central to an increasing amount of research, by the start of this new millennium there were very few texts specifically exploring the methodological issues facing youth researchers (Bennett et al., 2003; Heath et al., 2009; Heath and Walker, 2011) – although there were some exceptions such as Coles (2000). There were also a smaller number of texts where authors offered personal reflexive accounts of doing research with young people (Kehily, 2002). But these reflexive accounts and the more general textbooks covering research methods did 'not always reveal the issues which are characteristic of the field of youth studies' (Cieslik, 2003: 1). Traditionally, a way of conceptualising the methodological diversity in youth research has been through the distinction between 'quantitative' and 'qualitative' research approaches, although mixed methods approaches are becoming more popular and the extent of differences between the two approaches is a hot source of debate. Simplifying, quantitative research draws heavily on a 'scientific approach' and involves the collection as objectively as possible of numeric data (via tests and surveys involving structured interviews and questionnaires). Objectivity means the researcher is considered peripheral to data collection and analysis and the researcher will often never meet the young people involved in supplying data. Numerical data are analysed using statistical procedures, first, to test hypotheses about young people – hypotheses being predictions based on existing theory – and second, to explore broad trends and patterns among young people. An example of such quantitative research in youth studies is the Youth Cohort Study.

Qualitative research, on the other hand, is interested in life as it is lived and the meanings young people construct that frame their behaviours and practices (namely their subjective outlook). Qualitative research, therefore, usually involves the collection and analysis of mainly textual data (spoken or written language) through semi- or unstructured interviews, focus groups and observations with young people. The researcher therefore has a direct interaction with the young people involved in the research. Qualitative youth researchers analyse data to develop an explanation about lived experiences and everyday phenomena. They will attempt to ground this explanation in the voice of the young people involved in their research. They use different research designs, popularly ethnography, to research youth subcultures and biography to explore youth transitions. An example of this qualitative and biographical approach is Henderson et al.'s research (2007). A classic example of ethnography is Paul Willis's study, *Learning to Labour* (1977). Interestingly, through asking 'the lads' involved in his research to provide respondent validation of early drafts of his findings, Willis was an early proponent of a more participatory methodology that has become more popular in recent years (Sabo Flores, 2007). Some have suggested that merely combining 'quantitative and qualitative research methods is no longer adequate and research needs to be sensitive to the powerlessness of young people and to become more participatory – doing research with young people rather than on young people' (Roberts, 2003: 13).

The emergence of the European and UK youth research programmes mentioned earlier is evidence of how the 'youth industry' (Coles, 2000) is adding to the range and diversity of youth research. This variety is evidenced in a small number of more recent methodological texts which incorporate a discussion of case studies revealing a diversity of research approaches used with children and young people. Within such texts there is a focus on 'crucial issues' connected to actually planning, doing and disseminating research with young people. These include: involving young people in research and issues of power relations and representation; ethics; data collection and analysis; and dissemination (Heath et al., 2009; Tisdall et al., 2009). It is considered essential that youth researchers take heed of these issues if their 'research is to be in the best interests of … young people themselves' (Fraser et al., 2004: 1). 'A long-standing issue with youth researchers has been how one negotiates between the various parties and their respective interests involved in the research process' (Cieslik, 2003: 3).

There has been a growing recognition of the importance of researchers listening to young people and representing their views accurately. This is said to be key to researchers valuing the rights of young people. This is reflected in the adoption by many researchers of the United Nations Convention on the Rights of the Child that also applies to young people up to eighteen years of age. Therefore, increasingly there has been an attempt to make research inclusive of children and young people. To this end, youth researchers employ several different ethical codes of practice as guides. For example, the Statement of Ethical Practice of the British Sociological Association offers standards to help researchers ensure that the rights of young people are preserved when they become included in research projects (Heath et al., 2009: 24).

However, while ethical practices will strengthen some aspects of the research with young people, 'we cannot take it for granted that participation in research is always in their interests' (Alderson and Morrow, 2004: 7). For example, in youth research there can be a number of parties involved in the research process and each will have their respective interests and exercise their power to influence the research process. The concern is that young people may lack the power to set the research agenda and therefore their 'authentic voice' may not be heard. 'The conflicting interests of different organisations may be very difficult to reconcile, and so the interest of young people (and also the researcher) can be subsumed in a maze of political and ideological debate' (Cieslik, 2003: 4). Moreover, the interests of young people will be neglected if researchers allow for the distancing of 'the products of research from the original research process and the lives of participants' (Cieslik, 2003: 4).

Through the dissemination of research, and in attempts to facilitate engagement of the wider community with research findings, it has been claimed youth researchers have allowed the mass media to influence public opinion by constructing stories based on the 'spectacular lives' of a minority of young people while the more routine existence of the majority is ignored (Kelly, 2000; Roberts, 2011). It is claimed, in this way the work of youth researchers has been used to misrepresent the lives of most young people by the media. This, in turn, is said to have serious implications because media misrepresentations have informed 'policy initiatives that result in punitive forms of regulation and surveillance of young people'. Examples include 'community curfews, new forms of school discipline and policing' (Cieslik, 2003: 5).

Therefore, in attempting to protect the interests of young people and to empower them through research, there has been a call for youth researchers to go beyond token involvement of young people and for them to adopt a participatory paradigm and methodologies (Sabo Flores, 2007: 10). But while there has been support for such a move in theory (Clark, 2004), developing such methodologies has been described as 'a struggle' and it raises several 'challenges' (Pascal and Bertram, 2010: 249). It involves researchers ensuring their 'design is ethically, politically and contextually aware and well piloted' (Pascal and Bertram, 2010: 259). Researchers face the challenge of being reflexive about how they interpret the 'authentic voice' of young people and also when exploring ways to make more effective interpersonal and intrapersonal dialogic processes as part of the research. They need to redistribute power allowing young people to have 'a sense of their strength and rights' (Pascal and Bertram, 2010: 259). Dentith et al. (2009: 165) summarise one such participatory methodology – 'Youth PAR [Participatory Action Research]'. They passionately advocate this methodology and note how it 'beckons us to move beyond inclusion and participation in contemporary research with youth into a new paradigm of meaningful intergenerational research that imagines collaborative, inclusive and empowering research for powerful ways'.

Therefore, issues around power relationships, empowerment and ethics have been central to debates about a more participatory youth research. This reflects repeated rallying cries for methodological innovation in the wider social sciences. Despite the challenges in operationalising the participatory paradigm there is evidence of innovation. For example, Heath and Walker (2011) have identified new methods and approaches which have become increasingly popular in recent years among youth researchers. These include a wide range of imaginative and creative methods – for instance, music elicitation, mental mapping, blog analysis, visual methods, arts-based methods and mobile methods. These methods are being used across broad disciplinary and methodological backgrounds and they all foreground the pervasive influence of participatory and mixed methods approaches within much contemporary youth research (Heath and Walker, 2011).

REFERENCES

Alderson, P. and Morrow, V. (2004) *Ethics, Social Research and Consulting with Young People*. 2nd edn. Ilford: Barnardos.

Arnett, J.J. (2004) *Emerging Adulthood: The Winding Road from the Late Teens through the Twenties*. Oxford: Oxford University Press.

Bennett, A., Cieslik, M. and Miles, S. (2003) (eds), *Researching Youth*. Basingstoke: Palgrave Macmillan.

Cieslik, M. (2003) 'Introduction: contemporary youth research: issues, controversies and dilemmas', in A. Bennett, M. Cieslik, and S. Miles (eds), *Researching Youth*. Basingstoke: Palgrave Macmillan, pp. 1–10

Clark, J. (2004) 'Participatory research with children and young people: philosophy, possibilities and perils', *Action Research Expeditions*, 4: 1–18.

Coles, B. (2000) *Joined-Up Youth Research, Policy and Practice: A New Agenda for Change*. Leicester: Youth Work Press.

Dentith, A.M., Measor, L. and O'Malley, M.P. (2009) 'Stirring dangerous waters: dilemmas for critical participatory research with young people', *Sociology*, 43 (1): 158–68.

Feerick, S. (2009) *European Research on Youth: Supporting Young People to Participate Fully in Society*. Brussels: European Commission: Directorate General for Research.

Fraser, S., Lewis, V., Ding, S., Kellett, M. and Robinson, C. (eds) (2004) *Doing Research With Children and Young People*. London: Sage.

Furlong, A. (ed.) (2009) *Handbook of Youth and Young Adulthood: New Perspectives and Agendas*. London: Routledge.

Heath, S., Brooks, R., Cleaver, E. and Ireland, E. (2009) *Researching Young People's Lives*. London: Sage.

Heath, S. and Walker, C. (eds) (2011) *Innovations in Youth Research*. Basingstoke: Palgrave Macmillan.

Henderson, S., Holland, J., McGrellis, S. and Thomson, R. (2007) *Inventing Adulthoods. A Biographical Approach to Youth Transitions*. London: Sage.

Jones, G. (2002) *The Youth Divide: Diverging Paths to Adulthood*. York: Joseph Rowntree Foundation.

Kehily, M.J. (2002) *Sexuality, Gender and Schooling: Shifting Agendas in Social Learning*. London: Routledge.

Kelly, P (2000) 'Youth as an artefact of expertise: problematising the practice of youth studies in an age of uncertainty', *Journal of Youth Studies*, 3 (3): 301–16.

Pascal, C and Bertram, T. (2010) 'Listening to young citizens: the struggle to make real a participatory paradigm in research with young children', *European Early Childhood Education Research Journal*, 17 (2): 249–62.

Roberts, K. (2003) 'Problems and priorities for the sociology of youth', in A. Bennett, M. Cieslik and S. Miles (eds), *Researching Youth*. Basingstoke: Palgrave Macmillan, pp. 13–28.

Roberts, S. (2011) 'Beyond "NEET" and "tidy" pathways: considering the "missing middle" of youth transition studies', *Journal of Youth Studies*, 14 (1): 21–39.

Sabo Flores, K. (2007) *Youth Participatory Evaluation*. New York: Jossey-Bass.

Tisdall, K., Davies, J. and Gallagher, M. (eds) (2009) *Researching with Children and Young People: Research Design, Methods and Analysis*. London: Sage Publications.

Willis, P. (1977) *Learning to Labour: How Working Class Kids Get Working Class Jobs*. Farnborough: Saxon House.

7
Theorising Youth

A well-known television manufacturer in 2005 used the spectacle of millions of small coloured balls bouncing down the famous hills of San Francisco as a means of advertising its wares (Sony Bravia, 2005). Such an awe-inspiring sight serves as a wonderful metaphor for the complexity of life – each of us like a single ball bouncing into so many others. The difficulty we face as social scientists is trying to make sense of this complexity. The theories we use in youth studies therefore emerge out of this need to make very complex empirical social processes amenable to investigation. Theories can take many different forms. They can be models of reality that abstract from much of the detail of everyday life, explaining the mechanisms behind young people's social identities, **youth cultures** and **transitions** to adulthood and key problems such as poverty and unemployment. Theories can also be much more descriptive, offering insights into relatively mundane features of young people's lives such as their friendship groups and use of technology, for example. Concepts and theories can be inductive – the fruits of research such as the metaphors of transition used by some investigators (Evans and Furlong, 1997) or they may be deductive, created prior to projects that allow youth researchers to interpret the messy world they are researching. Concepts such as social and cultural capital developed by Bourdieu (1986) or the notion of 'fateful moments' used by Giddens (1991: 143) to describe a key turning point in a person's life are examples of theoretical ideas and frameworks that allow researchers to interpret and make meaningful their research with young people.

Youth professionals such as policy-makers, researchers and practitioners are not always explicit about the theories they use but theories inevitably reflect the research design that frames research projects. The sorts of theories that are chosen and how they are used are an expression of the research questions driving projects as well as the political, cultural and biographical characteristics of researchers themselves. It is important to develop the skills that allow you to interrogate how theories work in youth studies as these will enable you to identify the omissions and the biases in the accounts produced by youth studies professionals. In recent decades in the UK, for example, a generation of researchers have been schooled in qualitative approaches producing a wave of ethnographic studies into the biographies and lifestyles of young people (Hodkinson, 2002; Roberts, 2011). Whereas in the USA and parts of Europe there are still strong traditions of large-scale quantitative research into youth transitions (Bradley and Van Hoof, 2005). Such developments have consequences for how youth research has evolved in these different societies. Qualitative research tends to provide very detailed narratives of young people's lives that can emphasise their creativity and agency. Whereas quantitative methods can sometimes generate research that produces accounts where young people appear to be more constrained by the institutions and processes (such as labour markets) that enmesh them in their daily lives. In addition, the organisations that fund youth research (government agencies, charities and businesses) can often set quite narrow limits for research agenda that reflect the immediate political, economic and policy concerns of funders and which can preclude the development of 'alternative' research projects into young people. Much youth research and practice focuses on the 'problems' of young people such as unemployment, delinquency and educational under-achievement, which can marginalise other areas of investigation into the ordinary and mundane experiences of young people (Cieslik, 2003). These biases in youth research, policy and practice may unintentionally contribute to the popular impression of young people's lives as 'problematic' rather than ordinary and mundane.

Since the Second World War there has been considerable development in the theoretical approaches used by youth professionals driven by the growth of youth studies and wider processes of social change and theoretical innovation. One major theme has been the shift from models that conceive young people's lives as heavily structured by economic or cultural forces to ones where more subtle forms of co-option and incorporation are employed. The decades after the war were viewed as ones where class and gender divisions were prominent and the political power of the state could be coercive and oppressive. In more recent decades youth studies have drawn on different theoretical influences to understand the many changes brought by declining cultural traditions, economic restructuring and growing affluence and consumerism that shape young people's lives. As we saw with the fall of communism in Eastern Europe young people have had new freedoms and spaces in which to carve out their identities, yet economic, cultural and moral divisions remain and have similarly been remade in these new times (Roberts et al., 2000). As Western youth have experienced for some time, behind the appearance of choice and personal control in Western consumerist democracies may lie new forms of domination and exploitation. Youth researchers have drawn on the work of Foucault (1991) and others such as Nicolas Rose (1999) and Judith Butler (1997), for example, to understand how state agencies though ostensibly working to promote the welfare of young people may at the same time create forms of monitoring and surveillance that regulate young people's lives (Kelly, 2000). Kelly suggests that state organisations employ forms of language such as 'risk' to construct popular notions of young people that produce policies, practices and outcomes for young people that are marginalising rather than empowering (Kelly, 2009). Hence the language and ideas used by organisations can structure the ways that young people see themselves and the social world. Liz Frost (2001) has used this approach to illustrate how the mass media and state organisations promote normative conceptions of young **bodies** that can lead to forms of body hatred and body dysmorphia among young people. Other researchers have similarly drawn on this critical discourse theory to study the ways that young people's masculinities and **sexualities** and issues such as **disability** and 'difference' are structured in contemporary societies (Allen, 2007; Kehily, 2002). The key development in much of this recent theory is the movement from the focused external control of young people's lives (emanating from the labour market or political forces) to more dispersed forms of power that also work through language and culture to establish forms of self-regulation or oppressive 'technologies of the self' (Rose, 1999).

Since the 1990s one of the most influential theoretical approaches in youth studies has been developed by Beck (1992) and Giddens (1991) around the ideas of risk society and reflexive modernity. Long-term social change linked to globalisation – such as de-traditionalisation, individualisation, de-politicisation and the growth in instrumental rationality – has created societies where people experience their lives much more in terms of personal narratives than through older languages of collective solidarities. Beck talks of 'choice biographies' today rather than older 'normal biographies' where individuals are compelled to reflect on how they might navigate their way through life's journey. The restructuring of the key institutional fabric of families, jobs and communities creates uncertainties around social identities and life course transitions that open up new freedoms and simultaneously create new challenges and dangers. These theories have been used in many studies around the world to examine the changing lives of young people – how transitions to adulthood have moved from structured pathways to navigations (Furlong and Cartmel, 2007) and from predominantly classed social identities to youth identities framed by fluid, consumerist forms of sociability (Miles, 2000). Though some note that Beck has been used in a way that can over-emphasise the creativity and agency of young people, downplaying the role that socio-economic forces continue to have over the lives of the young (Woodman, 2009).

The question that remains is what makes for a good theory when working in youth studies? In one sense the concepts one uses in research need to be appropriate for the overall research design – in other words there needs to be a logical fit between research questions, methods, theory and forms of analysis and dissemination. If one is researching small-scale interaction one might employ more grounded concepts drawn from symbolic interactionism as we see, for example, in the work of Bloomer and Hodkinson (2000) rather than more general theory (such as Beck) that is used by researchers examining broader processes and trends in youth transitions, for example (Heinz, 2009).

Another way in which theory has come to be evaluated in the social sciences in recent years has been in relation to the issue of structure and agency. This debate has emerged as researchers tend to emphasise one set of research questions, theories and methods over others. So, for example, some qualitative projects that focus on youth identities and cultures will highlight the agency of young people, while more quantitative research will emphasise the structuring of young people's lives by social forces. The key point when evaluating youth research is to ask whether the theoretical approaches used have allowed for the analysis of both the active, creative characteristics of individuals and groups as well as the structuring or conditioning powers of social processes such as culture, economics and the moral order. To develop research and to employ theories that emphasise one aspect at the expense of the other may produce research findings which suggest that either young people are overly determined in their lives and have little control over them, or conversely that they are relatively free agents able to remake their lives as they wish without regard to social constraints. Both sorts of accounts are deficient, as they tend to offer inaccurate empirical depictions of how young people live their lives that can have punitive political and policy consequences for the young people themselves (Cieslik, 2001).

As a result of these theoretical concerns many youth studies professionals and research programmes have employed a more holistic, mixed methods approach that synthesises the strengths of different methodological perspectives (Henderson et al., 2007; Jones, 2002; Jones and Wallace, 1992). The work of Bloomer and Hodkinson (2000), for example, has explored young people's learning careers and is an example of research that tries to explore interaction and identities using Goffman's (1963) theories, while at the same placing such concerns in a wider context of structured power relationships that draw on Bourdieu's (1986) concepts of capitals, habitus and fields.

REFERENCES

Allen, L. (2007) 'Young people's agency in sexuality research using visual methods', *Journal of Youth Studies*, 11 (6): 565–78.

Beck, U. (1992) *Risk Society: Towards a New Modernity*. London: Sage.

Bloomer, M. and Hodkinson, P. (2000) 'Learning careers: continuity and change in young people's dispositions to learning', *British Educational Research Journal*, 26 (5): 583–97.

Bourdieu, P. (1986) 'The forms of capital', in J. E. Richardson (ed.), *Handbook of Theory of Research for the Sociology of Education*. New York: Greenwood Press, pp. 241–58.

Bradley, H. and Van Hoof, J. (2005) *Young People in Europe: Labour Markets and Citizenship*. Bristol: Policy Press.

Butler, J. (1997) *The Psychic Life of Power*. Stanford: Stanford Press.

Cieslik, M. (2001) 'Researching youth cultures: some problems with the cultural turn in British Youth Studies', *Scottish Youth Issues Journal*, 2: 27–48.

Cieslik, M. (2003) 'Introduction: contemporary youth research, issues controversies and dilemmas', in A. Bennett, M. Cieslik and S. Miles (eds), *Researching Youth*. Basingstoke: Palgrave Macmillan, pp. 1–10.

Evans, K. and Furlong, A. (1997) 'Metaphors of youth transitions: niches, pathways, trajectories or navigations', in J. Bynner, L. Chisholm and A. Furlong (eds), *Youth, Citizenship and Social Change in a European Context*. Aldershot: Ashgate Press, pp. 17–41.

Foucault, M. (1991) *Discipline and Punish: The Birth of the Prison*. London: Penguin.

Frost, L. (2001) *Young Women and the Body: A Feminist Sociology*. London: Palgrave.

Furlong, A. and Cartmel, F. (2007) *Young People and Social Change: New Perspectives*. 2nd edn. Maidenhead: Open University Press.

Giddens, A. (1991) *Modernity and Self-Identity: Self and Society in the Late Modern Age*. Cambridge: Polity.

Goffman, E. (1963) *Stigma: Notes on the Management of Spoiled Identity*. London: Penguin.

Heinz, W. (2009) 'Youth transitions in an age of uncertainty', in A. Furlong (ed.), *Handbook of Youth and Young Adulthood: New Perspectives and Agendas*. London: Routledge, pp. 3–13.

Henderson, S., Holland, J., McGrellis, S., Sharpe, S. and Thomson, R. (2007) *Inventing Adulthoods: A Biographical Approach to Youth Transitions*. London: Sage.

Hodkinson, P. (2002) *Goth: Identity, Style and Subculture*. Oxford: Berg.

Jones, G. (2002). *The Youth Divide: Diverging Paths to Adulthood*. York: Joseph Rowntree Foundation. www.jrf.org.uk/sites/files/jrf/1842630814.pdf (accessed 2 July 2012).

Jones, G. and Wallace, C. (1992), *Youth, Family and Citizenship*. Buckingham: Open University Press.

Kehily, M.J. (2002) *Sexuality, Gender and Schooling: Shifting Agendas in Social Learning*. London: Routledge.

Kelly, P. (2000) 'Youth as an artefact of expertise', in J. McLeod, and K. Malone (eds), *Researching Youth*. Hobart: Australian Clearing House for Youth Studies, pp. 83–94.

Kelly, P. (2009) *The Risk Society and Young People: Life @ the Intersection of Risk, Economy and Illiberal Governmentalities*. Behavioural Studies Working Paper Series, Monash University. http://arts.monash.edu.au/behaviour/working-papers/documents/bhs-working-paper-2009-02 (accessed 7 July 2012).

Miles, S. (2000) *Youth Lifestyles in a Changing World*. Buckingham: Open University Press.

Roberts, K., Clarke, S., Fagan, C. and Tholen, J. (2000) *Surviving Post-Communism: Young People in the Former Soviet Union*. Cheltenham: Edward Elgar.

Roberts, S. (2011) 'Beyond "NEET" and "tidy" pathways: considering the "missing middle" of youth transition studies', *Journal of Youth Studies*, 14 (1): 21–39.

Rose, N. (1999) *Governing the Soul: The Shaping of the Private Self*. 2nd edn. London: Free Association Books.

Sony Bravia (2005) www.youtube.com/watch?v=oP5J4W5GQ3w (accessed 7 July 2012).

Woodman, D. (2009). 'The mysterious case of the pervasive choice biography: Ulrich Beck, structure/agency, and the middling state of youth', *Journal of Youth Studies*, 12 (3): 243–56.

8
The History of Youth

As we discussed in **definitions of youth,** the concept of youth is culturally and historically specific – young people vary through time and between different societies. A historical perspective can help us to better understand continuity, social change and contemporary issues and problems such as poverty and inequality. A historical focus, as some suggest, 'is perhaps especially important now, with the accelerating pace of cultural change that has taken place around the world in recent decades due to the influence of globalization' (Arnett, 2009: xiv). Yet as Mitterauer (1992: vii) notes, 'the historical study of youth is a relatively new discipline' encompassing a broad focus on social and political history, the study of urban/rural youth and anthropological studies into changing rites and ritual in different cultures. This work documents the role of young people shaping the history of their countries. The Cultural Revolution in China was driven by the activities of the young (Red Guard Groups) from 1965 onwards (Chan et al., 1980: 397). The recent history of the Indian state has been influenced by the young who make up the majority of its population (Chowdhry, 1988).

The concept of youth features in accounts from early Western societies such as ancient Greece (fourth and fifth centuries B.C.), where 'both Plato and Aristotle viewed adolescence as the third distinct stage of life after infancy (birth to age 7) and childhood (ages 7 to 14)' (Arnett, 2009: 5). Adolescence derives from the Latin verb 'adolescere', which means to grow into adulthood. Both Plato and his student Aristotle framed adolescence as extending between the ages of fourteen and twenty-one and both also felt it was the stage of life 'in which the capacity for reason first developed' (Arnett, 2009: 5). Moving on from the classical age, historical records are limited in regard to the Middle Ages but young people feature in incidents such as 'The Children's Crusade' in 1212 – although there is some debate and disagreement about the exact nature of this 'crusade' and the age of those taking part from France and parts of what is now Germany. But it is claimed the 'crusade' was an attempt to appeal to the Muslim population living in what Christians describe as the 'Holy Land' and it was inspired by a

the history of youth

45

belief in the Christian **religion** that Jesus Christ decreed these lands could be settled only through the innocence of youth (Arnett, 2009: 6). Within early English literature the image of youth as an exciting and desirable phase in the life cycle is evident. In his sonnet *The Passionate Pilgrim*, Shakespeare wrote, 'age I do abhor thee, youth I do adore thee'. But in *Twelfth Night* he laments on the shortness of youth – 'youth's a stuff will not endure'.

Up until the Middle Ages the youth phase was 'associated with the ability to be self-sufficient and responsible for others' (Jones, 2009: 3). This understanding of the terms youth and adolescence was therefore based 'on a very different construction from that of the present day' (Jones, 2009: 3). Focusing on early French literature, Aries (1962) noted how during the Middle Ages the conditions of childhood and youth did not exist in the way they are understood within Western societies today. Rather, up until the Middle Ages children – once weaned – and youths were viewed as immature adults. But from the seventeenth century onwards a new ideal of childhood and youth was emerging associated with dependence. This was especially the case with regard to upper-class children and youth (at least the males) as is evident through the development of public schools in England – specialist institutions set up to cultivate the 'elite'.

For the majority of children, coming from working-class backgrounds, 'it was not until the nineteenth century, when child protection laws in England began to prohibit child employment and education was extended, that [they] came to be distinguished from dependent adulthood' (Jones, 2009: 3). Several authors therefore connect current understandings of childhood and youth in Western societies to the process of industrialisation that emerged from the eighteenth century onwards (Aries, 1962; Gillis, 1974).

The twentieth century in many respects was the century of young people, where adolescence and the young became more visible (Stainton Rogers, 1997). Growing populations in industrialising societies and expansion of 'welfare capitalism' into education, health and youth justice all focused attention on the place of young people in society (Jones, 2009: 3). The growth of cinema, print media, television and advertising all promote images of young people and the idea of youth. The young are film and pop stars, they model new products and are idealised as visions of beauty, fitness and health. Yet as we grow older we all pay a price for the fetishisation of youth, lamenting this loss of our own youth and struggling fruitlessly to find ways of staying young – through diets, cosmetic surgery and self-help guides.

The young were also the key actors in much of recent history: The young men in their millions who gave their lives in the First and Second World Wars, the countless young civilians caught up in conflict and the tens of millions of young migrants who travelled the world during the century. Young people fleeing from wars, or seeking work, freedoms and a better life are at the heart of much contemporary history – the rise of the USA, the fall of communism, struggles in the Middle East and diasporas from Africa.

In recent decades the young have also been at the heart of debates about social justice and quality of life for citizens in late modernity. As developed societies have de-industrialised and poverty and inequality have grown, so have collapsing opportunities for the young been at the forefront of concerns over the nature of Western capitalism (Brown et al., 2011). Though some have cited over-regulation and the growth in welfare dependency as the root cause of societies' ills and neo-liberal market policies as solutions (Murray, 1990), others have called for social-democratic policies and greater state intervention to ease the burden on youth (Toynbee, 2003).

How best to promote economic growth while ensuring social justice has been a major concern for developing nations during the twentieth century. And so similar arguments about young people's lives and the balance of welfare intervention and market discipline have been played out in the developing nations around the world (Hansen, 2008; Roberts et al., 2000). Here too we see young people, often in the majority, being the engine for social change, progress and conflict. Yet despite the transformations of late modernity there are continuities with the past, with the young in recent times still often portrayed as 'troublesome' or 'at risk' (Griffin, 1997). For example, contemporary concerns over the violence and criminality of gangs in the Brazilian Favelas (Covey, 2010) echo the panics over social unrest seen in nineteenth-century London over its many street gangs (Pearson, 1983). Across the centuries the media of the time from nineteenth-century newspapers to twenty-first-century websites made much of the trials and tribulations of young people and the threats they posed to themselves and the rest of society.

REFERENCES

Aries, P. (1962) *Centuries of Childhood*. New York: Vintage Books.

Arnett, J.J. (2009) *Adolescence and Emerging Adulthood*. 3rd edn. London: Pearson Education Limited.

Brown, P. Lauder, H. and Ashton, D. (2011) *The Global Auction: The Broken Promises of Education, Jobs and Incomes*. Oxford: Oxford University Press.

Chan, A., Rosen, S. and Unger, J. (1980). 'Students and class warfare: the social roots of the Red Guard Conflict in Guangzhou (Canton)', *The China Quarterly*, 83: 397–446.

Chowdhry, D.P. (1988) *Youth: Participation and Development*. Delhi: Atma Ram.

Covey, H. (2010) *Street Gangs Throughout the World*. 2nd edn. Springfield, IL: Charles C. Thomas Publishing.

Gillis, J. (1974) *Youth and History: Tradition and Change in European Age Relations 1770–Present*. New York: Academic Press.

Griffin, C. (1997) 'Representations of the young', in J. Roche, and S. Tucker (eds), *Youth in Society*. London: Sage, pp. 10–18.

Hansen, G. (2008) *Youth and the City in the Global South*. Indiana: Indiana University Press.

Jones, G. (2009) *Youth*. Cambridge: Polity Press.

Mitterauer, M. (1992) *A History of Youth*. Oxford: Blackwell Publishers.

Murray, C. (1990) *The Emerging British Underclass*. London: Institute of Economic Affairs.

Pearson, G. (1983) *Hooligan: A History of Respectable Fears*. London: Macmillan.

Roberts, K., Clark, S., Fagan, C. and Tholen, J. (2000) *Surviving Post-Communism: Young People in the Former Soviet Union*. Cheltenham: Edward Elgar.

Stainton Rogers, R. (1997) 'The making and moulding of modern youth: a short history', in J. Roche and S. Tucker (eds), *Youth in Society*. London: Sage, pp. 1–19.

Toynbee, P. (2003) *Hard Work: Life in Low Pay Britain*. London: Bloomsbury Press.

9
Young People, Divisions and Inequality

The study of young people by social scientists invariably involves the investigation of social divisions and inequality. The enduring, structured patterns of experiences in society that frame the identities and life chances of young people are at the heart of many of the debates in youth studies. Very often researchers regard social divisions and inequality as pathological as they have a deleterious effect on quality of life – they are social problems that need to be reduced. Wilkinson and Pickett (2009) point to how growing differences in the income and wealth within societies is associated with poorer health and educational outcomes for young people. Though some suggest that many social divisions are inevitable and reflect the competitive ethos of capitalist societies – some of their more harmful aspects may be reduced but not eradicated. Researchers focus on the economic, cultural and social engines of divisions often understood in relation to social class, gender, 'race', sexuality and ethnicity and concepts such as discrimination, prejudice and exclusion (Braham and Janes, 2002: xi). In the key institutional domains of society (such as education, family, leisure and employment) young people will come up against powerful forces that condition their lives, limiting some avenues of action while enabling others. Young people themselves are sometimes conscious of these conditioning processes and work against them to manage and subvert these constraints as they pursue their own projects. There are usually divisions between youths and older citizens but there are also cultural, social and economic differences between young people globally, between young people who live in different parts of the world. The study of social divisions then raises important questions about the different sorts of lives lived by different groups of youths, the causes of these divisions and how young people themselves and government policy are implicated in the enduring patterns of difference. Public policies and the strategies of the young may at times work to mitigate the negative consequences of inequalities and divisions, though at others these same forces are intimately implicated in the processes of domination – where some enjoy privileged lives while others suffer exclusion and disadvantage.[1]

Researchers have focused much attention on the ways economic divisions are produced leading to structured patterns of youth inequality within and between different societies. In affluent societies the incidence of youth poverty and social exclusion has been examined illustrating the vulnerability of young people to unemployment and under-employment. In the USA, UK and other Western European countries during the recent recession (2008 onwards) unemployment for those aged between sixteen and twenty-four was twice the rate for adults at over 20 per cent (Eurostat, 2009; Institute for Employment Studies, 2009; United States Department of Labour, 2009). More recent data show youth unemployment rates in Europe reaching between 30 and 40 per cent (Eurostat, 2010). Research points to how even before the recent recession the flexible labour market policies across Europe were polarising **employment** experiences for young people, with some doing well and many others subject to poor quality, vulnerable jobs (Bradley, 2005: 101). Evidence points to how early experience of educational underachievement and unemployment can have a lasting effect on life chances and identities, leading to further problems such as mental and physical ill health, drug use and **homelessness**. Important longitudinal research in the UK (Thomson, 2011) and Canada (Anisef et al., 2000) illustrates the relatively predictable relationships between childhood experiences of poverty and subsequent transitions into poor quality jobs and social and cultural disadvantage as adults. Youth researchers therefore raise some difficult questions about the responsibility of state agencies to support young people in their **transitions** to adulthood. However, in many affluent societies recently the prevailing neo-liberal policies have created relatively punitive approaches to young people that have tended to blame youth themselves for their disadvantage, offering only limited support for long-term training and employment initiatives (Mizen, 2004; Savelsberg and Martin-Giles, 2008). One consequence of this may be the marked increase in the incidence of mental health problems among young people and the continuing problems with long-term unemployment, homelessness and drug use in many societies (*The Guardian*, 2010). In all of these cases there is the suggestion that the state is doing too little to mitigate the deeply ingrained patterns of disadvantage associated with economic and cultural divisions.

In this context of the social and economic marginalisation of many young people, governments have developed forms of surveillance and control of young people's activities that reflect concerns (moral panics) about youth **crime** and deviance. In the UK, for example, there has been the expansion of the use of closed circuit television (CCTV), stop and search powers and anti-social behaviour orders to monitor and regulate young people's use of public spaces (Muncie, 2009). These policies, which often infringe on the liberties of young people, together with the continuing media portrayal of young people as 'trouble' suggest very real social and ideological divisions in society between young people and older citizens.

Chatterton and Hollands (2001) document how British cities are increasingly experienced as key sites for the playing out of young people's identities and practices as part of the night-time economy. Different sorts of young people (locals, students, gays, marginal youth) use different parts of the city as their venues and manage the increasingly commercialised nightlife in a multiplicity of ways. Here then we see quite explicit cultural divisions between young people, which have an important spatial dimension. Just as young people from different social backgrounds will live in different communities, so they attend different schools and often pursue different leisure activities and so youth divisions contribute to the wider social segregation often seen in contemporary societies. Such divisions are an obvious source of concern for those keen to promote the creation of tolerant and cohesive societies.

Many of the divisions experienced by young people will occur in their cultural lives, worked through their relationships in various domains and settings such as leisure, school and work. In their daily lives young people's views and experiences are often undervalued or misrecognised and their contribution to wider public debates and issues marginalised by media and government organisations. Recent research by the authors documented the importance of fluency of language use to the ways that young people accomplish the presentation of self in relationships with significant others. Where young people encountered problems with their spoken or written language skills (often originating in poor educational opportunities when young) they often experienced embarrassment, shame and stigma. Over many years such experiences come to shape young people's judgements about their academic abilities and employment prospects, creating subtle psychological barriers to self-advancement and constituting so-called hidden injuries of class (Sennett and Cobb, 1972).

In a similar way Aapola et al. (2005) explored the long-term construction of gendered identities and how young women are bombarded with contradictory messages about 'acceptable' ways of being a young woman – for example, working at appearing attractive to 'fit in' with one's peers yet avoiding being 'too' attractive in case one stand outs and attracts unwanted attention. The **body** is seen as a key site for the representation of gendered identities, and young women are compelled to learn complex practices and scripts that frame acceptable forms of self-identity. There are enduring normative assumptions about heterosexuality and of being able bodied, for example, that frame the language, ideas and practices of young people that can set up at times subtle and at others very conspicuous patterns of division and inequality. Recent research by Croghan et al. (2006) explored some of these issues in relation to style and young people's identities and cultural practices.

Following the work of Steve Miles (2000) they document the increasing significance of **consumerism** to young people's presentation of self and how 'fitting in' with peer group cultures relies on the purchase of key markers of youth identity such as clothes, technology, music and makeup. To be unable to purchase these items because of low income can lead to forms of symbolic and cultural exclusion or 'style failure' and in turn patterns of divisions between youth cultural groupings. In this way economic divisions rooted in socio-economic processes can produce further related cultural divisions. Though being affluent doesn't always ensure popularity – the authors note how young people have to work at 'fitting in', acquiring a sensitivity to group norms so that fluency and skills (humour, for example) or so-called forms of identity capital are also key to understanding youth friendship relations. As with earlier writings in this area, Croghan et al. (2006) document the sustained effort that is required from young people to navigate the complex terrain that are youth identities, peer groups and social practices – much of which involves self-policing and bodily management to ensure compliance with dominant rules of behaviour.

NOTE

1 It is important to acknowledge that social divisions are a feature of human societies. Though often seen as problematic and linked to social injustices, at the same time notions of difference can also be associated with rich cosmopolitan communities that celebrate and promote difference as a marker of healthy societies.

REFERENCES

Aapola, S., Gonick, M. and Harris, A. (2005) *Young Femininity: Girlhood, Power and Social Change*. London: Palgrave.

Anisef, P., Axelrod, P., Baichman-Anisef, E., James, C. and Turrittin, A. (2000) *Opportunity and Uncertainty: Life Course Experiences of the Class of 73*. Toronto: University of Toronto Press.

Bradley, H. (2005) 'Winners and losers: young people in the new economy', in H. Bradley and J. Van Hoof (eds), *Young People in Europe: Labour Markets and Citizenship*. Bristol: Policy Press, pp. 99–114.

Braham, P. and Janes, L. (2002) 'Social differences and divisions: introduction', in P. Braham and L. Janes (eds), *Social Differences and Divisions*. Oxford: Blackwell/Open University, pp. ix–xxii.

Chatterton, P. and Hollands, R. (2001) *Changing Our 'Toon': Youth Nightlife and Urban Change in Newcastle*. Newcastle: Newcastle University Press.

Croghan, R., Griffin, C., Hunter, J. and Phoenix, A. (2006) 'Style failure: consumption, identity and social exclusion', *Journal of Youth Studies*, 9 (4): 463–79.

Eurostat (2009) 'Five million young people unemployed in the EU27 in the First Quarter of 2009', press release, 23 July. http://epp.eurostat.ec.europa.eu (accessed 18 November 2009).

Eurostat (2010) 'Euro area unemployment rate at 10%', press release. http://epp. eurostat.ec.europa.eu/cache/ITY_PUBLIC/3-31032010-BP/EN/3-31032010-BP-EN.PDF (accessed 30 January 2012).

The Guardian (2010) 'Suicide rates on the rise, figures show', 28 January. www.guardian. co.uk/news/datablog/2010/jan/28/suicide-rates-data-ons (accessed 30 January 2012).

Institute for Employment Studies (2009) *The Real Impact of Youth Unemployment*, 14 October. www.employment-studies.co.uk/press (accessed 17 November 2009).

Miles, S. (2000) *Youth Lifestyles in a Changing World*. Buckingham: Open University Press.

Mizen, P. (2004) *The Changing State of Youth*. Basingstoke: Palgrave.

Muncie, J. (2009) *Youth and Crime*. 3rd edn. London: Sage.

Savelsberg, H.J. and Martin-Giles, B.M. (2008) 'Young people on the margins: Australian Studies of Social Exclusion', *Journal of Youth Studies*, 11 (1): 17–32.

Sennett, R. and Cobb, J. (1972) *The Hidden Injuries of Class*. New York: W.W. Norton.

Thomson, R. (2011) *Unfolding Lives: Youth, Gender and Change*. Bristol: Policy Press.

United States Department of Labour (2009) *Employment and Unemployment Among Youth Summary*. www.bls.gov/news.release/youth.nr0.htm (accessed 17 November 2009).

Wilkinson, R. and Pickett, K. (2009) *The Spirit Level: Why Equality Is Better for Everyone*. London: Penguin.

10

Representations of Youth

The ways in which young people are represented – through images and language – can have a powerful effect on the lives of young people as well as wider society. Social scientists are keen to interrogate forms of representation (such as the mass media), as these do not always reflect, in neutral ways, the reality of people's lives. Inevitable processes of interpretation can lead to distortion or bias in modes of representation that may intentionally or unintentionally further the interests of some groups over others (Thompson, 1991). We often think of representation in terms of modern notions of the mass media and how advertising, television, magazines and cinema construct dominant or stereotypical images of young people. However, one can also see the ways that a written and oral culture in the eighteenth and nineteenth centuries produced distinctive images of young people that reflected the concerns of the time and powerfully shaped the lives of youth. For example, Pearson (1983) notes how street youths in England during the late nineteenth century were often seen as symbols of the wider unruly, lower orders who were often violent, intoxicated and criminal, threatening the order of more civilised society. The term hooligan was coined in 1898 after one bank holiday in London led to many male youths being brought before the courts for disorderly behaviour and drunkenness (Pearson, 1983: 74). Such representations, Pearson suggests, were more a function of the anxieties of the affluent in society rather than an accurate depiction of the poor. Pearson suggests how this misrepresentation of the lives of disadvantaged young people seems a common theme in modern societies. Writing during the early 1980s when the popular press were whipping up alarm over the social unrest in many British cities, he notes how the modern anxieties over moral and social decline echo those made repeatedly since the nineteenth century. Common to all of these examples are the ways that the spotlight on the aberrant behaviour of a minority of young people are taken as representative of youth more generally and seen to herald the advent of a wider moral and social decline. Young people are often constructed by nostalgic adults as harbingers of unwelcome social change and blamed for the loss of a traditional comfortable way of life.

Mannheim (1952) and Talcott Parsons (1942) locate this emergence of generational conflict in the widely differing socialisation that different age groups experience. Key to their analysis was the profound shift in Western societies that resulted from the experiences of the First World War. Those that had lived through the war were forever marked by its horrors yet those born after it were immersed in new possibilities, hopes and ideas. There different experiences sowed the seeds of cultural tensions between the generations during the 1920s and 1930s. This was a pattern of experience and social change leading to generational conflict that was echoed just a few short decades later following the 1939–1945 war. For the young people of the late 1950s and 1960s who had never known war these former conflicts were just history and their lives of growing aspirations, music and consumerism seemed very alien to the older 'war generations'. It is this social and cultural dissonance between the generations rooted in different experiences that for many sociologists explain why it is that young people are so often represented as threatening or troublesome or radical.

The history of the representation of youth shows commons themes of how the young are often seen in pejorative ways as the source of 'trouble' and in need of control or as the victims of 'trouble' and in need of protection. Researchers highlight how these pathological depictions of youth, though often presented as neutral, factual accounts of reality, contain subtle and often not so subtle messages that can shape public opinion, policy agendas and wider cultural understandings in society. Significantly this circulation of distinctive ideas about young people can have a profound impact on the life chances and social identities of young people themselves. Jock Young (1971) famously explored this impact of media representations on young people, noting how the growing power of the mass media coupled with increasing social segregation means that people today are much more likely to be influenced by mediazed accounts of young people than in earlier times. Stan Cohen's (1973) seminal work on the moral panics and folk devils around Mods and Rockers fighting on the beaches during bank holidays in England classically illustrates the process by which young people are portrayed and the wider effects of such representations. These moral panics usually involve the exaggerated depiction of youth activities as threatening, which prompts the intervention of a moralising discourse from authority figures and mobilisation of expert commentators and then the development of new laws and initiatives aimed at solving this 'youth problem' (Critcher, 2003: 9). In recent years we have seen numerous examples of such moral panics in action. Critcher identifies the murder of Jamie Bulger as a case in point, where the two children responsible for the crime were said to have been influenced by watching so-called 'video nasties'. Following this incident there was a media campaign that focused on the growing threat of violent films to the young and the apparent link between such media and the purported rise in the incidence of violent crimes in the UK (Thomas, 2005). At the time of writing there are other moral panics in the UK centred on the threat posed by youth gangs and the carrying of knives and the links with supposed rising levels of violent offences in many British cities (*The Guardian*, 2012).

Many studies of media representations draw on neo-Marxian theories of ideology (Abercrombie et al., 1980) and particularly the concept of hegemony. This understands the production of media images as reflecting the underlying, unequal power relationships in capitalist societies. Hence the biased images, particularly of working-class young people, originate in the control that the affluent have over media production and their use of such agencies to protect their economic and political interests. Young people themselves are powerless to challenge the popular construction of working-class youth as 'trouble' and 'threatening' to the social order as it is others who set the media agenda and control the mass media. Hall et al.'s book, *Policing the Crisis* (1978) illustrates this approach, combining a neo-Marxian analysis with the deviancy amplification models developed by writers such as Cohen (1973). As with other moral panics the media furore over a relatively small number of offences committed by black youths elicited calls from the media and other commentators to get 'tough on crime', which led to increasing police regulation of black youths (through stop and search practices) and harsher sentences for youth offenders. Though such 'get tough' policies may themselves then amplify deviance, Hall et al. were also keen to present the 'mugging crisis' as a wider political struggle where the capitalist state is using its powers to manage potential challenges to its authority.

More recently writers have drawn on the work of Foucault (1979) and Baudrillard (1983) to understand the working of media representations suggesting that power is much more dispersed through language and culture and creates a much more fragmented yet still inequitable patterning of representations than theorised in earlier neo-Marxist accounts. Christine Griffin (1993) uses Foucault's notion of discourses to describe the ways that distinctive forms of language and culture come to define the ways in which society and young people can conceptualise the youth phase. How young people relate to one another, explore intimate relationships and understand their classed, gendered and racialised identities are all made possible through the language operating in societies. Such lingual tools set limits to what is possible for young people to think and do and so the opportunities that young people have to realise their potential – their **employment**, **leisure**, families and relationships – can be enabled and constrained by the operation of power through ideas and language.

In recent years researchers have developed ways of understanding how information technology such as the Internet, mobile phones and computer games can impact on the ways that young people are represented (Lui, 2011). There are familiar moral panics about the influence that the content of these technologies may have on young people's identities and behaviour that echo those earlier concerns seen in the nineteenth and twentieth century (Mesch and Talmud, 2010). Hence the prevalence of pornography and violence online has prompted calls for greater monitoring and regulation of children's access to this material. Websites that promote unrealistic or idealised ways of living are also seen as problematic and a possible threat to young people's way of life. Researchers have documented, for example, the growth in the popularity of 'Pro-Ana' sites that promote dieting and their links to conditions such as anorexia and bulimia (Halse et al., 2008). There has also been much commentary on the proliferation of a 'celebrity culture' across the mass media and how this can have a deleterious influence on the lives of young people, creating unrealistic materialist expectations of life (Cashmore, 2006).

REFERENCES

Abercrombie, N., Hill, S. and Turner, B.S. (1980) *The Dominant Ideology Thesis*. London: Harper Collins.

Baudrillard, J. (1983) *Simulations*. Boston: MIT Press.

Cashmore, E. (2006) *Celebrity Culture*. London: Routledge.

Cohen, S. (1973) *Folk Devils and Moral Panics*. St Albans: Paladin.

Critcher, C. (2003) *Moral Panics and the Media*. Milton Keynes: Open University Press.

Foucault, M. (1979) *Discipline and Punish: The Birth of the Prison*. New York: Vintage, Random House.

Griffin, C. (1993) *Representations of Youth: The Study of Youth and Adolescence in Britain and America*. Cambridge: Polity Press.

The Guardian (2012) 'Gang expert and police commander warn of "toxic expansion"', 26 January. www.guardian.co.uk/society/2012/jan/26/gangs-toxic-expansion-warning (accessed 30 January 2012).

Hall, S., Critcher, C., Jefferson, T. Clarke, J. and Roberts, B. (1978) *Policing the Crisis: Mugging, the State and Law and Order*. London: Macmillan.

Halse, C., Honey, A. and Boughtwood, D. (2008) *Inside Anorexia: The Experiences of Girls and their Families*. Philadelphia: Jessica Kinglsey.

Lui, F. (2011) *Urban Youth in China: Modernity, the Internet and the Self*. London: Routledge.

Mannheim, K. (1952) 'The problem of generations', in P. Kecskemeti (ed.), *Essays on the Sociology of Knowledge by Karl Mannheim*. New York: Routledge and Kegan Paul (1st edn 1927).

Mesch, G. and Talmud, I. (2010) *Wired Youth: The Social World of Adolescence in the Information Age*. London: Routledge.

Parsons, T. (1942) 'Age and sex in the social structure of the United States', *American Sociological Review*, 7, October: 604–16.

Pearson, G. (1983) *Hooligan: A History of Respectable Fears*. London: Macmillan.

Thomas, M. (2005) *Every Mother's Nightmare: The Killing of Jamie Bulger*. 2nd edn. London: Pan Books.

Thompson, J.B. (1991) *Ideology and Modern Culture: Critical Social Theory in the Era of Mass Communication*. Stanford: Stanford University Press.

Young, J. (1971) *The Drug Takers: The Social Meaning of Drug Taking*. London: Paladin.

Major Concepts, Issues and Debates

11
Young People and Leisure

Young people in most societies tend to have more leisure time than adults so how young people use their free time has been the subject of much research. Leisure is usually understood as that free time outside of the obligatory activities (such as formal education, domestic work and responsibilities and waged employment) that structure young people's lives (Roberts, 1983). Leisure activities for young people are important as they are often seen as playing a key role structuring the later life course **transitions**, social identities and **youth cultures** of adolescents (Hendry, 1983). The emergence then of distinctive classed, racialised and gendered adult selves is seen to flow in part from the activities, interests and relationships that make up young people's leisure pursuits. The patterning of opportunities and resources that are so important for the routes that we take through life can also be traced to these earlier leisure activities. As we go on to show, social scientists suggest that leisure activities can have both positive and negative influences; helping to foster interpersonal skills and **informal learning** on the one hand or promoting anti-social behaviour and delinquency on the other. Much research has focused on trying to understand the causes of these different outcomes from leisure activities and how **policy** and professional practice might influence young people's leisure. A further theme in leisure research documents the long-term commercialisation of leisure and how this contributes to processes of individualisation in contemporary societies (Furlong and Cartmel, 2007: 72; Rojek, 1985). Leisure can be a key way young people develop a unique sense of self but one that involves consumerist lifestyles that generate huge profits for global corporations.

The work of thinkers such as Freud, Mead and Piaget all stressed the significance of free time and play to cognitive development and so many commentators viewed the expansion of young people's leisure during the twentieth century as a positive development. The growth in incomes, consumption and changing patterns of employment also contributed to post-war debates about the emergence of a leisure society (Davis, 1990; Rojek, 2009: 21). The discussion during this period was that new free time available to young people allowed for their experimentation with new counter-cultural ways of life that gave rise to Psychedelic and Hippy subcultures in the 1960s. Involvement in new forms of music, drugs, politics and style during this time all hinged on the expansion of leisure opportunities for some young people. Seminal studies in the social sciences documented the lives of young people's leisure, where the street corner (Whyte, 1993), home (Deem, 1986) and youth club (McRobbie, 1978) are the locus of distinctive youth peer relations and socio-cultural identities. Early studies documented different leisure activities because of class background – the wider more varied and consumerist pursuits of affluent youth contrasted with the less commercialised and narrower activities of working-class youth (Clarke and Critcher, 1985: 177; Roberts, 1999). Researchers also documented how young women tended to occupy domestic spaces listening to music with friends and reading while males spent more time outside of the home playing sports and 'hanging out' with friends on the street (Deem, 1986; Frith, 1978). Hendry et al. (1993) noted that around three quarters of boys (aged thirteen to twenty) played sport each week whereas less than half of girls did. The authors suggest such differences originate in boys associating competitive sport with emerging masculine identities while many young women see such sports as unfeminine. Studies of sports activities illustrate the role of football in particular in the UK underpinning patterns of socialisation where young males acquire a sense of local and class cultural identity and are introduced to the drinking and physical violence that is often associated with working-class masculinities (Nayak, 2003). Studies have also noted the changing pattern of leisure activities as children mature into young people and into adulthood – moving from organised activities when young through to casual and commercialised leisure as teenagers and young adults (Hendry, 1983). When young, children tend to be supervised by adults, involved in structured leisure moving to more independent peer-based pursuits as young teens and into more commodified activities as they approach adulthood, shaped by the onset of intimate relationships and increasing disposable income.

In recent decades there have been several themes to research in young people's leisure. There has been the continuing concern and moral panics about the ways young people occupy public spaces – the street, shopping precincts and parks. The media often document the incidence of substance misuse (alcohol, drugs, smoking), violence and anti-social behaviour associated with young people's use of free time in public spaces (France, 2009). Attention has focused not only on the problems that young people may cause for residents but also for themselves in terms of health problems and the possible drift into youth offending. In the UK governments have introduced much more punitive policing and criminal justice approaches to young people, lowering the age of criminal responsibility and employing street surveillance such as CCTV and street warden schemes (Newburn and Hayman, 2002). Commentators have suggested that young people's use of drink and drugs in their leisure time may simply be reflecting wider changes in society and the shift to more liberal attitudes towards such behaviours. The growth in the night-time economy in the UK together with relatively cheap alcohol from supermarkets have also fuelled what some see as a predictable increase in young people's misuse of alcohol (Chatterton and Hollands, 2001; Hall and Winlow, 2006).

Some research has also suggested that shifts in Western culture and changing notions of masculinity and femininity have impacted on young people's leisure participation. Research has pointed to greater numbers of children and young people developing more home-based leisure interests with the growth of computer technology (Livingstone, 2003). Most young people now spend several hours a day surfing the web and playing TV and computer games and less time in more traditional sports-based pursuits (ONS, 2005). Predictable concerns have been raised by researchers about the growth of this more sedentary way of life and the associated health problems this may bring to new generations of young adults. Data in Western societies show an increasing number of young people and adults with obesity and weight-related health problems such as diabetes. In the USA, for example, almost 20 per cent of children and young people are obese – the suggestion being that such problems in part are associated with the sedentary lives of young people today (Ogden and Carroll, 2010).

Sweeting and West (2003) also point to significant numbers of young women now spending more time outside of the home, involved in street-based free time activities compared to earlier generations of young women. Free of the surveillance that frames domestic activities the authors point to increased alcohol and smoking among young women. Griffin et al. (2009) have also suggested greater numbers of young women are now using pubs and clubs and drinking greater amounts of alcohol than in the past – forms of adolescent behaviour that tended to be associated more with male rituals of growing up than those of young women. Such research poses some interesting questions, as one might suggest that the breakdown of traditional gendered leisure pursuits offer greater equality for women to experience public leisure pursuits. Or conversely, one might argue that the greater misuse of drink and the risks that this brings should not be applauded as young women are mimicking the least desirable aspects of an old fashioned muscular masculinity. The mass media have also documented how alcohol misuse can be linked to incidences of young women's vulnerability to assault and violent offences (*The Guardian*, 2012). There is the question therefore about the balance between greater freedoms to enjoy leisure and the increase in risk and wider social costs (such as anti-social behaviour) associated with these freedoms.

Commentators also point to an expansion of leisure opportunities promoted through various government policies in the UK. Aiming High schemes and funding such as the Youth Opportunities Fund have encouraged many more young people, particularly from disadvantaged backgrounds, to participate in a wider range of leisure activities (DCSF, 2009). The Cultural Olympiad associated with the 2012 Olympic Games in the UK also promoted widespread participation in leisure and cultural activities for young people between 2010 and 2012 (Cultural Olympiad, 2012). Many of these recent initiatives drew on technological advances such as Facebook, Twitter and other online technologies to encourage young people to engage in drama, video, music and dance projects. Though often designed as simply fun activities these projects also offered deeper, creative possibilities for young people to explore their social identities, relationships with peers and their place in the world (Arts Council England, 2011).

Nevertheless, at the same time surveys also point to the fact that many young people from poorer backgrounds are experiencing relatively narrow leisure careers, where 'hanging about doing nothing' is a key component together with watching significant amounts of TV and watching sport (MacDonald and Marsh, 2005). Though commentators talk of the transformative potential of recent social change to impact positively on young people's leisure careers, there is much evidence that points to the persistence of quite traditional patterns of leisure participation that are structured by class, gender, 'race' and region.

REFERENCES

Arts Council England (2011) *West Midlands Culture Programme for London 2012*. Birmingham: Arts Council England.

Chatterton, P. and Hollands, R. (2001) *Changing Our 'Toon': Youth, Nightlife and Urban Change in Newcastle*. Newcastle: Newcastle University Press.

Clarke, J. and Critcher, C. (1985) *The Devil Makes Work: Leisure in Capitalist Britain*. London: Macmillan.

Cultural Olympiad (2012) www.london2012.com/cultural-olympiad (accessed 7 July 2012).

Davis, J. (1990) *Youth and the Condition of Britain: Images of Adolescent Conflict*. London: Continuum Press.

Deem, R. (1986) *'All Work and No Play?' The Sociology of Women and Leisure*. Milton Keynes: Open University Press.

Department for Children, Schools and Families (DCSF) (2009) *Aiming High for Young People*. London: DCSF.

France, A. (2009) 'Young people and anti-social behaviour', in A. Furlong (ed.), *Handbook of Youth and Young Adulthood: New Perspectives and Agendas*. London: Routledge, pp. 430–35.

Frith, S. (1978) *The Sociology of Rock*. London: Constable.

Furlong, A. and Cartmel, F. (2007) *Young People and Social Change: New Perspectives*. 2nd edn. Maidenhead: Open University Press.

Griffin, C., Bengry-Howell, A., Hackley, C., Mistral, W. and Szmigin, I. (2009) '"Every time I do it I absolutely annihilate myself": loss of (self)-consciousness and loss of memory in young people's drinking narratives', *Sociology*, 43 (3): 457–76.

The Guardian (2012) 'Enduring myths about rape victims lead to acquittals', 30 January. www.guardian.co.uk/society/2012/jan/30/rape-victims-acquittals-chief-prosecutor (accessed 7 July 2012).

Hall, S. and Winlow, S. (2006) *Violent Night: Urban Leisure and Contemporary Culture*. London: Berg.

Hendry, L. (1983) *Growing Up and Going Out: Adolescents and Leisure*. Aberdeen: Aberdeen University Press.

Hendry, L., Shucksmith, J., Love, J.G. and Glendinning, A. (1993) *Young People's Leisure and Lifestyles*. London: Routledge.

Livingstone S. (2003) 'Children's use of the Internet: reflections on an emerging research agenda', *New Media and Society*, 5 (2): 147–66.

MacDonald, R. and Marsh (2005) *Disconnected Youth? Growing Up in Britain's Poor Neighbourhoods*. London: Palgrave Macmillan.

McRobbie, A. (1978) 'Working class girls and the culture of femininity', in Women's Studies Group: Centre for Contemporary Cultural Studies, University of Birmingham, *Women Take Issue: Aspects of Women's Subordination*. London: Hutchinson, pp. 96–108.

Nayak, A. (2003) *Race, Place and Globalisation: Youth Cultures in a Changing World*. Oxford: Berg.

Newburn, T. and Hayman, S. (2002) *Policing, Surveillance and Social Control: CCTV and Police Monitoring of Suspects*. Cullopton: Willan Publishing.

Ogden, C. and Carroll, M. (2010) *The Prevalence of Obesity Among Children and Adolescents. United States Trends 1963–65 through 2007–08*. www.cdc.gov/nchs/data/hestat/obesity_child_07_08/obesity_child_07_08.pdf (accessed 7 July 2012).

ONS (2005) *Social Trends 35*. London: Office for National Statistics.

Roberts, K. (1983) *Youth and Leisure*. London: George Allen and Unwin.

Roberts, K. (1999) *Leisure in Contemporary Society*. Wallingford: CABI Publishing.

Rojek. C. (1985) *Capitalism and Leisure Theory*. London: Routledge.

Rojek, C. (2009) *The Labour of Leisure*. London: Sage.

Sweeting, H. and West, P. (2003) 'Young people's leisure and risk-taking behaviours: changes in gender patterning in the West of Scotland during the 1990s', *Journal of Youth Studies*, 6 (4): 391–412.

Whyte, W.F. (1993) *Street Corner Society: The Social Structure of an Italian Slum*. 4th edn. Chicago: University of Chicago Press.

12
Youth and Crime

Social scientists tend to make the distinction between crime and deviance, where the former is understood as acts that contravene legal principles that govern behaviour (using hard drugs, for example) and the latter as acts that contravene moral or cultural rules of behaviour (wearing outlandish clothes or sporting a facial tattoo). Such simple distinctions become more complicated when we acknowledge that the power of the media, politicians, law enforcement agencies and public opinion can greatly influence how these categories are constructed. The media focuses attention on violent crime against the person, though in England and Wales it only accounts for around 6 per cent of recorded offences, and although 60 per cent of indictable crime is committed by people over twenty-one years of age, the media focuses a great amount attention on youth offending (Muncie, 1999: 14). More recent surveys suggest that around 20 per cent of recorded crimes in England and Wales involve violence against the person and 40 per cent of first time offenders are young adults (Natale, 2010: 2). In other countries such as the USA surveys suggest that though significant numbers of young people are involved in offending they make up a minority of those arrested – 16 per cent of arrests for violent crimes and 26 per cent for property crimes in 2008 (CDC, 2010: 2). Nevertheless despite these data there are regular moral panics about rising youth crime (*The Telegraph*, 2008), which result in the general public developing inaccurate perceptions of the incidence of youth offending. Recent examples in the UK have centred on youth gangs and knife crime, whereas overall incidents of knife crime were falling against a media campaign that suggested significant increases in young people using knives against each other (British Crime Survey, 2008; Silvestri et al., 2009).

Around 40 per cent of indictable offences in England and Wales are committed by young people under twenty-one years of age and some three quarters are committed by males (Muncie, 1999: 14). The majority of offences involved theft and handling stolen property. One international study of crime found that in England and Wales incidents of young people (aged fourteen to sixteen) convicted or cautioned for a violent crime rose from 360 per 100,000 in 1986 to 580 per 100,000 in 1994 but, like crime more generally in the UK and other societies, youth offending fell after 1994 (NACRO, 2003; Pitts, 2008). Though as Pitts (2008) notes, citing data from the 1992 British Crime Survey that uses qualitative interviews with householders, the spatial distribution of crime has been changing with a greater concentration in poorer areas in UK. Hence those living in disadvantaged areas of the UK now run a far greater risk of victimisation, particularly for offences against the person and property than those who reside in more affluent parts of the UK.

Youth researchers, the media and government alike have an interest in youth crime as it is connected to wider debates about the 'health' of society and around ideas of social order, regulation and integration. The incidence of delinquency therefore is seen as a marker of a dysfunctional society and as an index of social and moral decline involving assumptions about youth offenders developing careers as adult criminals. The focus by commentators in the press and government is inevitably on patterns of working-class offending and so reflects the **class** biases in the representations and construction of youth crime in contemporary societies (White, 2009).

There are influential psychological perspectives in youth studies that understand youth crime in relation to the developmental process in adolescence. Young people's identity formation and the storm and stress of maturation have been seen to make young people vulnerable to delinquency (Rutter et al., 1998). The youth stage affords young people the **leisure** time to experiment with different friends, behaviour and interests and with it the chance to test the boundaries of deviance and criminality. Classic social science accounts of delinquency have also focused on the social disorganisation (poor housing and low incomes) of urban areas as a breeding ground for youth offending (Park and Burgess, 1925), or the emergence of street gang culture in disadvantaged areas as the basis for delinquency (Shaw and McKay, 1942). Others such as Merton (1938) employed the Durkheimian concept of anomie in youth offending, where expectations that young people have of pursuing a 'good life' are dashed by the reality of poor opportunities for many young people in poor urban areas of industrial societies. One way in which young people manage such a mismatch between aspirations and legitimate opportunities is to adapt to poor opportunities by creating 'alternative' criminal careers that offer a route into some form of adult way of life. This form of cultural innovation to structural problems of poverty developed by Merton influenced later subcultural theories of delinquency that explored the complex values and peer group relationships of young people's deviance and criminality (Cloward and Ohlin, 1961; Cohen, 1955; Matza, 1964). Later research pointed to the power of the state and social organisations (such as the media and businesses) to construct definitions of youth crime and how the process of labelling can occur so that crime appears as an objective neutral process but is in reality reflective of unequal power relationships in societies that are biased against the working classes and young people in particular (Becker, 1963; Lemert, 1967).

The 1970s witnessed the development of a radical criminology that combined the work of Interactionist and Marxist thinking to argue that capitalist societies inevitably position young working-class people and ethnic minorities as potential offenders (Hall et al., 1978; Parker, 1974; Taylor et al., 1973). Industrial societies for the most part create poor opportunities for many working-class young people and the criminal justice system defines most crime as a working-class phenomenon – under such circumstances it is hardly surprising that many working-class youth come to be labelled as deviant and delinquent. These accounts then are more interested in the criminalisation process in contrast to earlier positivist criminology that understood crime in terms of the causes of offending behaviour. The 1970s also witnessed feminist writers examining **gender** relationships and criminality, whereby the power of males in societies was seen to account for the incidence of violent crimes against women and also the way that such crimes were often rendered invisible (Millet, 1970; Oakley, 1972). These writers spoke of the ways that violent behaviour of men was often excused as it was seen as an inevitable feature of masculinity. In recent decades others (Barry, 2006) have drawn on concepts of masculinity developed by Connell (1995) to account for the patterning of crime as the loss of traditional male employment in affluent societies has prompted a 'crisis in masculinity'.

Over the last twenty years the dominance of neo-liberal philosophies has meant that many governments and the mass media have created a climate whereby increasingly young people's behaviour is viewed as problematic and risky. In contrast to radical criminology that was sympathetic to the plight of impoverished young people in de-industrialising societies, writers such as Charles Murray (1984; 1990) sought to shift responsibility for youth offending in the USA and UK onto young people and their families. He argues that the collapse of working-class job opportunities and expansion of welfare dependency has created a generation of young people culturally distinct from their working-class ancestors, who see it as morally acceptable to become single parents and who pursue 'alternative careers' in the informal economy, drugs and petty crime.

Criminal justice policy in recent decades has similarly focused on the issue of young people's responsibility for their behaviour rather than the structural processes that may condition their actions. The result being an explosion of punitive laws and policing such as the Zero Tolerance schemes established in New York, where once petty offences such as graffiti painting would have gone unnoticed but subsequently became the subject of police interventions. In the UK too, a raft of new measures have been introduced that are aimed at managing the perceived growth in anti-social behaviour among young people (Squires and Stephen, 2005). There are child curfews, dispersal orders, fixed penalties for minor offences and also anti-social behaviour orders. Despite these tougher approaches to youth crime there has been no significant fall in offending and crucially around three quarters of young people convicted in England and Wales reoffend within a year (Natale, 2010: 7). As France (2009: 432) writes, recent criminal justice initiatives blur the boundaries between civil and criminal law and produce a situation whereby young people's freedoms and access to public spaces are being illegally restricted. Instead of maintaining public safety these schemes and laws have created new routes into criminal careers and have contributed to a growing demonisation of young people by the mass media, state agencies and public opinion, constructing **representations of youth** that are at odds with the reality of most young people's lives today.

REFERENCES

Barry, M. (2006) *Youth Offending in Transition*. London: Routledge.

Becker, H. (1963) *Outsiders*. New York: Free Press.

British Crime Survey (2008) *Crime in England and Wales*. London: Home Office.

CDC (2010) *Youth Violence: Facts at a Glance*. Atlanta, GA: Centre for Disease Control and Prevention.

Cloward, R. and Ohlin, L. (1961) *Delinquency and Opportunity: A Theory of Delinquent Gangs*. London: Routledge and Kegan Paul.

Cohen, A. (1955) *Delinquent Boys: The Culture of the Gang*. Glencoe, IL: Free Press.

Connell, R. (1995) *Masculinities*. Cambridge: Polity Press.

France, A. (2009) 'Young people and anti-social behaviour', in A. Furlong (ed.), *Handbook of Youth and Young Adulthood: New Perspectives and Agendas*. London: Routledge, pp. 430–5.

Hall, S., Critcher, C., Jefferson, T., Clarke, J. and Roberts, B. (1978) *Policing the Crisis: Mugging, the State and Law and Order*. London: Macmillan.

Lemert, E. (1967) *Human Deviance, Social Problems and Social Control*. Englewood Cliffs, NJ: Prentice Hall.

Matza, D. (1964) *Delinquency and Drift*. New York: Wiley.

Merton, R. (1938) 'Social structure and anomie', *American Sociological Review*, 3: 672–82.

Millet, K. (1970) *Sexual Politics*. New York: Doubleday Press.

Muncie, J. (1999) *Youth and Crime*. London: Sage.

Murray, C. (1984) *Losing Ground: American Social Policy 1950–1980*. New York: Basic Books.

Murray, C. (1990) *The Emerging British Underclass*. London: Institute of Economic Affairs.

NACRO (2003) *Youth Victimisation: A Literature Review*. Community Safety Practice Briefing. London: NACRO.

Natale, L. (2010) *Factsheet: Youth Crime in England and Wales*. London: Civitas, Institute for the Study of Civil Society.

Oakley, A. (1972) *Sex, Gender and Society*. New York: Harper and Row.

Park, R. and Burgess, E. (1925) *The City*. Chicago: University of Chicago Press.

Parker, H. (1974) *View from the Boys*. Newton Abbot: David and Charles.

Pitts, J. (2008) 'The changing shape of youth crime', *Youth and Policy*, 100: 165–85.

Rutter, M., Giller, H. and Hagell, A. (1998) *Anti-Social Behaviour by Young People*. Cambridge: Cambridge University Press.

Shaw, C.R. and McKay, H.D. (1942) *Juvenile Delinquency and Urban Areas*. Chicago: University of Chicago Press.

Silvestri, A., Oldfield, M., Squires, P. and Grimshaw, R. (2009) *Young People, Knives and Guns: A Comprehensive Review, Analysis and Critique of Gun and Knife Crime Strategies*. Kings College London: Centre for Crime and Justice Studies.

Squires, P. and Stephen, D. (2005) *Rougher Justice: Anti-Social Behaviour and Young People*. Devon: Willan Publishing.

Taylor, L, Walton, P. and Young J. (1973) *The New Criminology*. London: Routledge.

The Telegraph (2008) 'Violent youth crime up a third'. www.telegraph.co.uk/news/uknews/1576076/violent-youth-crime-up-a-third.html (accessed 7 July 2012).

White, R. (2009) 'Young people, crime and justice', in A. Furlong (ed.), *Handbook of Youth and Young Adulthood: New Perspectives and Agendas*. London: Routledge, pp. 444–51.

13
Youth Training

Training is often used in conjunction with **education** and the terms are even sometimes interchanged. But while they both involve learning and the acquisition of knowledge and skills, the two concepts are distinctive and have different meanings. Education is generally considered to be about providing wide-ranging learning with the purpose of inculcating a broad understanding of 'facts', concepts, events, people, things – i.e. declarative knowledge ('knowing what and why') and acquaintanceship knowledge ('knowing who and what') – as well as a critical and self-reflective capacity. However, traditionally, training has a tighter definition and is generally considered to be preparation for specific tasks or roles involving a narrower focus upon the learning of skills that lead to improved competencies (procedural knowledge and 'knowing how to'). As such, many young people have undergone training as preparation for **employment** and during the course of working. Alongside an extension of education, within the UK and in other Western countries, training opportunities have also been increasing dramatically since the 1970s. Ironically given the link mentioned above between training and employment, this coincided with what is regarded as the collapse of the youth labour market from the 1970s onwards. Indeed, training initiatives have become more synonymous with youth unemployment. The term 'training state' has been used to capture these developments and highlights the emerging importance of training as a feature of the transition of many young people from school, particularly those minimum age school leavers at greater risk of unemployment (Mizen, 2004).

A widely promoted policy response to high levels of youth unemployment in Western societies has therefore been the design of 'training schemes' (Dwyer and Wyn, 2001). Although collapsing youth labour markets happened at different times and with varying intensity across Western countries, the labour markets in many of these countries have remained stagnant (Brooks, 2009). Significantly, youths undertaking training are not considered to be officially unemployed and consequently, despite stagnant youth labour markets in many Western societies, youth unemployment rates actually declined from the 1990s onwards as young people took up training opportunities. But there has been a significant rise again over the last few years in youth unemployment as a further economic downturn has materialised and so youth unemployment has risen across Europe. The German Statistical Office figures reveal how, in total, 20.5 per cent of young people between fifteen and twenty-four were seeking work across the twenty-seven nation states making up the European Union by August 2011. This rose from 15.7 per cent in the summer of 2008. This overall percentage though masks significant differences between nations – for example, by the summer of 2011 there was 46 per cent in Spain, 27 per cent in Ireland and 20 per cent in the UK (Federal Statistical Office, 2012). In this gloomier context training initiatives continue to be seen as a key element across Europe in addressing youth unemployment.

At the 1997 Luxembourg Summit on Employment a common set of principles for use across the European Union was agreed and this effectively represented a 'guarantee' of education, employment and training for youths aged sixteen to eighteen years olds (Furlong and Cartmel, 2007). This agreement and newer arrangements such as a matrix of common initiatives for training across the European Union have led some to talk about the 'Europeification' of training policy (Antunes, 2006). Indeed, UK training policies in recent decades have also, like European policy, become more vocational. Vocationalism advocates as the central purpose of training the importance of occupational utility and 'employability' as a form of human capital. UK training is also demonstrative of emerging 'activation policies' popular across the rest of Europe. These policies aim to provide individuals with 'more responsibility for their own social inclusion' (Pohl and Walther, 2007). However, while a flow of ideas across borders is influencing training policies, nation states continue to have a role in shaping these policies via their ideological preferences, notably in regard to how they conceptualise 'youth' within their initiatives (Iannelli and Smyth, 2008; Pohl and Walther, 2007).

In the UK youth training policies are applied to a wide range of young people under twenty-five years (Mizen, 2004: 61). For younger people up to school leaving age of sixteen years old, there has been an increase in employment-related training usually in low skill work (Mizen et al., 1999). In schools in the UK, young people have received training on vocational initiatives such as 'junior intermediate labour markets'. A new 'diploma' qualification across several employment areas for fourteen to nineteen year olds was launched in 2009 and attempted to integrate more traditional aspects of schooling with employment-focused training. The aim was to enhance the standing of vocational training as, unlike many other European countries, the UK has a long history of valuing academic education above more vocational training (Wolf, 2011). Traditional 'A-level' examinations in England and Wales continue to be regarded as 'the gold standard qualification' by the middle classes and elite universities. Vocational qualifications and non-traditional A-levels are their poor relation but tend to be preferred in comprehensive schools (*The Guardian*, 2010). However, these efforts were short lived as these diplomas were scrapped in 2010 when the UK's Coalition government came to power.

Recent UK governments have restricted unemployment benefits to sixteen to eighteen year olds, encouraging the young instead to be in employment, education or training. Thus young people receive little direct state support other than modest education support grants (formally educational maintenance allowance) or undertake funded training places such as Modern Apprenticeships (MAs). MAs were introduced in 1994 and in 1997 became an entitlement for all sixteen-year-old school leavers. They are now simply termed apprenticeships and operate at several levels. They were also made open to those beyond the age of eighteen and there is some concern that as such most apprenticeships are now offered to older youths and adults. For example, the Institute for Public Policy Research (2011) has called for a 'rethinking' of apprenticeships, having identified how less than a quarter of these schemes in 2010 went to young people aged under twenty-five. Under New Labour, training for those over eighteen in the UK was also provided via the introduction of a scheme known as New Deal for Young People (NDYP) – although the options of taking employment or education were also offered. NDYP was compulsory for young people aged eighteen to twenty-four who had been unemployed for six months or more.

Mirroring wider European-level agreements, the previous UK New Labour government launched a September Guarantee for minimum aged school leavers. The introduction of 'guarantees' of work, education or training to young people effectively changed the vocabulary used to describe the situation of young people who are not in 'appropriate' activities (Furlong and Cartmel, 2007). The term NEET (not in education, employment or training) is now part of UK policy parlance and is used to collect statistical information on young people aged sixteen to twenty-four. Those considered within this category are the unemployed and those young people previously described as 'inactive' – including young mothers and those with disabilities. Taking the lead from other countries where similar arrangements are in operation, the September Guarantee also placed an obligation on young people to accept work, education or training places offered to them.

With youth unemployment increasing the UK Coalition government announced in November 2011 a £1 billion fund to help 500,000 unemployed young people complete a 'placement' with employers. Known as the Youth Contract this scheme continues to place an obligation on young people to complete temporary work placements or face losing their welfare payments. Despite the temporary nature of much of this training the general public believe it offers valuable opportunities for young people. Recent research by the European Commission in all twenty-seven member states found 75 per cent of respondents believe vocational education and training offers 'high quality learning' (TNS Opinion and Social, 2011: 7).

However, there are concerns among youth scholars about the direction of this work-based training policy, in particular that it focuses too much on the supply (i.e. the quality of employees) rather than demand side of the labour market (job creation) and will lead to the 'warehousing' of young people in temporary training schemes. Research shows that most would prefer to make transitions towards adulthood in more traditional ways such as through permanent waged employment (MacDonald and Marsh, 2005). Critics of recent 'youth activation' policies such as apprenticeships, New Deal for Young People, Jobs Fund and the Youth Contract question whether at times of economic crisis employers can offer sufficient numbers of training positions to young people that lead on to permanent employment. These views echo earlier criticisms of training schemes developed during the 1980s when we also saw economic restructuring and high rates of young unemployment (Lee et al., 1990). Then researchers found that repeated work/training placements that failed to lead on to permanent employment created 'cultural resistance amongst young people and their families to the idea that training or vocational preparation was a necessary pre-requisite to work' (Bynner, 2001: 12).

Accordingly, during the 1990s several youth researchers exploring the experience of young people completing training in the UK pointed to 'the mismatch between official rhetoric about the benefits of youth training and the dismal experience often observed on the ground' (Bynner, 2001: 13). For young people aged sixteen to nineteen completing training 'became a period of marking time' or 'warehousing' until jobs opportunities became available or unemployment benefits could be claimed at eighteen years old (Bynner, 2001). More recently research found that many young people on training schemes such as apprenticeships and later NDYP did little to enhance their chances of obtaining and staying in rewarding and secure employment. Rather, their biographies were characterised by recurrent periods of poor work, unemployment and then participation in training schemes, so called 'cyclical careers' (Furlong et al., 2003). This highlighted that training may be useful in times of economic boom and/or in local labour markets with many opportunities, but in neighbourhoods where there has been continuing stagnation following de-industrialisation training has less effectiveness (Furlong et al., 2003; Webster et al., 2004).

REFERENCES

Antunes, F. (2006) 'Globalisation and Europeification of education policies: routes, processes and metamorphoses', *European Educational Research Journal*, 5 (1): 38–55.

Brooks, R. (ed.) (2009) *Transitions from Education to Work: New Perspectives from Europe and Beyond*. Basingstoke: Palgrave Macmillan.

Bynner, J. (2001) 'British youth transitions in comparative perspective', *Journal of Youth Studies*, 4 (1): 5–23.

Dwyer, P. and Wyn, J. (2001) *Youth, Education and Risk: Facing the Future*. London: Routledge.

Federal Statistical Office (2012) 'Youth unemployment in Germany one of the lowest in the EU', press release. www.destatis.de/EN/PressServices/Press/pr/2011/GenTable_2011.html?cms_gtp=74006_unnamed%253D16 (accessed 11 July 2012).

Furlong, A. and Cartmel, F. (2007) *Young People and Social Change: New Perspectives*. 2nd edn. Maidenhead: Open University Press.

Furlong, A., Cartmel, F., Biggart, A., Sweeting, H., and West, P. (2003) *Youth Transitions: Patterns of Vulnerability and Processes of Social Inclusion*. Edinburgh: Scottish Executive.

The Guardian (2010) 'A-level results: top universities secretly list "banned" subjects – teachers', 20 August. www.guardian.co.uk/education/2010/aug/20/a-level-subjects-blacklist-claim (accessed 14 December 2010).

Iannelli, C. and Smyth, E. (2008) 'Mapping gender and social background differences in education and youth transitions across Europe', *Journal of Youth Studies*, 11 (2): 213–32.

Institute for Public Policy Research (IPPR) (2011) *Rethinking Apprenticeships*. London: IPPR.

Lee, D., Marsden, D., Rickman, P. and Duncombe, P. (1990) *Scheming for Youth: A Study of YTS in the Enterprise Culture*. Milton Keynes: Open University Press.

MacDonald, R. and Marsh, J. (2005) *Disconnected Youth? Growing Up in Britain's Poor Neighbourhoods*. London: Palgrave Macmillan.

Mizen, P. (2004) *The Changing State of Youth*. Basingstoke: Palgrave.

Mizen, P., Bolton, A. and Pole, C. (1999) 'School-age workers: the paid employment of children in Britain', *Work, Employment and Society*, 13 (3): 423–38.

Pohl, A. and Walther, A. (2007) 'Activating the disadvantaged: variations in addressing youth transitions across Europe', *International Journal of Lifelong Learning*, 26 (5): 533–53.

TNS Opinion and Social (2011) *Attitudes Towards Vocational, Education and Training: Special Eurobarometer 369*. Strasbourg: European Commission.

Webster, C., Simpson, D., MacDonald, R., Abbas, A., Cieslik, M., Shildrick, T. and Simpson, M. (2004) *Poor Transitions: Social Exclusion and Young Adults*. Bristol: Policy Press.

Wolf, A. (2011) *Review of Vocational Education: The Wolf Report*. London: Department of Education.

14
Young People and Housing

The concept of housing is related to but at the same time different from the concept of home. Definitions of home evoke physical, social, cultural and psychological meanings – the expression 'home is where the heart is' illustrates some of this (Henderson et al., 2007: 124). A young person therefore can occupy a house, a flat or a friend's settee and not necessarily think of it as 'home'. In contrast, housing can refer to the actual physical building for residency purposes of a young person or group of young people. Housing can also be conceptualised as a physical object affected by wider social structures and processes that in turn can profoundly influence young people and their lives.

Research into young people's housing highlights the importance of **social class, gender, ethnicity, education** (in particular higher education and its organisation across contexts), participation (or not) in the labour market (**employment**), housing supply and demand across contexts and provision for the disabled (Holdsworth and Morgan, 2005). A distinction also needs to be drawn between 'living away' and actually 'leaving the family home'. Increasingly many young people in the UK tend to live away from the family home before returning (Furlong and Cartmel, 2007), so-called 'yo-yo careers' (Biggart and Walther, 2006). Iacovou (2001) and Mulder (2009: 205–6) have pointed to geographical differences in patterns of leaving home among young people across the world. They highlight 'large-scale patterns' and 'a North versus South and East divide'. In Northern Europe (Nordic countries) and North America young people often leave the parental home early 'to live alone or with roommates, either for independence or for enrolment in education' (Mulder, 2009: 205). By age twenty-one or twenty-two in Northern European societies 50 per cent of young people had left home, whereas in Southern states such as Spain and Portugal the 50 per cent mark is reached only by age twenty-six or twenty-seven (Iacovou, 2001). In contrast, the authors suggest the Southern pattern is characterised by later home leaving as many Southern youth leave home with marriage. Despite these trends there are exceptions, for example, Mulder found delayed housing transitions related to marriage in parts of Northern Europe such as Flanders, Belgium. Indeed, other European research exploring the timing, sequencing and synchronisation of leaving home found a large range of differences between countries. The complex interplay between the present economic situation of young people and long-term institutional and cultural factors are thought to be 'the main driving factor' (Billari et al., 201: 339). The significance of religious values and the importance of marriage in Southern Europe mean that many young people will remain in their families of origin much longer than less religious Northern youth who may tend to leave home earlier to cohabit with partners (Iacovou, 2001). Other smaller scale qualitative **youth research** has also documented in detail the meanings young people attach to their residency experiences and these are linked to family and other **social networks** and interactions with peers (Heath and Kenyon, 2001; Samtoro, 2006).

'Within the UK there is a clearly recognised "youth" housing market, characterised by cheap and transitional housing mainly based within the private and social rented sector' (Holdsworth and Morgan, 2005: 17). This is similar to the position in several Northern European countries but contrasts with other countries such as Spain where there is relatively little demand and supply for 'youth' housing because as noted the trend in these Southern European countries is to buy a house on leaving the family home to marry. Therefore in Spain young people leave home at a later age than those in other Western societies (Holdsworth and Morgan, 2005).

The availability of affordable housing for young people is one key factor influencing the age at which young people move from the family home. As we see elsewhere in Europe relatively poor wage rates coupled to high cost of housing can shape the delayed housing transitions in Southern European states (Iacovou, 2001). In the UK and elsewhere the rising cost of housing has meant home ownership has remained only an aspiration for most young people. Rental costs have also risen in recent years and demand for social housing has outstripped supply, so many young people have to remain dependent on parents and remain living at home (Iacovou, 2001). Indeed, a recent review of literature concerning the 'housing choices' that young people make noted how there is greater 'risk' attached to all young people finding housing, with concerns about rising number of homeless youth (Heath, 2008).

With rising unemployment and poor social housing provision research shows how significant economic resources are to the structuring of housing transitions (Heath, 2008). Heath found that in the UK young people are moving later into independent housing – while simultaneously they are also remaining longer in education and starting employment at an older age. Social class inequalities and the unequal distribution of economic, cultural and social capital strongly influence the pattern of residency of young people across the housing market. 'Differing levels of access to practical and financial help, as well as sources of support and guidance, are key factors in understanding different housing outcomes' for young people (Heath, 2008).

Ford et al. (2002) explored this relationship between resources and housing transitions in great detail suggesting a model of five 'pathways' made by young people once they entered the housing system. At one extreme was the 'chaotic pathway' characterised by 'an absence of planning, substantial economic constraints and an absence of family support'. Other pathways were less constrained as greater resources allowed young people to achieve their desired housing aspirations (Ford et al., 2002: 2464–5).

Changes in the housing market over the final decades of the twentieth century were observed by Ford et al. and they indicated that their typology of pathways highlighted how housing transitions of young people had become more complicated over the years. They alluded to a possibility that young people can 'plan and control' their housing transition, usually when they could also draw on other resources such as parental support and therefore be more creative. But they also added that 'the chances that a young person follows one pathway rather than another is still largely a function of structural factors'. So planned pathways 'can only be forged by those with more resources' and chaotic pathways 'are associated with instability, poor conditions, limited choice and exclusion' (Ford et al., 2002: 2466).

With continuing social change there has been recognition that 'young adults' domestic and housing transitions remain an under-researched theme in youth studies' (Heath, 2009: 214). Indeed, recently in the UK a new research programme has been announced (Young People and Housing: Identifying Policy Challenges and Solutions for 2020) involving collaboration between housing charities, government departments and research organisations. The aim of the programme is to identify some of the key drivers of change in young people's housing choices and aspirations and how best to develop new policies that accommodate the changing needs of young people's housing careers (Joseph Rowntree Foundation, 2009).

REFERENCES

Biggart, A. and Walther, A. (2006) 'Coping with yo-yo transitions: young adults struggle for support between family and state in comparative perspective', in C. Leccardi and E. Ruspini (eds), *A New Youth? Young People, Generations and Family Life*. Aldershot: Ashgate Press, pp. 41–62

Billari, F., Philipov, D. and Baizan, P. (2001) 'Leaving home in Europe: the experience of cohorts born in 1960', *International Journal of Population Geography*, 7 (5): 339–56.

Ford, J., Rugg, J. and Burrows, R. (2002) 'Conceptualising the contemporary role of housing in the transition to adult life in England', *Urban Studies*, 39 (13): 2455–67.

Furlong, A. and Cartmel, F. (2007) *Young People and Social Change: New Perspectives*. 2nd edn. Maidenhead: Open University Press.

Heath, S. (2008) *Housing Choices and Issues for Young People in the UK*. York: Joseph Rowntree Foundation. www.jrf.org.uk/sites/files/jrf/2327.pdf (accessed 14 May 2011).

Heath, S. (2009) 'Young, free and single? The rise of independent living', in A. Furlong (ed.), *Handbook of Youth and Young Adulthood: New Perspectives and Agendas*. London: Routledge, pp. 211–16.

Heath, S. and Kenyon, E. (2001) 'Single young professionals and shared household living', *Journal of Youth Studies*, 4 (1): 83–100

Henderson, S., Holland, J., McGrellis, S., Sharpe, S. and Thomson, R. (2007) *Inventing Adulthoods: A Biographical Approach to Youth Transitions*. London: Sage.

Holdsworth, C. and Morgan, D. (2005) *Transitions in Context: Leaving Home, Independence and Adulthood*. Maidenhead: Open University Press.

Iacovou, M. (2001) *Leaving Home in the European Union*, Working Papers of the Institute for Social and Economic Research, paper 2001–18. Colchester: University of Essex.

Joseph Rowntree Foundation (2009) www.jrf.org.uk/funding/calls-for-proposal/young-people-housing (accessed 14 July 2009).

Mulder, C.H. (2009) 'Leaving the parental home in young adulthood', in A. Furlong (ed.), *Handbook of Youth and Young Adulthood: New Perspectives and Agendas*. London: Routledge, pp. 203–210.

Samtoro, M. (2006) 'Living with parents: a research study on Italian young people and their mothers', in C. Leccardi, and E. Ruspini (eds), *A New Youth? Young People, Generations and Family Life*. Aldershot: Ashgate Press, pp. 146–63.

15
Young People, Social Networks and Social Capital

Human beings are always connected to others in some way and so all of us are members of social networks of some form or another. 'The briefest glance at cultural and academic representations of "young people" reveals that they are very rarely portrayed or talked about as alone' (Marshall and Stenner, 1997: 183). Social networks are made up of individuals or groups who are linked together through one (or more) social relationship(s). The relationships can exist at different levels from the micro such as family and friends through to macro complex relations such as **religion**, beliefs, **gender**, **ethnicity** and **social class**. In youth studies the concept of social networks is often associated with social capital (Bassani, 2009: 74). Despite being a somewhat slippery concept, social capital is usually seen as 'networks together with shared norms, values and understandings that facilitate co-operation within or among groups' (Cote and Healy, 2001).

The work on social capital by Coleman (1988; 1990) Putnam (2000) and Bourdieu (1986) illustrates how norms of reciprocity, trust and resources are distributed through social relationships and can structure the life chances of young people. Coleman, Putnam and Bourdieu viewed social networks as a source of social capital which itself 'creates a framework for the transfer of other forms of capital between individuals' – in particular, cultural and economic capital (Jones, 2009: 125). Coleman (1988), for example, shows how social capital formed in family and educational settings can be converted into cultural and economic capital and has a strong influence on levels of educational achievement. As such the concept of social capital has been influential in youth studies as it allows us to interrogate how different resources are transmitted within families and other settings and how patterns of division and exclusion may occur (Helve and Bynner, 2007: 1). The links between social capital and social exclusion have been developed further through the distinctions between bridging and bonding capital. In some communities young people may have dense social networks (and often strong cultural identities) and so high levels of bonding capital. However, such networks may lack relationships with significant others outside of the community (bridging capital) that might offer educational and employment opportunities. Hence young people who lack bridging capital may be vulnerable to marginal employment careers and associated disadvantages (MacDonald and Marsh, 2005).

Bourdieu focuses on the unequal distribution of resources and how social capital is monopolised by some classes of people who use it to dominate or exclude others (Roberts, 2009: 16). Bourdieu implicates young people's participation in social networks and their associated social capital in wider processes of social reproduction and the sustaining of **divisions** in society. He suggests that middle-class children and young people participate in kinship networks that endow them with social, linguistic and cultural competencies which give them a better chance of succeeding both at school and at work. Whereas the social networks of the working classes largely deny them access to such social and cultural capital and they are therefore less likely to succeed academically and in the labour market. Educational success results in higher paid employment and thus social and cultural capital are converted to higher levels of economic capital for the middle classes. For Bourdieu this is how intragenerational and intergenerational reproduction of class differences and inequalities are maintained (Bourdieu, 1986).

One weakness of the social capital literature is that it fails to acknowledge the role of gender and racial relationships in social networks. For example, young women are often excluded from more powerful networks of trust and reciprocity that are dominated by males (Onyx and Bullen, 2001). Feminist authors have noted how the concept of social capital ignores power relations in networks and the hidden role of young women (Quinn, 2005). Quinn espouses the notion of 'imagined social capital' – benefits coming from symbolic and imagined communities that allow young women to construct a sense of belonging in the face of exclusion. For example, Anne Campbell's (1984) classic study investigated young women's role in gangs in New York and she observed how they were often marginalised by the activities of male gang members but continued to participate. Focusing on friendship networks involving girls, Hey (1997) notes how 'the so-called private, marginal realm of schoolgirl friendships is a significant place where the "social" is indexed. It is between and amongst girls as friends that identities are variously practised, appropriated, resisted and negotiated' (Hey, 1997: 30).

Moreover, some youth researchers note how, 'young people in their move towards autonomy and independence from their parents transfer their allegiance increasingly to peer groups' (Helve and Bynner, 2007: 1). Several studies have shown how intergenerational conflict can result from this change in allegiances as this can involve the adoption of new practices and the contesting of family and wider community values and behaviour codes (Whyte, 1943). As such, networks of friends and peers and the social and other forms of capital within them have also become of particular interest to youth researchers (Thomson and Taylor, 2005). As indicated through the discussion around the concept of **youth cultures**, relationships within friendship and peer networks are pervaded by ideas, values, attitudes, norms and social practices that strongly influence young people in their everyday lives. Through social networks young people establish relationships and it is often in these collective ways with peers and friends that they are able to experiment with cultural resources and develop their identities (Cote, 2002). First experiences of intimate relationships beyond the family are often encountered via social networks of peers and it is here that experimentation and development of **sexualities** can occur. Relationships within social networks with friends and peers have been viewed as a double-edged sword – with positive and negative ramifications. They can be the source of mutual support in difficult times and circumstances but, paradoxically, membership of networks can close off possibilities and limit horizons – for example, being the source of anti-school feelings. Relationships feature recurrently, whether in talk of the effects of 'peer pressure'; of an epidemic of teenage pregnancies and terminations; of the danger of youth cultures such as the 'rave scene'; of networks of illegal drug takers; and in relation to youth **crime** and disorder (Marshall and Stenner, 1997: 183; Webster et al., 2004).

As the new millennium began the involvement of young people in social networks witnessed significant change stemming from developments in information and communication technologies (ICTs). Indeed, since the start of the twenty-first century there has been a significant growth in the involvement of young people in virtual social networks via the Internet. This online social networking has grown since the emergence of MySpace in 2003, and Facebook and Bebo in 2005 (alongside a range of other niche Social Network Sites (SNSs) that have developed over the period). By 2008 it was reported that 'over 60 % of 13–17 year olds had profiles on SNSs. Many young people are spending upwards of two hours a night on online social networking activities' (Davies and Cranston, 2008: 5) although those from socially disadvantaged backgrounds have less frequent and regular access to social networking sites. Some are concerned about perceived risks attached to youth involvement in such networks (Davies and Cranston, 2008). But others have noted how these concerns should be set against the opportunities offered to young people to access bridging capital via expanded networks, 'for example, in formal and non-formal education, employment, cultural expression, political engagement and social life' (Helve and Bynner, 2007: 2).

REFERENCES

Bassani, C. (2009) 'Young people and social capital', in A. Furlong (ed.), *Handbook of Youth and Young Adulthood: New Perspectives and Agendas*. London: Routledge, pp. 74–80.

Bourdieu, P. (1986) 'The forms of capital', in J. Richardson (ed.), *Handbook of Theory and Research for the Sociology of Education*. New York: Greenwood Press, pp. 241–58.

Campbell, A. (1984) *The Girls in the Gang*. Oxford: Blackwell.

Coleman, J. (1988) 'Social capital and the creation of human capital', *American Journal of Sociology*, 94: S95–S120.

Coleman, J. (1990) *Foundations of Social Theory*. Cambridge: Harvard University Press.

Cote, J.E. (2002) 'Sociological perspectives on identity formation: the culture–identity link and identity capital', *Journal of Adolescence*, 19 (5): 417–28.

Cote, S. and Healy, T. (2001) *The Well Being of Nations: The Role of Human and Social Capital*. Paris: Organisation for Economic Co-operation and Development.

Davies, T. and Cranston, P. (2008) *Youth Work and Social Networking: Final Research Report*. Leicester: National Youth Agency.

Helve, H. and Bynner, J. (eds) (2007) *Youth and Social Capital*. London: The Tufnell Press.

Hey, V. (1997) *The Company She Keeps: An Ethnography of Girls' Friendship*, Buckingham: Open University Press.

Jones, G. (2009) *Youth*. Cambridge: Polity Press.

Marshall, H. and Stenner, P. (1997) 'Friends and lovers', in J. Roche and S. Tucker (eds), *Youth in Society*, London: Sage, pp. 183–9.

MacDonald, R. and Marsh, J. (2005) *Disconnected Youth? Growing Up in Britain's Poor Neighbourhoods*. London: Palgrave Macmillan.

Onyx, J. and Bullen, P. (2001) 'The different faces of social capital in NSW Australia', in E.M. Uslaner (ed.), *Social Capital and Participation in Everyday Life*. London: Routledge, pp. 45–58.

Putnam, R. (2000) *Bowling Alone: Collapse and Revival of American Community*. New York: Simon & Schuster.

Quinn, J. (2005) 'Belonging in a learning community: the re-imagined university and imagined social capital', *Studies in the Education of Adults*, 37 (1): 4–18.

Roberts, K. (2009) 'Socio-economic reproduction', in A. Furlong (ed.), *Handbook of Youth and Young Adulthood: New Perspectives and Agendas*. London: Routledge, pp. 14–21.

Thomson, R. and Taylor, R. (2005) 'Between cosmopolitanism and the locals: mobility as a resource in the transition to adulthood', *Young: Nordic Journal of Youth Research*, 13: 327–342.

Webster, C., Simpson, D., MacDonald, R., Abbas, A., Cieslik, M., Shildrick, T. and Simpson, M. (2004) *Poor Transitions: Social Exclusion and Young Adults*. Bristol: Policy Press.

Whyte, W.F. (1943) *Street Corner Society: The Social Structure of an Italian Slum*. Chicago: University of Chicago Press.

16
Young People and Wellbeing

Happiness and wellbeing have been the topic of recent widespread debate (Bauman, 2008; Layard, 2005) though the issue of how to flourish through life, balancing the fleeting pleasures with a more enduring contentment, has a long history dating to Socrates and Plato (McMahon, 2006). Contemporary writers view wellbeing as having both subjective and objective components; those aspects that reflect a young person's thoughts and emotional experiences around their life (subjective wellbeing) and then more concrete characteristics such as income, physical health, education, housing, etc. (Argyle, 2004: 14). The study of adolescent wellbeing is complicated by the physiological and psychological changes associated with the maturation process, and also the changes in resources and relationships that come with adulthood so that with age people tend to have better wellbeing than when they were young (Helson and Lohnen, 1998). National governments and institutions such as the World Health Organization are keen to promote the wellbeing of young people and have worked with social scientists to define and measure wellbeing in their efforts to develop policies to enhance the quality of life of young people. Wellbeing programmes developed by governments usually involve several quality of life benchmarks such as good mental and physical health, safety, opportunity for achievement and personal development, social participation and economic resources (Department for Education and Skills, 2003; Happy Planet Index, 2009). When trying to assess quality of life researchers measure the subjective and objective elements of wellbeing most commonly through social surveys (see Diener and Suh, 1997). This also involves some calculation of the balance of positive characteristics (such as good educational attainment) with negative characteristics (such as ill health) to produce some overall wellbeing score (UNICEF, 2007). In this way data from social surveys can be used to compare the wellbeing of young people in different societies and also assess how wellbeing changes over time. Policy-makers, practitioners and researchers are keen to know what are the key factors that explain differences in young people's wellbeing. Is quality of life rooted in material processes so that deprivation is the key cause of poor wellbeing as economists might argue? Or is the quality of social relationships more important to wellbeing – divorce and family conflict, for example, being a key barrier to good wellbeing as some sociologists suggest? Or, as psychologists claim, are some people genetically predisposed to develop certain personality traits that frame their wellbeing irrespective of their social resources and opportunities in life? Recent commentators suggest that all of these processes (and others) may be relevant to an understanding of wellbeing and contemporary research tries to accommodate this complexity in the analysis of quality of life (Layard and Dunn, 2009).

In developing societies the issues that frame young people's wellbeing are rather more transparent than those in richer societies. Material deprivation, poor nutrition, limited access to health, **education**, welfare provision and a dangerous environment structure the lives of children and youth in emerging societies. Three quarters of the children who are obese in the world (some 20 million under five years of age) live not in rich societies as one might expect but in poor countries marked by inadequate diets (World Health Organization, 2004). Of the children under five years of age who die in these countries, 35 per cent do so because of malnutrition (World Health Organization, 2009). A half of children who die each year, over one million, are through injury (95 per cent of childhood deaths through injury occur in poor societies) and a further quarter succumb to communicable diseases, most of which are preventable (World Health Organization, 2009). Though there have been improvements in recent decades, the disparities between the lives of children and young people in rich societies and those elsewhere are stark. Infant mortality rates in poorer societies can reach 100–150 deaths per thousand compared to 7–10 per thousand in affluent countries so one realises that many children around the world do not live to become teenagers (World Health Organization, 2005: 8). Clearly the continued poverty and exploitation of young people around the world raises serious questions about the possibility of universal human rights and wellbeing for young people. Improving the lives of children and young people in poorer and richer societies alike is accordingly central to the United Nations Development strategy (United Nations, 2007) as well as many other agencies, charities and governments around the world. For most this involves reducing the suffering experienced by young people by ensuring adequate nutrition, safe environments and access to health, education and welfare services.

The picture of adolescent wellbeing in richer societies is more complex than that in developing societies. There are worrying epidemiological trends, with increases in the incidence of anxiety and depression among young people and significant growth in the use of anti-depressants among the young (Martin, 2007). Suicide rates for those under twenty-four years of age in Western societies have tripled in the last fifty years even as rates for adults have declined in this period (Cutler et al., 2001), and suicide is one of the major causes of death for young people and particularly young men (Wasserman et al., 2005). As one might expect growing up in low income homes and in societies marked by social inequality can undermine the quality of life of young people – as we see in the UK and the USA (UNICEF, 2007). Young people's lives have become commodified to such an extent in recent years that to lack the money to participate in consumerist lifestyles has a profoundly exclusionary effect on both the social identities and everyday life chances of adolescents. But the UNICEF report notes that other factors are also significant when explaining how counties such as the UK and the USA score poorly for adolescent wellbeing. Family conflict and breakdown, friendship networks that are more adversarial than supportive and schooling experiences marked by hostility and violence all take their toll on the lives of young people in these countries. By contrast young people in Scandinavian societies such as Sweden and Denmark enjoy better lives in part because there is greater social equality but also as they experience institutions and relationships characterised more by trust, respect and mutual support. Recent studies into the poor wellbeing of children in the UK (Layard and Dunn, 2009) note that further problematic behaviours emerge that can compound the difficulties such young people experience. Countries at the bottom of the adolescent wellbeing league table (such as the UK, USA, Hungary and Austria) have significant percentages of their young people who drink alcohol, smoke cannabis, are sexually active at an early age and who are involved in violent behaviour. Taken together these early childhood experiences and patterns of behaviour condition the subjective wellbeing and social identities of adolescents as well as the sorts of **transitions** they make through childhood, adolescence and into adulthood. Layard and Dunn (2009) offer what appear to be rather straightforward solutions to the problem of poor wellbeing – loving, secure families; good friendships; non-commercialised healthy lifestyles; lives built on solid values and morals; supportive, high quality education; good mental health organisations; and sufficient material resources to offer decent standard of living. Behind such aims, however, lie ambitious goals – reducing social inequality; tempering the individualism and competitiveness of modern societies; enhancing the integrity of families; curbing the power of the mass media, new technology and the attractiveness of consumerism and so on. Some societies do raise their children to be happy adolescents and adults but it remains to be seen whether other societies can implement such profound social change.

Despite defining wellbeing as the spectrum of positive and negative experiences had by young people, commentators tend to focus attention on the problems of young people and how this suffering may be alleviated? This interest in poor wellbeing is fuelled by popular mediazed constructions of young people as being 'troublesome' or 'at risk'. In affluent societies there have been frequent moral panics that have focused attention on young people's drug and alcohol use, mental ill health, injuries, accidents, violence, obesity and sexual health. In developing societies concern also focuses on diet, nutrition and their impact on morbidity and mortality rates in later life. When exploring wellbeing therefore we have to be sensitive to the social construction of young people. For the issue of wellbeing may be used by differing interest groups to pursue their own agenda rather than to simply illuminate the factors that shape the quality of life of young people. As Veenhoven (2006) has argued there may be a neglect of the actual growth in happiness in recent decades – the joy, pleasure and fun that characterises most young people's lives may be obscured by the miserablist fixation with young people's 'troubled lives'.

The topic of wellbeing is revealing as it illustrates many of the differing ways that young people are constructed as 'problem youth'. The examples of poor wellbeing (such as anxiety, depression and associated behaviours such as binge drinking, unsafe sex and smoking) can show how cultural assumptions and moral guidelines function to create social boundaries that police the behaviour of young people, disempowering young people in the process (Furedi, 2004). To investigate wellbeing is to also study the unequal power relationships that link young people to other groups and social institutions.

Poor wellbeing is also at the heart of many academic disciplines that study the lives of young people; offending and criminology; poverty, disadvantage, inequality and sociology; illness and medicine; mental ill health and psychology; unemployment and economics and so on. In that the wellbeing of children and young people is seen to frame later quality of life, the issue of youth wellbeing is also at the heart of a number of key debates today. Social surveys suggest that in many affluent societies increasing prosperity in recent decades has not led to corresponding increases in wellbeing (Easterlin, 1974). Instead data suggest the incidence of poor wellbeing amidst affluence – so called affluenza (James, 2007). Many developed societies have seen growth in the rates of depression, anxiety, suicide and problematic drugs and alcohol use. Some commentators suggest then that behind the façade of 'successful' prosperous lives in affluent societies lies a darker hidden face of modernity. Though many people in rich countries have relatively comfortable lives they accumulate the hidden psychic injuries associated with life in competitive, consumer-driven capitalist societies. For some, the incidence of poor mental health and risky behaviours of young people in affluent societies points to the need for a fundamental debate about what constitutes a 'good society' and what makes a 'good life'. As Layard and Dunn argue (2009) if rich democratic societies are still marked by the widespread unhappiness of children and young people then one should begin to question the role of consumerism, individualism and secularism that frame our cultural lives and critique the economic policies and political ideologies that promote economic growth as *the* goal of public policy.

REFERENCES

Argyle, M. (2004) *The Psychology of Happiness*. London: Routledge.

Bauman, Z. (2008) *The Art of Life*. Cambridge: Polity Press.

Cutler, D., Glaeser, E. and Norberg, K. (2001) 'Explaining the rise in youth suicide', *Harvard Institute of Economic Research*, paper no. 1917.

Department for Education and Skills (2003) *Every Child Matters*. London: HMSO.

Diener, E. and Suh, E. (1997) 'Measuring quality of life: economic, subjective and social indicators', *Social Indicators Research*, 40: 189–216.

Easterlin, R.A. (1974) 'Does economic growth improve the human lot?' in P. David and M. Reder (eds), *Nations and Households in Economic Growth: Essays in Honor of Moses Abramovitz*. New York: Academic Press, pp. 89–125.

Furedi, F. (2004) *Therapy Culture: Cultivating Vulnerability in an Uncertain Age*. London: Routlege.

Happy Planet Index (2009) www.happyplanetindex.org/explore/global/index.html (accessed 7 July 2012).

Helson, R. and Lohnen, E.C. (1998) 'Affective colouring of personality from young adulthood to midlife', *Personality and Social Psychology Bulletin*, 24: 241–52.

James, O. (2007) *Affluenza*. London: Vermilion.

Layard, R. (2005) *Happiness: Lessons from a New Science*. London: Penguin.

Layard, R. and Dunn J. (2009) *A Good Childhood: Searching for Values in a Competitive Age*. London: Penguin.

Martin, R. (2007) 'Wellbeing', in M.J. Kehily (ed.), *Understanding Youth: Perspectives, Identities and Practices*. London: Sage/Open University Press, pp. 181–214.

McMahon, D. (2006) *Happiness: A History*. New York: Grove Press.

UNICEF (2007) *Child Poverty in Perspective: An Overview of Child Wellbeing in Rich Countries*. Florence: UNICEF.

United Nations (2007) *United Nations Millennium Development Goals Report 2007*. New York: United Nations

Veenhoven, R. (2006) 'Rising happiness in nations 1946–2004: a reply to Easterlin', *Social Indicators Research*, 79: 421–36.

Wasserman, D. Cheng, Q and Jiang, G. (2005) 'Global suicide rates among young people aged 15–19', *World Psychiatry*, 4 (2): 114–20.

World Health Organization (2004) *The Global Burden of Disease: 2004 Update*. Geneva: WHO.

World Health Organization (2005) *World Health Report 2005: Making Every Mother and Child Count*. Geneva: WHO.

World Health Organization (2009) *Child and Adolescent Health and Development 2008*. Geneva: WHO.

17
Young People and Gender

Gender is central to any attempt to make sense of young people's lives. When young people describe themselves, their maleness and femaleness is at the heart of their attempts to represent their social identities. Though our biological status as boy or girl seems unproblematic physiologically, the social significance of our sex – how it is played out culturally, politically and economically – is much more complex. Social scientists argue that these concepts of masculinity and femininity vary greatly historically and culturally and are linked to the unequal distribution of opportunities and resources. Because of this distinctive social construction of gender, young people's life chances and the quality of life they experience are profoundly shaped by the gendered nature of institutions and relationships in societies.

Early research into gender and young people tended to focus on young women as victims, documenting the incidence of educational under-achievement, poor employment opportunities, sexual harassment and the construction of femininities characterised by passivity, emotionality and fixation on appearance (Griffin, 1985; Wallace, 1987). This discrimination and prejudice could for some be challenged by 'women friendly' policies that would promote gender equality in **education**, at work and in wider society. Sexism in society for some feminists then could be overcome by equal pay acts, access to abortion and contraception, and new educational curricula. However, other writers such as Millet (1977) and Firestone (1990) argued that gendered inequalities are a structural feature of modern societies where culture, politics and economics are inherently biased against women. The system of patriarchy means that though new policies improve the lives of young women they still suffer a range of injustices and oppression. A more equal society can only come about with a deeper more profound reform of social structures in modern societies.

More recently work on gender in youth studies has acknowledged the messy dialectical relationship between men and women and how their lives are intertwined rather than simply focusing on women as victims. In recent decades the deindustrialisation of Western societies has raised questions about masculinities and femininities as traditional labour market opportunities for young men have declined while women's **employment** opportunities have expanded. Researchers have documented a 'crisis in masculinity' in developed societies as a relative decline of job opportunities in manufacturing industries has restricted traditional transitions that young men made into employment and associated adult identities (Dolby and Dimitriadis, 2004; Weis, 1991). The growth in information technology has also transformed the ways in which gender relationships can be mediated – the use of social networking supporting the friendships and activities of young people (Elm, 2009). The growing global flows of people, commodities and ideas in recent years have also opened up debates about what masculine and feminine can mean for young people around the world. Young women in developing societies and authoritarian states have become more conscious and politically active in efforts to challenge gendered inequalities in their societies. One feature of the so-called 'Arab Spring' – popular protests in Middle Eastern societies – has been the call for greater opportunities for women (Gumuchian, 2011).

A foundational debate in youth studies has been the critique of simple unitary conception of gender as developed by psychology and the argument for a stratified, conflictual gender relations. Connell (1995) proposed the idea of dominant or 'hegemonic masculinities' that has been explored in many studies. In recent years we have seen researchers explore the differing ways that young people live out ways of being boys and girls but that these ways of being involve shifting power relationships and the marginalisation and oppression of some of their peers. In many settings researchers point to a dominant form of masculinity rooted in 'football, fucking and fighting' (Mac an Ghaill, 1994: 56). A physicality, toughness, as well as efforts to subordinate young women are all played out in the lives of many young men, which for some then also leads to problematic relationships with formal learning (Barnes, 2011; Willis, 1977). Class cultural and 'racial' traditions that inform the use of language and style mediate these gender displays so forms of dominant masculinity can vary greatly. In upper/middle-class independent schools, for example, one would see significant differences in masculinity to an ethnically diverse working-class south London school setting (O'Donnell and Sharpe, 2000). Yet the 'dominant lads' in both settings might share the same homophobia, sexism and displays of toughness despite their **class** and racial differences. And in both sorts of schools those young men who did not display these forms of masculinity would be marginalised, struggling to 'fit in' with many of their peers and vulnerable to bullying.

Dominant forms of young femininity are usually represented in different ways to those of boys, with young women emphasising their physical and sexual allure, which can be read as attempts to promote their emerging adult female identities. A concern for one's appearance and one's 'bodily management' – use of cosmetics and familiarity with fashion and style codes – all feature in many young women's lives. There are then complex and subtle rules governing how young women represent themselves in developed societies (Aapola et al., 2005: 136). Researchers also point to the continuing centrality of romance, friendships and emotional intimacy – though the form this takes can vary according to the class, **'race'** and ethnic backgrounds of the women concerned (McLeod, 2002). If young women play out these dominant forms of young femininity they can access resources such as the social and symbolic capital that comes from prestige and having diverse social networks. As with dominant masculinities, if some young women fail to adopt some of the key features of young femininity they will be vulnerable to marginalisation from their peers. Researchers such as Valerie Hey (1997) have documented the ways that young women can police the behaviour of other girls (through note writing, gossip and even violence) ensuring compliance with dominant modes of conduct and appearance. To not worry about one's appearance, to be indifferent to heterosexual romance, to be ignorant of female celebrities is to run the risk of exclusion and isolation from one's peers.

There have been several strands to gender research over the past decade. One has been the continuing salience of dominant or hegemonic forms of masculinity and femininity. There has also been research into efforts of young women to assert their femininity in ways that offer them control over their **sexualities** and their **bodies** and resist the ways that the media and boys often objectify and infantilise young women. So-called 'girl power' or 'ladettes' draws on some of the ideas of the feminist movement whereby girls can create their own spaces to enjoy sport, technology, music and can reclaim words such as 'girl' for their own positive use (Aapola et al., 2005: 20). However, the positive potential of such movements can be undermined by a drift into behaviours that mimic the violence, sexism and racism of some young men. Or as Reay (2001) posits, 'girls with attitude' can also just recreate different ways for girls to organise their lives around traditional concerns of romance and boyfriends. Others suggest that 'girl power' offers limited real freedoms for young women to shape their lives, particularly working-class women who face poor job and training opportunities as they leave school and move into adulthood (Walkerdine et al., 2001). Aapola et al. (2005: 36) suggest that the girl power movement may reflect processes of individualisation in late modernity and hence offer more of an illusion of self-determination than a reality of greater freedom and autonomy. In neo-liberal Western societies, they argue, individuals are offered numerous 'choices' about how to construct consumerised identities and countless routes through training into employment. Yet the underlying quality of these jobs are often poor and the myriad youthful identities that are on offer often reproduce those unequal relationships where young women are defined via their role as an object of the male gaze.

Research into young masculinities has explored some of the ways that young men may be adapting to the economic and social changes of the twenty-first century. Nayak (2006), for example, charts how young men respond to the decline of traditional jobs and their involvement in 'feminised' office employment. Instead of waged work offering spaces for the playing out of traditional cultural forms of working-class maleness it is now **leisure** spaces that provide an arena for displays of toughness, physicality and the honing of practical skills. Young men's involvement in football and drinking in particular come to be the sites where working-class masculinities can be reproduced, celebrating those older traditions of working-class leisure while at the same time offering ways of bonding and experimentation that allow young men to feel masculine and be valued. Other commentators have noted how traditional forms of working-class masculine display centred around toughness and manual skills have become fetishised in the lives of some young men in a way that Connell (1995) has referred to as 'protest masculinity'. The playing out of elements of working classness can also be interpreted as threatening and disruptive in educational settings and by authority figures such as the police, and so these forms of masculine display have for many now become associated with forms of deviance and emerging criminality (McDowell, 2009). Economic insecurities and tensions stemming from the 'war on terror' in recent years have also combined with these constructions of class to frame patterns of marginalisation of ethnic minority and particularly Muslim young men and women (Archer, 2003). The popular media have also come to associate some of the contemporary aspects of masculine and feminine display with cultures of worklessness representing such behaviour as causes of disadvantage rather than as responses to economic and cultural insecurity. Writers such as Reay (2005) and Jones (2011) document how working-class masculinities/femininities have become caught up with wider processes of class prejudice – the vilification of class cultural traditions and the demonising of young men and women. Such **representations of young people** as 'a problem' can be seen as a wider struggle over ideas that tends to obscure the underlying social changes that are reshaping young people's lives today.

REFERENCES

Aapola, S., Gonick, M. and Harris, A. (2005) *Young Femininity: Girlhood, Power and Social Change*. London: Palgrave.

Archer, L. (2003) *Race, Masculinity and Schooling: Muslim Boys and Education*. Milton Keynes: Open University Press.

Barnes, C. (2011) 'A discourse of disparagement: boy's talk about girls in school', *Young: Journal of Nordic Youth Research Association*, 19 (1): 5–23.

Connell, R. (1995) *Masculinities*. Cambridge: Polity Press.

Dolby, N. and Dimitriadis, G. (eds) (2004) *Learning to Labour in New Times*. London: Routledge.

Elm, M.S. (2009) 'Young women's creation of style in a Swedish Internet community', *Young: Journal of Nordic Youth Research Association*, 17 (3): 241–64.

Firestone, S. (1990) *The Dialectic of Sex: Case for Feminist Revolution*. London: The Women's Press.

Griffin, C. (1985) *Typical Girls: Young Women from School to Work*. London: Routledge and Kegan Paul.

Gumuchian, M. (2011) 'Arab Spring puts women's rights in the spotlight', Reuters Press Agency, 20 December. www.reuters.com/article/2011/12/20/us-arabs-women-idUSTRE7BJ0QW20111220 (accessed 7 July 2012).

Hey, V. (1997) *The Company She Keeps: An Ethnography of Girls' Friendship*. Buckingham: Open University Press.

Jones, O. (2011) *Chavs: The Demonization of the Working Class*. London: Verso.

Mac an Ghaill, M. (1994) *The Making of Men: Masculinities, Sexualities and Schooling*. Milton Keynes: Open University Press.

McDowell, L. (2009) 'New masculinities and femininities: gender divisions in the new economy', in A. Furlong (ed.) *Handbook of Youth and Young Adulthood: New Perspectives and Agendas*. London: Routledge, pp. 58–65.

McLeod, J. (2002) 'Working out intimacy: young people and friendship in an age of reflexivity', *Discourse: Studies in the Cultural Politics of Education*, 23 (2): 211–26.

Millet, K. (1977) *Sexual Politics*. 2nd edn. London: Virago Press.

Nayak, A. (2006) 'Displaced masculinities, chavs, youth and class in the postindustrial city', *Sociology*, 40 (5): 813–31.

O'Donnell, M. and Sharpe, R. (2000) *Uncertain Masculinities: Youth, Ethnicity and Class in Contemporary Britain*. London: Routledge.

Reay, D. (2001) '"Spice Girls, nice girls, girlies and tomboys": gender discourses, girls' cultures and femininities in the primary classroom', *Gender and Education*, 13 (2): 153–66.

Reay, D. (2005) 'Beyond consciousness: the psychic landscapes of class', *Sociology*, 39 (5): 911–28.

Walkerdine, V., Lucey, H. and Melody, J. (2001) *Growing Up Girl: Psychosocial Explorations of Gender and Class*. Basingstoke: Palgrave.

Wallace, C. (1987) *For Richer and Poorer: Growing Up, In and Out of Work*. London: Tavistock.

Weis, L. (1991) *Working Class Without Work*. Routledge: London.

Willis. P. (1977) *Learning to Labour: How Working Class Kids Get Working Class Jobs*. Farnborough: Saxon House.

18

Young People and Sexualities

Sexualities – the ways that people intimately relate emotionally and physically to one another – are at the heart of our identities and everyday practices. Exploring ones desires as we grow through puberty is a key part of the journey towards adulthood. And so any attempt to understand young people necessarily requires an insight into the role of sexualities in their lives. Yet much youth research tends to overlook sexualities focusing instead on what may seem the more pressing issues of say unemployment and education. These priorities may reflect the methodological challenges of research into sexualities that by their very nature delve into the unspoken and concealed worlds of young people. Yet our **cultures** are saturated with youth sexualities – corporations use young bodies in their advertising; young romance, sex and love is also the engine of much great music and art, from Shakespeare and *Breakfast at Tiffany's* to Elvis Presley and The Smiths. One might also argue that a 'good society' is one that offers young people the freedom to explore intimate relationships safe from prejudice and discrimination. Indeed research documents how important intimate relationships are to our overall **wellbeing** (Layard, 2005). In reality sexual practices are also often a site of oppression and marginalisation hence their importance to youth studies.

Although there were several landmark studies into sexualities during the mid-twentieth century (De Beauvoir, 1953; Kinsey et al., 1953; Schofield, 1968) it was not until the 1970s and 1980s that this issue took on a greater significance for social scientists. In particular concerns over the spread of HIV/AIDS was the catalyst for greater awareness of young people's sexual practices. Class, gender and racial equalities at this time were the subject of research and legislation whereas little progress was made advancing policies and research around the experiences of gays, lesbians, bisexuals and transgender individuals (GLBT). For much of the twentieth century GLBT were the subject of institutionalised discrimination condoned by the state as equalities legislation excluded sexualities (Weeks, 1985). Growing up as gay in the twentieth century meant that to get on in life, at work and in education one had to conceal one's sexuality and 'fit in' with a dominant heterosexual culture. Liberalisation of laws on sexuality in many Western societies took much of the twentieth century so that the rights enjoyed by heterosexuals were not conferred on young homosexuals for several accades. In Britain, for example, it was not until 2001 that the age of consent for homosexuals was lowered to sixteen years of age in parity with heterosexuals. Indeed in many countries even today (see, for example, Islamic Iran), the state is reluctant to promote gay rights and tackle homophobic cultures.

Social scientists tend to argue that sexualities are socially constructed, though sex drives and sex acts are universal, biological and psychological processes, the meanings these have for people and how they are valued varies through time and across societies. The work of Foucault (1978; 1984a; 1984b) illustrates these historical changes in sexual identities and practices. His work has been influential to youth studies, notably around how power relationships working through state institutions (such as hospitals and schools) and forms of language (such as binary oppositions) constitute sexualities, framing the marginalisation of GLBT individuals. Foucault helps us understand the subtle forms of language, crude categories such as abnormal–normal, gay–straight, whore–virgin, which carry implicit value judgements that label minorities and 'others' as deviant, ill or threatening. His work shows how official policies and language construct heterosexuality as universal and 'healthy' and how we are responsible for managing our sexualities as we work to regulate our sexual practices so they are acceptable to wider society. For Foucault then power works in diverse ways through institutions and individual practices and one can see therefore how all young people and particularly GLBT youth can experience the dissonance between their own sexual identities/practices and the dominant sexualities in wider society.

In contrast, Ken Plummer (1994) has offered a smaller-scale insight into the experiences of young people's sexualities and how GLBT learn about the playing out of sexual identities. Drawing on Interactionist concepts from Goffman, Plummer illustrates how corrosive heterosexist peer cultures can be for young gays and lesbians and how they manage and cope with everyday problems of 'fitting in' with friends and family. One way young gays and lesbians cope with hegemonic heterosexual culture (or 'hetero-normativity') is through the telling and retelling of their own personal stories of 'coming out' as gay or lesbian. When asked about 'coming out' by Plummer this young man responded:

> The question is inescapable. Every gay man has his story and his friends and lovers will, sooner or later, ask him to tell it. It is our common bond

with one another, uniting the different classes, races, educational backgrounds and other groups that make up the gay community. Whether or not our lives have shared the same experiences, a coming out story stirs a powerful empathy in each of us and brings to mind our own years of fear and pain… Coming out is not only a personal statement of worth and self-respect it is a statement of dissent – a voice raised in defence of diversity and democracy. (Wayne Curtis, quoted in Plummer, 1994: 49)

In recent years, however, some research has pointed to a possible weakening in the strength of hegemonic masculinities at least in some middle-class settings. Anderson's research (2009) into male college students in the USA suggested a greater acceptance of gay identities by traditional 'sports orientated' male peer cultures. In the last decade many more public figures in Western societies have also been open about their GLBT identities than in the past, which may suggest some changes in cultural attitudes towards sexualities.

Schooling has been a key focus of sexualities research, with studies showing a range of ways that formal organisation and peer **cultures** can shape sexual identities/practices (Frosh et al., 2002). Holland (2009) writes of how schools can reflect and reinforce societal norms and values around sexualities so that young people's early encounters of homophobia and heterosexism are vividly played out in the playground and classroom. Though as researchers such as Epstein and Johnson (1998) show, class, race and **gender** work through sexualities to frame the experiences of young people in schools. Their ethnographic research in a single-sex girl's school illustrates how the issue of sexuality becomes heightened as schools fail to acknowledge the centrality of sex, romance and the **body** to young people. The de-sexualised nature of modern schools means that the bodily and lingual displays of sexualities are a powerful currency that are then employed in the traditional struggles between teachers and pupils over control and resistance in the classroom and corridor. The authors write about the significance of makeup and revealing dress to young women – how they use these sexualised forms of display to challenge and provoke teachers and to 'fit in' with their peers. Yet echoing Paul Willis' (1977) arguments about working-class boys' educational experiences, Epstein and Johnson suggest that though some young women may accrue social advantage through a form of hypersexuality they also run the risk of labelling from other girls and from teaching staff. They may come to be seen as anti-school and their learning careers and educational attainment may suffer as a result.

Research into mixed sex schools illustrates how difficult it is for young women to navigate different ways in which they can display their sexuality (Nayak and Kehily, 2007). Here we see various double standards at work and the powerful use of binary oppositions. For women to openly discuss their sexual desire they run the risk of being labelled as 'loose' or 'sluts' yet for young men such talk is de rigueur for traditional forms of masculinity where promiscuity is 'heroic' for young males. Holland et al. (2004) talk of the 'male in the head', the ever present internalised male voice that polices the behaviour of young women, closing down spaces for the safe exploration of love, lust and longing. Aapola et al. (2005) discuss the moral gaze of young men and other young women in schools and the constant effort required by women to manage their sexualities so that they avoid the drift into disrespectability and stigmatisation. The winners it seems in these cultural struggles over identities/practices are heterosexual young men. As school peer cultures are sites of male power, sexualities are an important medium through which such power is exercised. And so we can see various rituals in school settings that reinforce the compulsory heterosexuality that underpins the values and relationships of young people.

In many contemporary societies there have been concerns about the sexual health of young people and in particular the rising incidence of sexually transmitted diseases (STDs). In developing societies the spectre of HIV/AIDs haunts the lives of young people who may have been orphaned because of AIDS or run the risk of infection themselves because of the high rates of infection among young people (World Health Organization, 2006). The World Health Organisation's report into HIV among young people found that three quarters of new infections were in young people, some 5000–6000 new cases of infection each day (World Health Organization, 2006). In the UK, for example, there are concerns over increasing incidence of STDs (chlamydia, herpes and gonorrhoea) with the majority of new infections (about 500,000 per year) in young people under twenty-five years of age (Health Protection Agency, 2010). For some this may be yet another example of the moral panics that can be constructed around young people's behaviour. Though for others such concerns over sexual health may reflect problematic changes to young people's sexual practices. Some commentators suggest that the rise of the Internet and social media has 'mainstreamed' pornography in youth cultures, which has distorted young people's attitudes and behaviours. Pornography tends to divorce sex from social relationships and emotional intimacy, presenting often extreme acts as part of everyday normality

(Dworkin, 1981). If young people's sexual practices and their sexual expectations are shaped by pornography they may end up leading more promiscuous yet unfulfilling and risky lives than earlier generations.

At the time of writing the global recession has led to the emiseration of countless millions of young people around the world that can have implications for their sexual practices/identities. Researchers point to the impact of growing poverty on the incidence of risky behaviours such as unsafe/early sex as well as early motherhood (Kabiru et al., 2010; Moloney et al., 2011). At times of economic hardship some young women and men may be forced to use their bodies as an economic resource – selling sex (Watson, 2011) or working as dancers in clubs (Colosi, 2010). However, the relationships between social disadvantage and sexual practices are complex, with some research showing how early sexual activity and motherhood are valued and seen as rewarding by young people (Henderson et al., 2007: 148). Yet such coping strategies may have profound long-term emotional and material consequences for the wellbeing of young people.

REFERENCES

Aapola, S., Gonick, M. and Harris, A. (2005) *Young Femininity: Girlhood, Power and Social Change*. London: Palgrave.

Anderson, E. (2009) *Inclusive Masculinity: The Changing Nature of Masculinities*. New York: Routledge.

Colosi, R. (2010) 'A return to the Chicago School? From the "subculture" of taxi dancers to the contemporary lap dancer', *Journal of Youth Studies*, 13 (1): 1–16.

De Beauvoir, S. (1953) *The Second Sex*. London: Jonathon Cape.

Dworkin, A. (1981) *Pornography: Men Possessing Women*. London: Women's Press.

Epstein, D. and Johnson, R. (1998) *Schooling Sexualities*. Buckingham: Open University Press.

Foucault, M. (1978) *The History of Sexuality Vol. One: An Introduction*. Harmondsworth: Penguin.

Foucault, M. (1984a) *The History of Sexuality: Vol. Two: The Use of Pleasure*. Harmondsworth: Penguin.

Foucault, M. (1984b) *The History of Sexuality: Vol. Three: The Care of the Self*. Harmondsworth: Penguin.

Frosh, S., Phoenix, A. and Patman, R. (2002) *Young Masculinities*. Cambridge: Polity Press.

Health Protection Agency (2010) 'Sexually transmitted infections reach almost half a million', press release, 25 August. www.hpa.org.uk/NewsCentre/NationalPressRele ases/2010PressReleases/100825STI/ (accessed 7 July 2012).

Henderson, S., Holland, J., McGrellis, S., Sharpe, S. and Thomson, R. (2007) *Inventing Adulthoods: A Biographical Approach to Youth Transitions*. London: Sage.

key concepts in youth studies

Holland, J. (2009) 'Understanding the sexual lives of young people', in A. Furlong (ed.), *Handbook of Youth and Young Adulthood: New Perspectives and Agendas*. London: Routledge, pp. 406–12.

Holland, J., Ramazanoglu, C., Sharpe, S. and Thomson, R. (2004) *The Male in the Head: Young People, Heterosexuality and Power*. 2nd edn. London: Tufnell Press.

Kabiru, C., Beguy, D., Undie, C.-C., Msiyaphaza Zulu, E. and Ezeh, A. (2010) 'Transition into first sex among adolescents in slum and non-slum communities in Nairobi, Kenya', *Journal of Youth Studies*, 13 (4): 453–71.

Kinsey, A., Pomeroy, W., Martin, C. and Gebhard, P. (1953) *Sexual Behaviour in the Human Female*. Philadelphia: Saunders.

Layard, R. (2005) *Happiness: Lessons from a New Science*. London: Penguin.

Moloney, M., Hunt, G., Joe-Laidler, K. and MacKenzie, K. (2011) 'Young mothers (in the) hood: gang girl's negotiation of new identities', *Journal of Youth Studies*, 14 (1): 1–19.

Nayak, A. and Kehily, M.J. (2007) *Gender, Youth and Culture: Young Masculinities and Femininities*. London: Palgrave.

Plummer, K. (1994) *Telling Sexual Stories: Power, Change and Social Worlds*. London: Routledge.

Schofield, M. (1968) *The Sexual Behaviour of Young People*. Harmondsworth: Penguin.

Watson, J. (2011) 'Understanding survival sex: young women, homelessness and intimate relationships', *Journal of Youth Studies*, 14 (6): 639–55.

Weeks, J. (1985) *Sexuality and its Discontents: Meaning, Myths and Modern Sexualities*. London: Routledge.

Willis, P. (1977) *Learning to Labour: How Working Class Kids Get Working Class Jobs*. Farnborough: Saxon House.

World Health Organization (2006) *Preventing HIV/AIDs in Young People: A Systematic Review of Evidence from Developing Societies*. Geneva: WHO.

19
Young People and Education

The concept of education and the formal management and organisation of knowledge and learning is central to the study of young people in contemporary societies (see also **informal learning**). Education is both a philosophical and theoretical concept and, over time, competing educational philosophies have influenced the organisation of schools and colleges, curricula and pedagogic techniques that have been developed for young people. Within the UK, the influence of competing educational philosophies is evident in the variety of schools and colleges that exist alongside one another such as elite (public schools); liberal (secondary schools); vocational (technology schools); and civic (community schools). This co-existence is unsurprising given the 'third way' political theory of the recent UK Conservative, Labour and Coalition governments and their willingness to contemplate a combination of public, private and non-profit provision when developing educational policy underpinned by market principles.

Educational systems in Western societies aim to promote 'equality of opportunity', widening access to provision to enhance the life chances of individuals and the competitiveness of increasingly knowledge-based economies in the global era. Though EU policies have encouraged common aims and objectives in education policy (Lawn, 2006) 'the nation state retains considerable autonomy in relation to education' (Brooks, 2009). The history of educational policy-making also reflects different cultural and political traditions that influence the character of education systems in different countries – more centralised systems in France and Germany compared to de-centralised systems in England and Wales (Archer, 1984). In 1997 the UK's former Prime Minister Tony Blair famously described the Labour Party's policy priorities as 'education, education and education'. These educational policies contrast with others across European countries in creating a 'liberal transition regime' valuing individual rights and responsibilities above collective provision by placing increasing responsibility on the individual for maximising their 'employability' (Brooks, 2009; Pohl and Walther, 2007).

From 1997 onwards the New Labour government in the UK was keen to develop a 'learning society' (Ranson, 1998) as a way of meeting the challenges of increasing **globalisation** and so supporting economic and social development (OECD, 2000; Spring, 2009). Within a 'learning society' all members of a population are encouraged to participate in formal, non-formal and informal learning. Though not a new idea, the suggestion is that globalisation requires constant upgrading of citizens' knowledge and skills as societies become more dynamic and technological. Widening access to learning across the life course, it is claimed, helps promote better life chances, social mobility and social cohesion within society (Brown et al., 2011). Recent governments around the world have invested heavily in the infrastructure to support the opportunities for learning across society. In the UK, for example, there has been unprecedented investment in early education and childcare and schooling for children and expansion in further and higher education for young and older adults. In many emerging societies such as China and India there has been extensive investment in education – from nurseries through to university education.

Surveys show how investment in education can produce positive results as data from the Youth Cohort Study in the UK show, in particular there have been continuing rises in attainment since 1997 in national GCSE examinations for sixteen year olds in England and Wales (Department for Education and Skills, 2010). But this trend masks continued patterns of differential attainment because of the **social class** and backgrounds of young people. 'Social class remains the strongest predictor of educational achievement in the UK, where the social class gap for educational achievement is one of the most significant in the developed world' (Halsey et al., 1980; Perry and Francis, 2010: 2). The Youth Cohort Study data (2010) shows in the UK that 82 per cent of those from professional classes achieved at least five A*–C grades at sixteen years of age whereas just 44 per cent of those from lower 'routine' background did (Department for Education and Skills, 2010: 10). There are also attainment differences because of **gender**, with 57 per cent of boys achieving five good GCSE passes whereas 66 per cent of girls did. **Ethnicity** is also significant for shaping educational attainment with 55 per cent of young people from Pakistani backgrounds achieving five good passes compared to 50 per cent for African Caribbean and 61 per cent for those students of white background (Department for Education and Skills, 2010: 10). These differences in educational attainment at sixteen years of age are also replicated in further and higher education, with working-class students and some ethnic minorities participating less and achieving less than those from white and more affluent backgrounds. International comparisons of educational attainment are not always straightforward but the OECD has conducted international surveys of competencies in maths, reading and sciences, through the programme for international student assessment (PISA) since 2000 (OECD, 2009). This shows marked variations in competencies between fifteen year olds from countries such as China, Japan, Finland and Hong Kong scoring highly and those doing less well such as the UK and the USA lower down the league tables.

Governments have developed numerous policies in an effort to narrow differences in attainment and the negative influence of social background on performance in education. Comprehensive schooling, Education Action Zones and the later introduction of more market-based schooling systems (such as academies) all aimed to raise the standards of provision in England and Wales. Financial support for students in schools and colleges was also introduced in England and Wales through the Educational Maintenance Allowance (EMA) in an attempt to encourage greater numbers of young people to remain in education and training beyond sixteen years of age. Through its September Guarantee, the UK Labour government planned by 2015 to ensure all young people participated in learning until they were at least eighteen years old (Department for Children, Schools and Families, 2006).

In 2010 the UK Coalition government continued the market approach to educational policies introducing the idea of Free Schools popularised in Sweden that allowed for local communities to establish their own local schools funded by the state but enjoying autonomy from local government. At a time of budget cuts, spending on education and programmes such as EMAs has been greatly reduced. At the time of writing we are yet to see the full impact of these reforms and cuts to funding on patterns of educational attainment. Though data already show a rise in the numbers of young people not engaged in any form of education, **employment** or **training** (NEET). After leaving compulsory schooling, being NEET has become synonymous with later failure and social exclusion. With austerity measures and the reduction in EMAs the NEET numbers have risen since the UK election in 2010 – indeed between July and September of 2011 almost one in five sixteen to twenty-four year olds in England (1,163,000) were NEET and this represented a 137,000 increase on the same period from 2010 (*The Guardian*, 2011: 16).

The implicit assumption in current UK educational policy is that young people must bear much of the responsibility for their failure in education, yet research suggests such failure has much more complex causes. Studies of school-to-work transitions have continued to highlight the importance of structural factors such as social class, gender and ethnicity in shaping inequalities of process and outcome in education for young people (Raffe, 2009). The theoretical persuasion of the author(s) tends to determine which explanatory factors are privileged, with Marxists emphasising class and feminists emphasising gender, for example. Several youth researchers illustrate how a poor level of educational attainment can then subsequently influence the labour market prospects of young people, which in turn conditions the sorts of **housing**, relationships, domestic and **leisure** careers young people experience through their twenties and thirties (Jones, 2002; MacDonald and

Marsh, 2005). Some recent studies have also documented the experiences of gay, lesbian and bisexual students in schools and how a culture of heterosexism has framed the experience of bullying, labelling and also educational under-achievement (Nayak and Kehily, 1996).

Classic studies of youth **subcultures** and identities also made an important contribution to wider understandings of the disaffection of young people with education. One of the key strengths of these studies (e.g. Willis, 1977) was to show how a focus upon the structuring of educational outcomes also needed to be accompanied by a focus upon the cultural context of the school/college peer-based **social networks**. The latter can frame engagement (the demand) for educational opportunities and help us understand the processes by which young people under-achieve in school and lead distinctive transitions into adulthood. Willis (1977) documented how selection processes in schools can influence the cultural responses of students that contribute to the development of anti-school, pro-school or 'ordinary' youth subcultures. His study illustrated different ways that young people experience education and the importance of style, language and music to peer group relationships. Drawing on insights emerging from wider developments in educational theory about forms of 'cultural capital' (Bourdieu, 1974), more recent youth studies show how young people from working-class backgrounds often struggle to acquire the appropriate cultural practices needed to succeed in formal education. But importantly, within these studies the youth subcultures identified drew their influences largely from key structural aspects of students' backgrounds – in particular, class, gender, race and ethnicity (Gillborn and Mirza, 2000).

Recently, some have challenged the structural models that emphasise socio-economic explanations of school-to-work transitions. They claim that research in the UK, Europe, North America and Australia 'indicates a growing mismatch between the established models of transition and the actual attitudes, choices and experience of young people themselves' (Dwyer and Wyn, 2001: 1). Those advocating this view highlight how changes in the socio-economic context since the 1970s have resulted in a 'de-structuring' of educational transitions as the latter are now characterised by 'elements of uncertainty, unpredictability and risk' (Dwyer and Wyn, 2001: 1). Transitions are no longer largely determined by class but rather young people are seen to have more choice today regardless of their social position, gender and ethnicity. Consequently, some youth researchers in Europe have developed the concept of 'learning biographies' to explore again the transition from education in this new context. They point to youths that can be creative in making rather than taking education-to-work transitions (du Bois Reymond and Chisolm, 2006). Others though remain sceptical – for example, pointing out that the scope to be creative or not which these new studies point to remains largely dependent upon class background (Brooks, 2009).

REFERENCES

Archer, M. (1984) *The Social Origins of Education Systems*. London: Sage.

Bourdieu, P. (1974) 'The school as a conservative force: scholastic and cultural inequalities', in J. Eggleston (ed.), *Contemporary Research in the Sociology of Education*. London: Methuen, pp. 32–46.

Brooks, R. (ed.) (2009) *Transitions from Education to Work: New Perspectives from Europe and Beyond*. Basingstoke: Palgrave Macmillan.

Brown, P., Lauder, H. and Ashton, D. (2011) *The Global Auction: The Broken Promises of Education, Jobs and Incomes*. Oxford: Oxford University Press.

Department for Education and Skills (DfES) (2010) *Youth Cohort Study: The Activities and Experiences of 16 Year Olds: England and Wales, 2009*. London: DfES Publications.

Department for Children, Schools and Families (DCSF) (2006) *Raising Expectations: Supporting All Young People to Participate Until 18*. Nottingham: DCSF Publications.

du Bois Reymond, M. and Chisolm, L. (2006) 'Young Europeans in a changing world', *New Directions for Child and Adult Development*, 113: 1–9.

Dwyer, P. and Wyn, J. (2001) *Youth, Education and Risk: Facing the Future*. London: Routledge.

Gillborn, D. and Mirza, H.S. (2000) *Educational Inequality: Mapping Race, Class and Gender*. London: HMSO.

The Guardian (2011) 'Clegg announces £1bn fund to help 500,000 young jobless into work', 25 November, 16. www.guardian.co.uk/society/2011/nov/25/nick-clegg-fund-youth-unemployment (accessed 30 December 2011).

Halsey, A.H., Heath A. and Ridge, A. (1980) *Origins and Destinations: Family, Class and Education in Modern Britain*. Oxford: Clarendon.

Jones, G. (2002) *The Youth Divide: Diverging Paths to Adulthood*. York: Joseph Rowntree Foundation.

Lawn, M. (2006) 'Soft governance and the learning spaces of Europe', *Comparative European Politics*, 4: 272–88.

MacDonald, R. and Marsh, J. (2005) *Disconnected Youth? Growing Up in Britain's Poor Neighbourhoods*. London: Palgrave Macmillan.

Nayak, A. and Kehily, M.J. (1996) 'Playing it straight: masculinities, homophobia and schooling', *Journal of Gender Studies*, 5 (2): 211–30.

OECD (2000) *Knowledge Management in the Learning Society*. Paris: OECD Publishing.

OECD (2009) *PISA Results 2009*. Paris: OECD.

Perry, E. and Francis, B. (2010) *The Social Class Gap for Educational Achievement: A Review of the Literature*. London: RSA Project.

Pohl, A. and Walther A. (2007) 'Activating the disadvantaged: variations in addressing youth transitions across Europe', *International Journal of Lifelong Education*, 26 (5): 533–53.

Raffe, D. (2009) 'Explaining cross-national differences in education-to-work transitions', in A. Furlong (ed.), *Handbook of Youth and Young Adulthood: New Perspectives and Agendas*. London: Routledge, pp. 105–13.

Ranson, S. (1998) *Inside the Learning Society*. London: Cassell.

Spring, J. (2009) *Globalization of Education: An Introduction*. New York: Routledge.

Willis, P. (1977) *Learning to Labour: How Working Class Kids Get Working Class Jobs*. Farnborough: Saxon House.

20
Young People and the Body

Over the last thirty years or so sociologists have been increasingly concerned with the ways in which the body is implicated in social identities, cultures and power relationships. Writers such as Foucault (1977) and Elias (2000) chart the long-term changes in societies and the self, suggesting that modernity is characterised by an increasing body consciousness. The body plays a greater role in how people experience their lives in terms of outward bodily appearance and internally through emotions and subjectivities. Featherstone (2000) and Crossley (2006) discuss the growth of an increasingly visual culture encouraged by technological advances (video, photography, the Internet) that has further promoted concerns with the body and appearance. Recent research points to the use of social media such as websites and blogs as a key medium for the exploration of bodily representation and the construction of youthful identities (Tara, 2010). In an average day in a modern city we are all bombarded with images of bodies – on the TV, computer screens, street advertising and shop windows.

Embodiment theory argues that our conceptions of who we are, are embodied as our emotional/psychological self exists internally and our physical self we experience everyday through our senses. We mostly communicate with others through bodily signs, others read us and we make sense of others through interpretations of our physical and emotional bodies. People make judgements, rightly or wrongly, about others because of the way their bodies appear, the size, shape, colour, movement can all signify particular meanings about the people who live in these bodies. Prejudice and discrimination through **class, 'race', gender** and other divisions can all be promoted by particular readings of the body. The body therefore can be understood as a key resource that enables or constrains people's efforts to get on in life (through work, **education** and family), to 'fit in', share with others or our attempts to carve out distinctive identities.

Classic studies in youth research from the 1970s and 1980s tended to abstract from detailed analyses of the body. Studies that explored 'race' (Gilroy, 1987), class (Hall and Jefferson, 1976) and gender (Griffin, 1985), though acknowledging the role of style and appearance in the shaping of youth identities, cultures and transitions, failed to unpack in any systematic way how different bodily processes are implicated in young people's lives. It is only in more recent years that youth studies have applied embodiment theory in their work, some emphasising how the body frames patterns of exploitation or domination, while others offering more optimistic accounts of youthful bodies as resources for identity work and careers into adulthood (Frost, 2001).

Some early studies from the 1990s documented the role of body art such as piercings and tattoos in the subcultural lives of young people (Widdicombe and Wooffitt, 1995). Goths, Punks and Hippies employed distinctive body art as ways of constructing subcultural styles and marking out their membership of their groups. In the 1990s such body modification also distinguished such group members from more mainstream ordinary youth. As Riley and Cahill (2005) discuss, body art is often valued by young people not just as a signifier of group membership but also as a subversive statement evoking links with primitive cultures and ancient traditions of identity construction and representation. Young people's unease with dominant forms of youth identity, **transitions** and roles therefore can be challenged through the creative use of their bodies. Young women can, for example, use body art to challenge the dominant cultural assumptions that they use makeup and conventional clothes to construct normative, heterosexual identities. Young men can use earrings and tattoos to resist the expectations that societies place on them to be smartly dressed young workers and learners. The body then in these instances can be a site not just of visual display but also of political activity. One recent example of this role of body art as politics was that of 'slut walks' (Greer, 2012). After a police officer in the USA suggested that the sexual assault of a young woman had been encouraged by what the woman had worn, thousands of young women demonstrated around the world, walking together in revealing clothes and with bodies adorned with slogans written in marker pen. Here then we can see, as Judith Butler (2011) has explored, young women wishing to take control of their bodies by subverting the traditional ways that bodies are read, challenging the everyday objectification they endure as young women.

Although writers in the 1990s documented the significance of body art to some young people, more recent commentators point to the normalisation of body art in **youth culture**. Writers such as Giddens (1991) and Shilling (2003) locate this normalisation within the recent transformations of contemporary societies, notably the restructuring of institutions such as the family, education and work and the associated growth in insecurity, risk and individualisation. In recent decades then the body has become an additional resource for young people in their efforts to develop identities and statuses in the face of uncertainties about how they represent their selves. Tattoos, piercings and other body modifications can be empowering as they are of great significance to young people's sense of self and self-worth, enabling a sense of uniqueness while promoting links to others (Sweetman, 1999). Riley and Cahill (2005: 265) discuss the sense of pleasure and freedom that can come from body art. Young people can use their bodies to create forms of subcultural capital that challenge and transgress boundaries around identities and life course transitions.

Though bodies are resources for young people, most social science research explores how bodies are implicated in the domination and exploitation of adolescents. In developing societies young people's bodies are a key source of labour power and many suffer modern slavery as a result (Bales et al., 2009). Young people are trafficked around the world and underpin the sex industries because of the allure of their bodies (Siddarth, 2010). Huge profits then accrue to businesses because of the exploitation of young people's bodies.

Bodies can constrain in other ways. If one thinks of physical and mental disability we can appreciate some of the limitations that we may all face because of how our bodies function – we have problems walking, talking or thinking. And as Goffman (1963) famously explored, others can add to our difficulties and exclusion by judging and stigmatising those whose bodies are different from the mainstream.

However, much research focuses on how apparently healthy young bodies can be involved in the experience of prejudice and discrimination. Crossley (2006) discusses the work of Bordo (1993) who noted the power the media and celebrity culture wield to define idealised notions of body images and how people enjoy fleeting pleasure from aspiring to these body types – thin women and muscular men in Western societies. The relentless use of 'ideal' bodies in advertising, film and online media demands that we monitor and work on our bodies yet these body ideals for most are unobtainable and so whatever pleasure young people experience in striving for better bodies is undercut by anxieties and insecurities about their bodies, their lifestyles and self-image. The result is a 'bulimic culture' where young people 'yoyo' from the experience of pleasure to angst about their bodies, which can encourage all manner of consumerist, quick-fix solutions to perceived problems about appearance and lifestyle such as dieting, cosmetic surgery and physical work-out regimes. As a result of this perverse, mediazed, body-centric culture research such as that by Liz Frost (2001) argues that large numbers of young people and women in particular experience hatred of their own bodies. In addition, in the UK the Bread for Life Campaign in 1988, for example, found only 25 per cent of the 900 young people they interviewed were happy with their weight, 20 per cent at any time were dieting and 61 per cent felt inadequate about their appearance. In more recent research in the USA, Taylor (2011) and Boyd et al. (2011) documented the pressures that young people are under to appear thin and how bullying around body size and body fat are a feature of everyday life in American schools. Such harassment causes distress for many young people, threatening their self-identities and self-worth.

Body image is also bound up with discourses around sexuality and forms of masculinity and femininity. Researchers point to how the media and large corporations can promote quite narrow conventions about acceptable forms of youth identities (Bordo, 2001; Connell, 2005; Mac an Ghaill, 1994). Overall many of these more pessimistic interpretations of young people's bodies suggest a closing down of the opportunities for young people to creatively explore their social identities. As Featherstone (2000) argues, the emergence of a visual culture and fixation on the body has hollowed out deeper more diverse and subtle ways of 'being' in contemporary societies. If one 'looks the part' and projects appropriate emotions then one 'is the part'. Foucault (1977) and Rose (1999) write of how this focus on the body and the self and the increasing work one has to do to maintain one's appearance and subjectivities is a key form of oppression in contemporary societies. This is a sophisticated form of oppression that is sustained not just by large corporations and state bureaucracies but also by young people themselves in their everyday lives.

REFERENCES

Bales, K., Trodd, Z. and Williamson, A.K. (2009) *Modern Slavery: The Secret World of 27 Million People*. Oxford: One World Publications.

Bordo, S. (1993) *Unbearable Weight*. Berkeley: University of California Press.

Bordo, S. (2001) *The Male Body*. New York: Farrar, Strauss and Giroux.

Boyd, E., Reynolds, J., Tilman, K. and Martin, P. (2011) 'Adolescent girls race/ethnic status, identities and drive for thinness', *Social Science Research*, 40 (2): 667–84.

Butler, J. (2011) *Bodies That Matter: On the Discursive Limits of Sex*. London: Routledge.

Connell, R. (2005) *Masculinities*. 2nd edn. Cambridge: Polity Press.

Crossley, N. (2006) *Reflexive Embodiment in Contemporary Society*. Milton Keynes: Open University Press.

Elias, N. (2000) *The Civilizing Process*. Oxford: Wiley-Blackwell.

Featherstone, M. (2000) *Body Modification*. London: Sage.

Foucault, M. (1977) *Discipline and Punish: The Birth of the Prison*. London: Allen Lane.

Frost, L. (2001) *Young Women and the Body: A Feminist Sociology*. London: Palgrave.

Giddens, A. (1991) *Modernity and Self-Identity: Self and Society in the Late Modern Age*. Cambridge: Polity.

Gilroy, P. (1987) *'There Ain't No Black in the Union Jack*. London: Routledge.

Goffman, E. (1963) *Stigma: Notes on the Management of Spoiled Identity*. London: Penguin.

Greer, G. (2012) 'These "slut walk" women are simply fighting for their right to be dirty', *The Telegraph*, 12 May. www.telegraph.co.uk/health/women_shealth/8510743/These-slut-walk-women-are-simply-fighting-for-their-right-to-be-dirty.html (accessed 29 June 2012).

Griffin, C. (1985) *Typical Girls: Young Women from School to the Job Market*. London: Routledge and Kegan Paul.

Hall, S. and Jefferson, T. (eds) (1976) *Resistance Through Rituals: Youth Subcultures in Post-War Britain*. London: Hutchinson.

Mac an Ghaill, M. (1994) *The Making of Men: Masculinities, Sexualities and Schooling*. Buckingham: Open University Press.

Riley, S. and Cahill, S. (2005) 'Managing meaning and belonging: young women's negotiations of authenticity in body art', *Journal of Youth Studies*, 8 (3): 261–80

Rose, N. (1999) *Governing the Soul: The Shaping of the Private Self*. London: Free Association Books.

Shilling, C. (2003) *The Body and Social Theory*. London: Sage.

Siddarth, K. (2010) *Sex Trafficking: Inside the Business of Modern Slavery*. Columbia: Columbia University Press.

Sweetman, P. (1999) 'Anchoring the postmodern self? Body modification, fashion and identity', *Body and Society*, 5 (2): 51–76.

Tara, C. (2010) 'Digital dressing up: modelling female teen identity in the discursive spaces in the fashion blogosphere', *Journal of Youth Studies*, 13 (4): 505–20.

Taylor, N. (2011) '"Guys she's humongous". Gender and weight based teasing in adolescence', *Journal of Adolescent Research*, 26 (2): 178–99.

Widdicombe, S. and Wooffitt, R. (1995) *The Language of Youth Subcultures: Social Identity in Action*. London: Harvester Wheatsheaf.

21

Young People and Place

In our everyday lives place has a powerful hold over us. Place can refer to an order of priority, outcome, occupation or vocation but is most commonly associated with physical space or location. Human geography talks of 'topophilia' as the love people have for physical places (Tuan, 1974). Beaches, mountains, rivers, even a street can all offer us powerful emotional experiences evoking memories of past lives. Football fans flock to their stadia as if temples or shrines, enjoying a sporting spectacle yet also communing with the traditions and rituals of their club. Over time a house becomes a home, the four walls accumulating the shared memories of family life. Therefore, place can be distinctive, personal yet also shared, imbued with meaning, symbolism and emotions shaping our social identities and practices as we grow through life.

Different sorts of young people may have different understandings of place and may conceptualise space differently from older people. Place therefore is also a mental or psychological construction where in our everyday lives we experience places in imagined ways. We can also talk of 'knowing your place', which implies a social ranking of people. Used in this sense place has some similarity to the concepts of 'field' and 'habitus' used by Bourdieu (1977). For Bourdieu 'fields' in Western societies include the arts, law, **class**, **politics**, economics, science and **education**. These fields are social spaces of conflict or competition representing external structural conditions of possibility in which people form complex social relations and have access to varying levels of economic, cultural and social capital (Jones, 2009: 40). For example, academic under-achievement of many working-class young people has been accounted for by their lack of cultural capital and their failure to master requirements expected within the field of education. Rather, they often adopt habitus – dispositions for social practice – that are felt to conflict with dominant values in this field. So the meaning they attach to education as a field (place) and their involvement within it makes a profound difference to their lives.

Through focusing on the places frequented by young people, youth researchers have sought to develop a better understand of their worlds. First, by exploring the importance of place in shaping young peoples' identities, opportunity structures, **transitions** into adulthood, **youth subcultures** and lifestyles. Second, by exploring how the environmental characteristics of places – such as neighbourhoods and communities – have meaning for the young people that reside within them (Hopkins, 2010). Such research has a long history in the social sciences as we see with the Chicago School whose 'social ecology of the city' linked the physical characteristics of neighbourhoods with the norms and values of its inhabitants. Hence Thrasher (1927) writes of the emergence of youth gangs that identify with their neighbourhood and how such associations arise out of the poverty and poor opportunities in these urban areas. Whyte's *Street Corner Society* (1943) explored the North Boston Italian community and its local street gangs, demonstrating how the identities of young people were bound up with **social networks** and relations at the street level. Whyte identified two groups of young men – 'corner boys' and 'college boys'. Whyte highlighted how 'college boys' were interested in education and social mobility while he showed the importance of places such as local street corners and shops in the socialisation of the 'corner boys'. The local relations he found were also linked to wider economic and **social policy** including opportunities structured via the New Deal programme. Research by J.B. Mays (1954) as well as Wilmott (1966) also illustrated how growing up in disadvantaged communities in England can influence the values of young people and in particular patterns of delinquency. In the UK, place and its intersection with youth subculture also featured in research undertaken by the University of Birmingham's Centre for Contemporary Cultural Studies (Hall and Jefferson, 1976). A key theme of their work was how local cultural influences (rooted in work and leisure) can frame the emerging cultures and social relationships of young people to create distinctive class-based youth subcultures.

More recently, **globalisation** has promoted research into spatial relationships as it is claimed that globalisation has recast the significance of place in contemporary societies. Anthony Giddens' (1990) work in this area suggests that globalisation has created dynamic, technologically driven social relationships and these relations connect geographically distant localities, meaning events happening locally are increasingly shaped by events taking place many miles away (Giddens, 1990: 64). In this context the capacity of local places to produce place-based **social networks**, meanings, affiliations and a sense of belonging is said to be reduced as families and individuals are increasingly open to influences from beyond their neighbourhoods. As such, social polarisation, divisions and individuated lives come to the fore as the influence of locality declines. As Thomson (2006: 81) has shown, some claim the local and traditional ideas of place 'no longer matter'. Yet other studies have demonstrated how place continues to matter in the context of globalisation. These include studies in developing societies and 'shanty towns' (Favelas) in Brazil and how young people's life chances and identities can be shaped by the deprivation and poor opportunities that characterise such areas (Ney dos Santos, 1996).

Ken Roberts and colleagues' research in the UK and the former 'Eastern Bloc' has also highlighted the importance of place and its impact on job opportunities and youth transitions of young people (Roberts, 2005; Roberts et al., 1999).

Longitudinal research undertaken in the Teesside area of the North East of England has also focused upon how place affects the transitions made by 'socially excluded' working-class young people (MacDonald et al., 2005; 2010; Shildrick et al., 2009). This research demonstrated how the places where these young people resided, in some of England's poorest local neighbourhoods, influenced their membership of place-based social networks. In neighbourhoods blighted by de-industrialisation, economic decline, place-based networks of family and friends offered crucial support and inclusion to young people as they made their transition into adulthood. Not surprisingly therefore, young people demonstrated a strong sense of attachment and belonging to these networks. But, membership of these local working-class networks also offered limited access to wider economic, cultural and social capital. As such, while these place-based networks offered support, paradoxically for young people membership and a strong loyalty and sense of belonging resulted in the closing down of opportunities and put a limitation on the possibilities of young people escaping the conditions of social exclusion (MacDonald et al., 2005; Webster et al., 2004).

Research based in several other areas in England with high levels of worklessness (Hull, Walsall and Wolverhampton) has further explored belonging and attachment to place-based social networks (Green and White, 2007). The authors found 'attachment to place is a very important factor in some young people's life choices' and that 'place-based social networks affect aspirations and behaviour' of young people. 'Reliance on family support can reduce ambition and limit choices to familiar options and locations.' But they found this was not always the case and that membership of locally based social networks gave 'some young people strong advantages in the labour market' (Green and White, 2007: viii). 'Some young people are "trapped by space" (either by circumstances or desire) whereas others "transcend" it' (Green and White, 2007: 91). Youth research then suggests that in the context of globalisation place continues to matter as a source of influence on young people and their lives. But this is in a way whereby aggregate characteristics (including globalisation) and social dynamics of place intersect and influence the lives of groups and individuals in complex ways. In this context the term 'glocal' has become popular and tries to capture the continued significance of local places on the lives of young people despite global influence (Robertson, 1992).

REFERENCES

Bourdieu, P. (1977) *Outline of a Theory of Practice*. Cambridge: Cambridge University Press.

Giddens, A. (1990) *The Consequences of Modernity*. Cambridge: Polity.

Green, A. and White, R. (2007) *Attachment to Place: Social Networks, Mobility and Prospects*. York: Joseph Rowntree Foundation.

Hall, S. and Jefferson, T. (eds) (1976) *Resistance Through Rituals: Youth Subcultures in Post-War Britain*. London: Hutchinson

Hopkins, P.E. (2010) *Young People, Place and Identity*. London: Routledge.

Jones, G. (2009) *Youth*. Cambridge: Polity Press.

MacDonald, R., Shildrick, T. and Blackman, S. (eds) (2010) *Young People, Class and Place*. London: Routledge.

MacDonald, R., Shildrick, T., Webster, C. and Simpson, D. (2005) 'Growing up in poor neighbourhoods: the significance of class and place in the extended transitions of 'socially excluded' young people', *Sociology*, 39 (5): 873–91.

Mays, J.B. (1954) *Juvenile Delinquency*. London: Jonathon Cape.

Ney dos Santos, O. (1996) 'Favelas and ghettos: race and class in Rio de Janeiro and New York City', *Latin American Perspectives*, 23: 82.

Roberts, K. (2005) 'Social class, opportunity structures and careers advice', in B.A. Irving and B. Malik (eds), *Critical Reflections on Careers Education and Guidance: Promoting Social Justice within a Global Economy, Abingdon*: Routledge/Falmer, pp. 130–42.

Roberts, K., Fagan, C., Tholen, J., Nemiria, G., Adibekian, A. and Tarkhnishvili, L. (1999) 'Young people and employment in the transition countries: evidence from Ukraine, Georgia and Armenia', *The Finnish Review of East European Studies*, 6 (1): 6–24.

Robertson, R. (1992) *Globalisation: Social Theory and Global Culture*. London: Theory, Culture and Society/Sage.

Shildrick, T., Blackman, S. and MacDonald, R. (2009) 'Young people, class and place', *Journal of Youth Studies*, 12 (5): 457–65.

Thomson, P. (2006) 'Miners, diggers, ferals and show-men: School-community projects that affirm and unsettle identities and place?' *British Journal of Sociology of Education*, 27 (1): 81–96.

Thrasher, F. (1927) *The Gang*. Chicago: University of Chicago Press.

Tuan, Y.F. (1974) *Topophilia: A Study of Environmental Perception, Attitudes and Values*. Englewood Cliffs, NJ: Prentice Hall.

Webster, C., Simpson, D., MacDonald, R., Abbas, A., Cieslik, M., Shildrick, T. and Simpson, M. (2004) *Poor Transitions: Social Exclusion and Young Adults*. Bristol: Policy Press.

Whyte, W.F. (1943) *Street Corner Society: The Social Structure of an Italian Slum*. Chicago: University of Chicago Press.

Wilmott, P. (1966) *Adolescent Boys in East London*. London: Routledge and Kegan Paul.

22
Young People and Religion

Religion has been considered to comprise three essential elements which are based on an idea of the sacred (Durkheim, 1912). First, beliefs in the supernatural such as a God(s) and/or divinities including angels; second, symbols such as a cross or iconography; and third, practices including rituals such as baptism or fasting. These elements can be the basis of a socio-religious community such as a church, temple or sect. Sacred things are categorised as protected and isolated by religious command within these communities. The sacred elements of the Christian religion are a supreme being labelled 'God', which is considered omnipotent, and his followers worship and praise him through established rituals (masculine characteristics are ascribed to the Christian God in the Bible). As Durkheim writes, religious beliefs usually involve the sacred with its emphasis on the extraordinary or other-worldly contrasted with profane beliefs with their emphasis on the common, the everyday and the secular. Religion is usually defined by the sacred rather than by a belief in God(s) because some religions such as forms of Buddhism do not actually include a supreme being. Max Weber held slightly different views, seeing religion as a set of coherent beliefs that arise out of the need to manage existential dilemmas such as birth and death. In this sense we are all religious as we all face these existential issues.

Collins-Mayo and Dandelion (2010: 1) suggest that youth studies has mostly neglected the role of religion in the lives of the young. Yet it is also 'an important source of values, life purpose and communal belonging and a vehicle for marking the transition from adolescence to adulthood'. Young people are viewed as being at the 'forefront of cultural and social change' and therefore 'it is their engagement with religion, religious ideas and institutions that tell us how resilient beliefs and practices are, and how religions might adapt, transform and innovate in regard to wider social and cultural trends' (Collins-Mayo and Dandelion, 2010: 2). Youth scholars have focused upon religiosity, which is a term that denotes the extent to which groups of young people or individuals are religious. This religiosity can be measured by the strength of belief or commitment to a faith or through participation in religious activities and rituals such as attending Mass or Mosque. In this latter sense, patterns of religiosity differ between regions of the world, between nation states, between groups within populations and between individuals – although unfortunately most data from large-scale surveys have only focused upon English-speaking countries.

Drawing on data from the National Study of Youth and Religion in the USA, Pearce and Lindquist Denton (2009: 414) identify how '84% of American teenagers (ages 13–17) believe in God, 12% are unsure, and only 3 per cent do not believe in God'. Indeed, 'between four and six out of ten American teenagers say they believe in angels, demons, divine miracles and life after death'. In contrast, within the UK in the mid-1990s a sample of thirteen to fifteen year olds attending school in England and Wales found '39% believe in God and 41% believe in life after death' (Pearce and Lindquist Denton, 2009: 414). Within the UK further research highlights how young people attend church less than older people although not going to church does not necessarily mean young people lack religious faith. The English Church Census identified how there was a rapid decline in the numbers of young people attending church during the 1990s. The average age of church goers increased from thirty-seven years in 1979 to forty-five years by 2006. This survey also revealed how 59 per cent of churches had nobody between the ages of fifteen and nineteen attending them in 2005 (Brierley, 2006). These data raise some intriguing questions about the spiritual, moral and cultural development of recent generations and their impact on wider British society.

Other European countries show a similar pattern of declining religiosity to the UK, though Davie (2002) does suggest that Europe is an 'exceptional case', as in other parts of the world significant numbers of young people are involved in religious practices. Around the globe young people are part of a growth in 'fundamentalism', a term used to describe an enthusiastic revival in religion which is occurring in several continents. There is also some evidence for the growth of fundamentalism in Europe and the UK within several religions (Almond et al., 2003). Indeed, the pattern regarding religiosity in the UK is more complex than it seems as evidence suggests that **'race' and ethnicity** can influence religious adherence. Survey research and census data reveal how there are higher levels of religiosity among all ethnic minority groups (apart from the Chinese) when compared with the majority 'white' population within the UK. However, among all ethnic groups in the UK younger people generally have lower levels of religiosity. **Gender** also shapes religiosity among the young with females being more religiously involved than males. Parental and family relationships also influence religious participation among young people. Further, findings from qualitative research raise doubts about the survey data that usually suggest that large numbers of people are religious in Western societies. The ethnographic data found that for many youths, 'faith operates in the background, not as a central feature of their everyday lives' (Pearce and Lindquist Denton, 2009: 415). Hence quantitative surveys do not always reveal the complexities of how faith operates in the lives of young people today.

Voas and Crockett (2005) attempt to explain the relatively low levels of religiosity among young people in the UK and considered three possibilities. First, they suggested age may be a reason, with people tending to become more religious as they get older and closer to death. Also religious beliefs might be affected by critical moments in the life course such as having children as often people wish to raise their children in a faith.

Second, the authors also indicated how religiosity was associated with particular historical periods marked by specific events or social upheaval. Linkages have therefore been drawn between **politics** and faith during times of social change across several societies. In Northern Ireland, for example, during the recent troubles (1960s–1990s) many young people identified with either the Catholic or Protestant Christian Church. This could be understood as a cultural as well as a religious act. At times of strife the different churches came to be associated with the wider cultural or sectarian identities as much as they did for their inherent religious activities (Mitchell, 2005). We witnessed a similar role for Christian churches during the Civil Rights movements in the USA during the 1960s and the 'liberation theology' expressed as resistance to oppressive regimes within Southern America and then beyond (Berryman, 1987). Thus Generation Y born in the UK during the 1980s and growing up in the relatively stable times since have 'little spiritual interest, being rather more focused on personal happiness' (Brierley, 2006: 118).

Finally Voas and Crockett (2005) suggest, drawing on data from the British Social Attitudes Survey, there is a progressive decline of religion across the country as the religiosity of each generation lessens (2005: 24). Some have questioned if this conclusion of Voas and Crockett applies throughout the life course and to non-conventional spiritual beliefs among the young. Spirituality refers to beliefs about immaterial reality and/or an inner path which allows a young person to find the essence of his or her being and also to the most profound values and meanings by which young people live (Sheldrake, 2007). Flory and Miller (2000) in the USA claimed Generation X born between 1960 and 1980 increasingly turned away from conventional religion and denominational loyalty as they moved from youth into adulthood to express religious spirituality through 'new religions' and youthful religious gatherings (including a Christian tattoo parlour). Research has also explored alternative youth religions including paganism and young witches. But spirituality outside of religion may reject notions of supernatural beings and metaphysical beliefs. For instance, forms of pantheism highlight a respect for nature but reject any notion of a God entity. Spirituality in pantheism is based on humanistic ethics and the universe and nature are held in wonder and awe. But this reverence for nature does not include an anthropomorphic worship or belief that nature has a mind or personality which can be influenced via prayer or ritual. In the UK Heelas et al. (2005) found non-religious spiritual beliefs in society are growing rapidly across both generations X and Y, although full active engagement with such spirituality often does not occur until young people become middle-aged.

The recent interest in culture and morals in the social sciences has led to some new projects into the religious lives of young people. In particular questions have been raised about the relationship between liberal values and religious beliefs. If young people increasingly hold more liberal views on the family (cohabiting, births outside of marriage) and sexuality (accepting of homosexuality) does this imply a decline in religiosity or do young people develop ways of accommodating conflictual moral positions? Research by Yip et al. (2011: 4) explored some of these cultural and moral complexities of young people's lives in a study of 693 'religious young adults, aged between 18 and 25. Specifically, it studied the sexual and religious values, attitudes, experiences and identities of young adults from different religious traditions, namely Buddhism, Christianity, Hinduism, Islam, Judaism and Sikhism'. The research also considered 'factors (for example, family, social and cultural expectations, religious institution) that inform their decision-making in these areas, and the diverse ways they managed their religious faith and sexuality' (Yip et al., 2011: 4). It found 'participants acknowledged the significant social dimension of religious faith which not only illuminated their personal lives, but also helped foster interpersonal and community connections. Some participants also emphasised the sense of ethnic and cultural belonging that their religious identification offered' (Yip et al., 2011: 4). In regard to the **sexuality** of these young people, 'participants were almost equally split on the idea that sex should only occur within marriage, suggesting that some religious young adults had moved from "sex in marriage" as the ideal to "meaningful or committed sexual expression" as the ideal (but in diverse relational contexts)' although 'monogamy within a partnered relationship was also highly valued' (Yip et al., 2011: 5).

Yip et al.'s research constitutes what has been described as, 'a growing body of research outlining the positive and protective relationships between religion and youth outcomes' (Pearce and Lindquist Denton, 2009: 417). This positive influence on youth is felt to come through 'moral orders', which offer guidance, 'learned competencies' including knowledge and skills and 'social and organisational ties', which offer access to valuable cultural and social capital (Smith, 2003). There is a long history of religious organisations attempting to have a positive influence through **working with young people** (for example, the YMCA). Faith-based youth work can be situated within various settings from local community halls to prisons. Youth scholars with an interest in religion and non-religious spiritual beliefs recognise how further exploration is required to develop understandings in several areas. For example, Pearce and Lindquist Denton (2009: 418) have called for research which provides 'better investigation of the factors that select families and youth into religious practice and identifies and support their continuation in order to produce more confident estimates of so called "effects" of adolescent religiosity'.

It is perhaps unsurprising there is a growing interest in religion and young people as religious beliefs are connected to the ways that moral issues are navigated by young people. And the young have been at the centre of widespread debates and moral panics about the place of work, family life and sexuality in society. For example, in the USA the emergence of neo-Conservativism is linked to extremist Christian beliefs concerning homosexuality and the issues of restricting abortion. The latter offer a threat to the citizenship rights of some young people. In the aftermath of the July 2007 bombings in London and moral panics over Islamic youth, research has also explored possible reasons for why the young perpetrators came to adopt such fundamentalist religious views. Lewis (2007) found that within British Muslim communities an intergenerational gap has developed which has resulted in a disconnection between many young Muslims and older members of the community including traditional Muslim religious leaders. In this context Lewis claimed a small minority turn towards radical groups as they sought somewhere to belong and something in which to believe. Another area of potential exploration is in regard to 'honour-related violence' (HRV) including 'honour killings'. No major religion condones 'honour killings' but it is reported that 25 per cent of victims are under eighteen years of age. Many perpetrators of HRV, who are often young males, attempt to justify their actions through reference to religious beliefs (Idriss and Abbas, 2011). Given the myriad ways that religion influences young people's lives it seems likely religion and belief will be a vibrant area of youth studies over the coming decades.

REFERENCES

Almond, G., Appleby, R. and Evan, S. (2003) *Strong Religion: The Rise of Fundamentalism Around the World*. Chicago: University of Chicago Press.

Berryman, P. (1987) *Liberation Theology: The Essential Facts about the Revolutionary Movements in Latin America and Beyond*. London: I.B. Tauris.

Brierley, P. (2006) *Pulling Out of the Nose Dive: A Contemporary Picture of Churchgoing*. London: Christian Research.

young people and religion

Collins-Mayo, S. and Dandelion, P. (eds) (2010) *Religion and Youth*. Farnham: Ashgate Press.

Davie, C. (2002) *Europe: The Exceptional Case. Parameters of Faith in the Modern World*. London: Darton, Longman and Todd.

Durkheim, E. (1912) *The Elementary Forms of the Religious Life*. New York: Collier Books.

Flory, R.W. and Miller, D.E. (2000) *Gen X Religion*. London: Routledge.

Heelas, P., Woodhead, L., Seel, B., Tusting, K. and Szersynski, B. (2005) *The Spiritual Revolution: Why Religion Is Giving Way to Spirituality*. Oxford: Blackwell.

Idriss, M.M. and Abbas, T. (2011) (eds.) *Honour, Violence, Women and Islam*. London: Routledge.

Lewis, P. (2007) *Young, British and Muslim*. London: Continuum Publishing.

Mitchell, C. (2005) *Religion, Identity and Politics in Northern Ireland*. Aldershot: Ashgate Press.

Pearce, L. and Lindquist Denton, M. (2009) 'Religiosity in the lives of youth', in A. Furlong (ed.), *Handbook of Youth and Young Adulthood: New Perspectives and Agendas*. London: Routledge, pp. 413–19.

Sheldrake, P. (2007) *A Brief History of Spirituality*. Oxford: Wiley-Blackwell

Smith, C. (2003) 'Theorizing religious effects among American adolescents', *Journal for the Scientific Study of Religion*, 42: 17–30.

Voas, D. and Crockett, A. (2005) 'Religion in Britain: neither believing nor belonging', *Sociology*, 39 (1): 11–28.

Yip, A.K.T., Keenan, M. and Page, S. (2011) *Religion, Youth and Sexuality: Selected Key Findings from a Multi-faith Exploration*. Nottingham: University of Nottingham.

23
Young People and Music

We set out here to examine what might be distinctive about young people's involvement with music, how this has evolved historically and some of the key insights made by researchers in this field.

Music is powerful as it has the ability to move us emotionally and physically as we listen or make music for ourselves. A song can transport us to other places, to our pasts or to futures yet to be lived. Music enables us to connect with others who are strangers or those who are dear to us. If we want to understand young people therefore, how they relate to one another, the things that are important to them, then music must be a part of that analysis. Researchers view popular music as a central feature of young people's cultural **identities** and practices – how they represent themselves, relate to each other and differentiate themselves from others (Bennett, 2009; Rentfrow et al., 2009). As the youth phase is seen as a time of 'storm and stress' and vulnerability (Erickson, 1968) music has a key role in helping young people manage these psychological explorations of the self. Popular music then can be empowering as it offers a vocabulary through which young people can express their feelings about their lives. If young people are marginalised as they have little 'voice' at school, or work or are unemployed then the creative possibilities of music are important for young people's self-esteem and general **wellbeing** (Bradley, 1992). As music allows people to share common interests and meet with others it can also be a catalyst for the establishment of friendship groups that are culturally distinctive, drawing in particular forms of dress, language and consumption (Bennett, 2000: 195; Willis, 1978). In many societies a young person's interest in music and the cultural displays associated with it are seen as a key 'rite of passage', marking one of the early steps in teenage life, away from the control of parents and an important one towards adult independence.

Youth studies regards the 1950s as a key point in the emergence of popular music and its role in **youth cultures**. Growing affluence in Western societies, the growth in radio and record formats and a baby-boom generation all combined to create the conditions for a youth market for music (Frith, 1983). Elvis Presley and other rock and roll stars set the scene for the arrival of global musical acts such as The Beatles and Rolling Stones, and genres such as Psychedelic/Hippy, Soul, and Rhythm and Blues of the 1960s and the Glam Rock and Reggae of the 1970s. Early commentators suggest that young people's involvement in these musical genres can be understood as a form of escapism from the drudgery and disempowerment of the everyday world of education and work (Frith, 1983). Writers talk of music-based cultural groupings being a focus for tensions and conflict with parental culture, working as an axis around which rebelliousness is played out (Willis, 1978: 68). The dress codes of Rock and Roll such as stylised work clothes of denim and leather, the coarse language of the street, the pounding beat of drums, bass and guitars all evoke this anger, frustration and pent up power of youth waiting to be vented. Young male Hippies with long hair and the androgynous image of David Bowie all subverted the everyday rules of dress in the 1960s and 1970s. It was common at the time for the press to depict these youth cultures as threatening the norms and values of wider society as the music and its stars were encouraging deviant behaviour – permissiveness, taking drugs, drinking alcohol to excess and violent acts. Rock and Roll in its time, like the Hippies, Punks and Rappers that followed, have all symbolised the threat posed by young people to the moral order and represent for older people at least a sign of moral and social decline. Popular musical genres during the twentieth century have all become involved at one time or another in moral panics about the 'youth of today' and what young people's values and behaviour signify about the state of wider society (Cohen, 1987; Malbon, 1999; Thornton, 1995).

Youth researchers have attempted to analyse how popular music and **youth cultures** can become embroiled in these moral panics that can create distorted impressions of young people's lives. Some have pointed to the power of the mass media and the need for newspapers and TV news to generate newsworthy stories. And so small skirmishes between Mods and Rockers during the summer months are heavily publicised which encourages more young people to get involved in such activity – so-called 'deviancy amplification' (Cohen, 1987). This focus on the behaviour of a minority can then lead to unjustified labelling of young people in general or a pathologising of youth as troublemakers. Though as some researchers note (Thornton, 1995) this public interest in the deviance of youth cultures may be welcomed by some youth, bolstering their self-esteem and standing among other young people and enhancing their 'subcultural capital'. Most researchers are critical of popular representations of youth cultures in the mass media, noting how only a minority of young people are actually involved in such behaviour and participate in these spectacular youth cultures (Roberts, 2011). Most ordinary young people in the UK during the 1960s and 1970s were neither Mods nor Rockers. Similar arguments could be made for involvement in later musical genres such as Psychedelia, Glam Rock, Punk and Rap.

The most influential analysis of musical tastes and youth cultures was developed by the Centre for Contemporary Cultural Studies (CCCS) in the English Midlands during the 1970s (Hall and Jefferson, 1976). Here they combined the insights of the Chicago School (the use of ethnography to study youth cultures in urban locations) with the Marxist interest in the historical development of class struggle. The ambition of the CCCS was not only to investigate the place of music and style in particular youth cultures but also to link such formations to deeper class relationships. Hence the dress codes and musical tastes of youth cultures are chosen not just because of an innate aesthetic or rhythmic appeal but also because they offer a cultural way of managing the tensions and frustrations that young people experience because of their position in the class system. Paul Willis (1978) suggests there is an homology between **social class** background and subcultural grouping hence working-class youth during the 1970s in England would tend to be more attracted to Rock and Roll and Biker culture, while more afflu-ent middle classes would participate more in Hippy youth cultures and Psychedelic music. Frith (1983) developed similar arguments in his analysis of music cultures in school age youth where middle-class sixth formers were interested in progressive rock while the younger working-class students were into more accessible mainstream pop music.

More recent research into popular music and youth cultures has tended to question the close relationship between socio-economic back-grounds, subcultural groupings and musical preferences (Bennett, 1999; Redhead, 1990). The last decades of the twentieth century saw young people develop more complex, ephemeral and shifting musical tastes, leaving behind the more enduring subcultural affiliations that may have characterised their parents' adolescence. This has been encouraged by technology such as the Internet that has globalised the music industry allowing for rapid movement/consumption of music around the world. The ability to quickly search for new music and download it electroni-cally allows consumers to assemble diverse portfolios of sounds. Advances in computing also allow young people to easily create and circulate their own music allowing for far more creative engagement in music than was possible for earlier generations (Charry, 2012). Researchers employ concepts such as lifestyles (Miles, 2000), 'neo-tribes' and 'scenes' (Bennett, 1999) to describe these new more fluid, creative cultural practices and the often 'pick and mix' approach to musical tastes adopted by many young people today. This is not to say that music has lost any of its power and influence in young people's lives. Research still points to the centrality of music to young people's social relationships and identities. Young people still connect to others through a shared interest in music, spend hours each day listening to music and watching music videos. Musicians are key features in a con-temporary celebrity culture, young people following the style and lives of current stars such as Lady Gaga, Beyonce, Adele and others.

Contemporary researchers have been keen to show how musical gen-res can travel around the globe, being combined to create distinctive local scenes as we see with the fusion of Rap and Bhangra (Bennett, 2000). Commentators such as Bennett (1999) and Muggleton (2000) view this emergence of post-subcultures as reflecting the more fluid, consumerist lives of young people today, yet some have been critical of this research for neglecting the relationships between youth cultures and political/economic processes (Griffin, 2010). Griffin writes that the significance of the CCCS approach was its attempt to link youth cultures (and associated musical tastes) with the educational, family and **employment** experiences of young people and to chart the political and cultural implications of these connections. In so doing one can develop an historical account of young people's cultural lives that is sensitive to their structural locations yet charts the creative ways they establish and maintain their friendships and identities. For Griffin and others (Cieslik, 2001) post-subcultural accounts have become perhaps too concerned with documenting the cultural creativity of young people's involvement in music to the detriment of the economic and political features of their lives that can also frame their participation in cultural activities.

REFERENCES

Bennett, A. (1999) 'Subcultures or neo-tribes? Rethinking the relationship between youth, style and musical taste', *Sociology*, 33 (3): 599–617.

Bennett, A. (2000) *Popular Music and Youth Culture: Music, Identity and Place*. London: Macmillan.

Bennett, A. (2009) 'Spectacular soundtracks: youth and music', in A. Furlong (ed.), *Handbook of Youth and Young Adulthood: New Perspectives and Agendas*. London: Routledge, pp. 263–8.

Bradley, D. (1992) *Understand Rock 'n' Roll: Popular Music in Britain 1955–1964*. Buckingham: Open University Press.

Charry, E. (2012) *Hip Hop Africa: New African Music in a Globalizing World*. Bloomington, IL: Indiana University Press.

Cieslik, M. (2001) 'Researching youth cultures: some problems with the cultural turn in British Youth Studies', *Scottish Youth Issues Journal*, 2: 27–48.

Cohen, S. (1987) *Folk Devils and Moral Panics: The Creation of the Mods and Rockers*. 3rd edn. Oxford: Blackwell.

Erickson, E.H. (1968) *Identity, Youth and Crisis*. New York: Norton.

Frith, S. (1983) *Sound Effects: Youth, Leisure and the Politics of Rock*. London: Constable.

Griffin, C. (2010) 'The trouble with class: researching youth, class and culture beyond the Birmingham School', *Journal of Youth Studies*, 14 (3): 245–59.

Hall, S. and Jefferson, T. (eds) (1976) *Resistance Through Rituals: Youth Subcultures in Post-War Britain*. London: Hutchinson.

Malbon, B. (1999) *Clubbing: Dancing, Ecstasy and Vitality*. London: Routledge.

Miles, S. (2000) *Youth Lifestyles in a Changing World*. Buckingham: Open University Press.

Muggleton, D. (2000) *Inside Subculture: The Postmodern Meaning of Style*. Oxford: Berg.

Redhead, S. (1990) *The End of the Century Party: Youth and Pop Towards 2000*. Manchester: Manchester University Press.

Rentfrow, P., McDonald, J. and Oldmeadow, J. (2009) 'You are what you listen to: young people's stereotypes about music fans', *Group Processes and Intergroup Relations*, 12 (3): 329–44.

Roberts, S. (2011) 'Beyond "NEET" and "tidy" pathways: considering the "missing middle" of youth transition studies', *Journal of Youth Studies*, 14 (1): 21–39.

Thornton, S. (1995) *Club Cultures: Music Media and Subcultural Capital*. Cambridge: Polity.

Willis, P. (1978) *Profane Culture*. London: Routledge and Kegan Paul.

24

Young People, 'Race' and Ethnicities

There is a lazy temptation to consider 'race' and ethnicity as interchangeable as if they mean the same thing. But although the two concepts are often linked together, 'race' and ethnicity are quite distinct. 'Race' and ethnicity are central to issues such as social change, **youth subcultures**, **youth transitions**, youth identities and a consideration of how **power, divisions and inequalities** are understood. But despite their ubiquity the two concepts have been the source of much debate. 'Race' is often associated with biological characteristics. For example, during both the eighteenth and nineteenth centuries, scientists in the field of comparative anatomy believed phenotypic traits such as skin colour, head shape, hair texture and facial characteristics could be used to categorise people racially. But since then further scientific research has revealed how physical traits do not relate to genotypic characteristics in a neat way. Indeed, there are genetic similarities between people with different physical traits and vice versa. A significant benefit of developments via the genetic science is to debunk the controversial view of racial supremacy which emerged alongside the use of phenotypic traits to define 'races' – although unfortunately there are young people in several countries who continue to naively subscribe to this view (Bartlett et al., 2011).

In this discussion inverted commas are placed around 'race' to highlight the problematic nature of the concept when it comes to defining people via some physical distinction. Within the sociology of 'race' there has been a focus upon how social groups come to be socially constructed via use of their own or others definitions of 'race'. So, as with the organisation of groups such as the Black Power movement in the USA in the 1960s, sociologists have been interested to explore the 'race relations' underpinning such racially defined groups. But recognition of the socially constructed nature of such groups has meant increasingly the term 'ethnicity' is preferred to 'race' in such discussions. Ethnicity refers to a group of people with distinct and shared cultural practices and identity. These groups of people are believed or believe themselves to share common traits differentiating them from other collectives in society. These traits are not simply based on biological factors relating to 'race' and they may or may not include language or **religion**.

An ethnic group differs to say a **social class** because it may include individuals from different socio-economic strata. Also ethnicity and ethnic groups evolve and are not static. New ethnic groups can be formed, for example, with the movement of populations between countries. So the population of migrants from India who have come to the UK are seen as a distinctive ethnic group. However, in India they would belong to different groups defined by caste, religion and language.

As Webster (2009: 67) notes, 'racial and ethnic group identity is subjectively experienced differently and perhaps less strongly than in the past among some individuals and groups while strengthening in others'. The bombings and attempted bombings planned and perpetrated by British Muslim youths in London during 2007 have resulted in a recent focus upon this particular ethnic group. For example, Lewis (2007) has noted how in British Muslim communities an intergenerational gap has developed which has resulted in a disconnection between many young Muslims and older members of the community including traditional Muslim leaders. This, claims Lewis, is dispossessing Islamic youth and leading a small minority to turn towards radical groups as they seek somewhere to belong and something in which to believe. Recently Sughra Ahmed's (2009) research, completed across the UK, illustrates how Muslim youths view themselves as British. These young people were quite happy 'negotiating their multiple identities' but some did feel disconnected from older generations, which they believed stereotyped them.

Other youth scholars have also noted how the children and youths of migrant populations in Western societies experience more 'difficulties adapting and assimilating to their adopted or host countries compared to their parents' (Webster, 2009: 68). In explaining the marginal transitions of young people from some ethnic minority groups they have pointed to 'the legacies and cultures of ethnic groups themselves' (Webster, 2009: 69). Webster is critical of an 'immigration and marginalisation thesis', which claims the children and youths of migrant groups have higher expectations of being accepted and culturally assimilated than their parents. But instead he suggests racism, hostility and a lack of opportunity thwart these expectations and lead to school failure and crime for some youths from ethnic minority groups.

The immigration and marginalisation thesis has focused on African American and Afro-Caribbean populations in the USA and UK suggesting that the cultural and economic legacies of slavery have influenced patterns of modern day lone parenthood, family breakdown and poverty. This means the young people in these groups fail to benefit from family and community networks in the same way as other disadvantaged young people from other ethnic minority groups. Conceptions of masculinities within African American and Afro-Caribbean communities in the USA and UK are also claimed to have resulted in a legacy potentially disadvantaging black youths in the schooling and education systems. For instance, Sewell (1997) focused upon 'Black Masculinities' in a secondary school finding 'conformists', 'innovators', 'retreatists' and 'rebels' – the latter boys were in a minority (18 per cent of the black boys in the secondary school Sewell visited) and they rejected the importance of education and the norms and values of the school. Sewell suggested these categories provided a potential explanation for under-achievement of black boys.

Critics, however, claim such explanations emphasising cultural deficit within certain ethnic minority groups divert attention from the racism in society which they view as the main reason for the negative transition experiences of some youths from certain groups. Those placing a stress on racism when **theorising youth** highlight power differences, divisions, differences and discrimination between different racial and ethnic groups (Skellington and Morris, 1992; Solomos and Back, 1996). Bogus debates around supposed 'racial supremacy' highlight these sorts of prejudice which can be directed at groups within a population because of their race. Within the UK the 1965 Race Relations Act has been amended several times and most notably by the New Labour government in 1999, a few years after the tragic murder in London of the black British teenager Stephen Lawrence in April 1993. The horror of the Lawrence murder was the indifference of the police to this serious crime and their failure to properly investigate the offence and prosecute the killers. After many years of campaigning by the Lawrence family the killers were eventually prosecuted in 2012, nineteen years after the offence. The subsequent reforms aimed to strengthen the law so that race hate crimes are adequately dealt with by the criminal justice system. Sadly, though, in the UK and elsewhere, there have continued to be many young victims of race hate crimes. Ethnicity can also be used as a basis for prejudice and social discrimination against young people. An obvious manifestation of the latter was the persecution of the Jews in Nazi Germany and there have been more recent cases of 'ethnic cleansing' and genocide affecting the lives of young people, for example, in Kosovo and Rwanda, respectively, during the late twentieth century. Demos have completed survey research exploring a rise in far-right political activity using new technologies online through social network sites across Europe. They found within the online social media following, support and sympathies from young people for these far-right political groups which tout anti-immigrant and Islamophobic sentiments 'dwarfs' their formal memberships (Bartlett et al., 2011).

Bhattacharyya and Gabriel (1997) note how 'racism refers generally to ideas and practices of inferiority and subordination and to the structuring of social relations between groups defined in racial terms'. Within the UK the authors talk about a 'contemporary racist culture' (1997: 68). Sociologists have pointed to racism and its negative effects on the learning careers of children and youths. Indeed, 'the area of schooling and education has been a key arena of debate about racism in society – particularly in relation to youth' (Bhattacharyya and Gabriel, 1997: 73). There has been a focus upon the racism of both some teachers and pupils directed at ethnic minority groups as an explanation for educational under-attainment. Statistics from the UK, however, relating to **education** and attainment reveal a complex pattern. The young from Chinese and Indian backgrounds consistently achieve results above the national average while those from Pakistani, Bangladeshi and Afro Caribbean backgrounds persistently achieve results below national average. Coard (1971) claimed the educational under-achievement of Afro-Caribbean pupils in mainstream schools was explained by teacher's racism, low expectations held by teachers and consequently black children being conditioned to feel inferior. Similar findings have been found by Richardson (2005), Gilborn and Youdell (2001) and Mirza (1992).

Research into racial discrimination stresses how ethnic groups are not free-floating social entities whose fate is determined simply by alleged deficits and internal processes. Studies also develop explanations about the experiences of young black and minority ethnic (BME) groups which recognise the possibility of racism but which also emphasise the distinctive location of young people from ethnic groups within the overall system of social stratification – particularly gender and social class. Connolly's (1998) research in an inner-city primary school has suggested how gender and ethnicity interact. This research claims teachers define gender and ethnic identities with reference to wider discourses and stereotypes in society (Connolly, 1998). It is claimed the differing ways in which young people live out being boys and girls can be understood by considering ethnicity alongside gender, social class and other potential contributory factors in an additive model of identity formation (Mac an Ghaill, 1999).

A study by Webster (2009: 66) notes how, 'suffice to say there is little doubt how within Britain and America the disproportionate presence of young African-Caribbean and African-American men in the youth and criminal justice system is both striking and even greater than in the past'. He also notes how young people from these ethnic minorities 'suffer disproportionately in respect to school failure, exclusion from school, being in the care system and joblessness'. However, he goes on to observe how 'these disadvantages are suffered by other groups too' – including the white working class. Indeed, Webster points out how different ethnic groups may share a common **social class** position and it is this which 'may be the overriding factor in determining transition outcomes' for all young people, regardless of ethnic identity. Others have also questioned the stand alone explanatory power of 'race' and ethnicity when it comes to transitions made by young people. Furlong and Cartmel (2007: 8) observe 'many of the disadvantages faced by members of minorities are a consequence of their position within the class structure, rather than being a feature of racial exclusion'. No doubt given the significance of prejudices and disadvantages experienced by BME young people and their lasting effect on their lives these debates will continue.

REFERENCES

Ahmed, S. (2009) *Seen and Not Heard: Voices of Young British Muslims*. Leicester: Policy Research Centre. http://policyresearch.org.uk/publications_reports-Seen-NotHeard.php (accessed 3 November 2011).

Bartlett, J., Birdwell, J. and Littler, M. (2011) *The New Face of Digital Populism*. London: Demos.

Bhattacharyya, G. and Gabriel, J. (1997) 'Racial formations of youth', in J. Roche and S. Tucker (eds), *Youth in Society*. London: Sage, pp. 68–80.

Coard, B. (1971) *How the West Indian Child Is Made Educationally Sub-normal in the British School System*. London: New Beacon Books

Connolly, P. (1998) *Racism, Gender Identities and Young Children*. London: Routledge.

Furlong, A. and Cartmel, F. (2007) *Young People and Social Change: New Perspectives*. 2nd edn. Maidenhead: Open University Press.

Gillborn, D. and Youdell, D. (2001) *Rationing Education: Policy, Practice, Reform and Equity*. Buckingham: Open University Press.

Lewis, P. (2007) *Young, British and Muslim*. London: Continuum Publishing.

Mac an Ghaill, M. (1999) *Contemporary Racisms and Ethnicities*. Buckingham: Open University Press.

Mirza, H. (1992) *Young, Female and Black*. London: Routledge.

Richardson, B. (ed.) (2005) *Tell it Like it Is: How Our Schools Fail Black Children*. Stoke-on-Trent: Trentham Books.

Sewell, T. (1997) *Black Masculinities and Schooling*. Stoke-on-Trent: Trentham Books.

Skellington, R. and Morris, P. (1992) *'Race' in Britain Today*. London: Sage.

Solomos, J. and Back, L. (1996) *Racism and Society*. London: Macmillan.

Webster, C. (2009) 'Young people, "race" and ethnicity', in A. Furlong (ed.), *Handbook of Youth and Young Adulthood: New Perspective and Agendas*. London: Routledge, pp. 66–73.

.... 25 ....

Young People and Informal Learning

Learning is widely understood to be the act or process of acquiring knowledge or skills. Several learning theories have been developed to outline the way young people learn but there are two broad theoretical models. First, the behaviourist model points to the importance of conditioning and learning from experience, for example, when young people are on a placement in the work place. Conditioning is the process of learning behaviours associated with environmental stimuli. Second, the theoretical model emphasises the process of cognition or the way information is mentally processed to form items of knowledge or belief (i.e. cognitions). For example, cognition and information management ('mental housekeeping') are involved when young people complete study/reading as part of a higher education programme. A key aim of these learning processes can often be the goal of making young people 'independent' and 'lifelong learners'. These learning processes are categorised by the European Centre for the Development of Vocational Training (2009) as formal, non-formal and/or informal. Formal learning is learning undertaken by young people as students usually through tuition from a teacher when they participate in schooling and college systems. Whereas informal learning is that learning which occurs outside of these settings in the home and peer group, for example.

For generations young people were regarded as passive acquirers of learning via this formal process but they are now expected to be more active and engage in the learning process to a much greater extent. This can involve non-formal learning. Non-formal learning takes place alongside mainstream education and training but does not typically lead to formalised qualifications. Non-formal learning might involve young people collaborating with others usually with a similar interest or for a similar purpose. This might be at an international youth event or within a local youth club. Both formal and non-formal learning are characterised by organisation and a degree of directive control of learning. In contrast, informal learning has been defined as 'any activity involving the pursuit of understanding, knowledge or skill which occurs without the presence of externally imposed curricular criteria', and is evident 'in any context outside the pre-established curricula of educative institutions' (Livingstone, 2001: 206). Livingstone goes on to suggest that, 'basic terms of informal learning (e.g. objectives, content, means and processes of acquisition, duration, evaluation of outcomes, applications) are determined by the individuals and groups that choose to engage in it' (Livingstone, 2001: 206).

This definition is careful not to over-emphasise the importance of social context, suggesting that informal learning can be undertaken in formal educational contexts and beyond in the work, home and leisure environments. Indeed, informal learning occurs through socialisation via youth **subcultures** and participation within kinship and **social networks** (Pais and Pohl, 2003). It is therefore very important to the construction of both collective and individual **identities** of the young and how social solidarity and integration comes about. As Durkheim (1956) and Parsons (1961) have explored in the past, informal learning is a key part of how we perform roles in schools, the workplace and in other social contexts. Indeed, use of new technologies and social media is an increasingly important source of informal learning as we have seen recently with its role in the 'Arab Spring' and the development of **political protest** movements within societies with oppressive regimes.

Despite a claim that informal learning is 'an ill-defined and messy concept' (Cullen et al., 2000), it is linked to notions of a 'learning society' that have become an important part of government policy in recent decades. The idea of a learning society views education as broadly promoting learning informally across institutions beyond schools and colleges and across individuals' 'learning biographies'. Governments in the UK and EU have invested in online learning resources, family learning and literacy programmes which all encourage informal learning in different settings. The notion of a learning society is also connected to other concepts such as 'knowledge economy' in which young people are viewed as lifelong learners who participate in informal learning across different strands of their lives and throughout their life course. Indeed, this has been identified as an 'overarching trend' affecting the lives of all young people in Europe – 'the rapidly increasing importance of education and informal learning processes to prepare the young generation for life in knowledge economies' (du Bois Reymond and Stauber, 2003).

Consequently, in the first decade of the twenty-first century informal learning has become part of wider European Union policy (European Centre for the Development of Vocational Training, 2009) and the policy of the UK government (Cullen et al., 2000). There is a growing appreciation that formal learning for young people in schools and colleges sits alongside non-formal and informal learning and that the latter is particularly important (Somekh et al., 2002). Informal learning is said to potentially 'increase individual's self-confidence and social skills and also contributes to their 'citizenship, social identity and social capital' (Cullen et al., 2000). In 2008 the UK government decided to consult on the future role of informal learning in post–compulsory education and training and within wider social policy areas (Department for Innovation, Universities and Skills, 2008a). The response of the UK's previous New Labour government to this consultation was to reiterate its continuing commitment to 'ensuring the strength and sustainability of informal learning' (Department for Innovation, Universities and Skills, 2008b).

In the UK recent Coalition government policy has placed less emphasis on informal learning and restated its commitment to raising standards of more traditional formal learning and qualifications (e.g. via the 'English Baccalaureate'). There is a long-standing tradition in the UK of producing reports that acknowledge the importance of informal learning to citizens and wider society then failing to translate this interest into new policy and practice (Coffield, 2000). Such commentators note that the neglect of informal learning is often due to government's instrumental approach to education and the pursuit of training policies that concentrate on the needs of employers and the goal of enhancing employability of workers. What is lost in this narrow promotion of formal learning is the opportunity to offer young people more self-directed and creative learning that can support personal development and the longer-term creation of lifelong learners. If government embrace more ambitious education policies that support informal learning these can help all learners but particularly those who are likely to under-achieve and are at risk of developing marginal transitions into poor work, unemployment and criminal careers (McNeil and Smith, 2004; Simpson and Cieslik, 2007).

Some researchers have been strong advocates for informal learning and the contribution it can make in regard to young people and their wider social development. The UK's Economic and Social Research Council established a Research Programme into 'The Learning Society: Knowledge and Skills for Employment' in 1994 comprising several research projects, and one of the programme's major summary reports highlights 'the necessity of informal learning'. Despite its importance though, the report claims that 'the case for informal learning has still to be won; indeed, it has scarcely begun to be heard' (Coffield, 2000). Other youth researchers – particularly in other European countries beyond the UK – have in the last decade linked informal learning as a central concept in their explanations for **youth transitions**. Focusing on the 'learning biographies' of young people, this research highlights how 'informal and non-formal learning' is important and can be central to enabling young people 'to change from disengagement to re-engagement'. Indeed, these researchers have called for transition policies that strive for a better integration of different modes of learning (du Bois Reymond and Stauber, 2003; Pais and Pohl, 2003).

REFERENCES

Coffield, F. (2000) *The Necessity of Informal Learning*. Bristol: Policy Press.

Cullen, J., Batterbury, S., Foresti, M., Lynos, C. and Stern, E. (2000) *Informal Learning and Widening Participation*. Research Brief No. 191. Nottingham: Department for Education and Employment Publications.

Department for Innovation, Universities and Skills (DIUS) (2008a) *Informal Adult Learning: Shaping the Way Ahead*. London: DIUS Publications. www.dius.gov.uk/consultations/adult_learning (accessed 10 July 2009).

Department for Innovation, Universities and Skills (DIUS) (2008b) *Informal Adult Learning – Shaping the Way Ahead*. Consultation Response Analysis Report, London: DIUS Publications. www.dius.gov.uk/consultations/adult_learning.

du Bois Reymond, M. and Stauber, B. (2003) 'Biographical turning points in young people's transitions to work across Europe', RC34 Publication, Aldershot: Ashgate Press.

Durkheim, E. (1956) *Education and Sociology*. Toronto: The Free Press.

European Centre for the Development of Vocational Training (2009) *European Guidelines for Validating Non-formal and Informal Learning*. Luxemburg: Office for Official Publications of the European communities. www.ecvet-team.eu/sites/default/files/european_guidelines_validating_nfil_en.pdf (accessed 11 July 2012).

Livingstone, D. (2001) *Adults' Informal Learning: Definitions, Findings, Gaps and Future Research*. Toronto: Research Network for New Approaches to Lifelong Learning. www.oise.utoronto.ca/depts/sese/csew/nall/res/21adultsifnormallearning.htm (accessed 11 July 2009).

McNeil, B. and Smith, L. (2004) *Success Factors in Informal Learning: Young Adults' Experiences of Literacy, Language and Numeracy*. London: NRDC.

Pais, J.M. and Pohl, A. (2003) 'Of roofs and knives: the dilemmas of recognising informal learning', in A. López Blasco, W. McNeish and A. Walther (eds), *Young People and Contradictions of Inclusion: Towards Integrated Transition Policies in Europe*. Bristol: Policy Press, pp. 223–43.

Parsons, T. (1961) 'The school class as a social system: some of its functions in American society', in A.H. Halsey, J. Floud and J. Anderson (eds), *Education, Economy and Society*. New York: Free Press, pp. 434–55.

Simpson, D. and Cieslik, M. (2007) 'The role of basic skills in transitions to adulthood', *YOUNG*, 15 (4): 395–412.

Somekh, B., Lewin, C., Mavers, D., Harrison, C., Haw, K., Fisher, T., Lunzer, E., McFarlane, A. and Scrimshaw, P. (2002) *ImpaCT2: Pupils' and Teachers' Perceptions of ICT in the Home, School and Community*. Nottingham: DfES.

26
Youth and Social Class

Conceptually class can feature in a straightforward way within youth studies by simply denoting a population of cases that are connected because they are similar in some way such as classes of **housing** transitions as we see in the work of Ford et al. (2002). Yet social class is more often understood as a form of social stratification drawing on the works of Marx and Weber. Class as used in youth studies tends to employ either the Marxist or Weberian models of analysis. For Marx (1986) class positions arise through specific historical conditions and through one's relationship to the means of production – one either sells one's labour or employs labour. Productive relations or the experience of work is key here to how we understand patterns of exploitation and struggle and how our subjectivities (identities) are shaped in everyday life. Weber's model (1978) differs somewhat in not just focusing on economic relationships but also on the struggle for prestige (status) and political resources (party). Hence for Weber owning capital was only one source of market position in his stratification system as other capacities such as higher skill and education levels were important in creating classes, as these individuals are more able to command higher rewards for their labours. So social class is defined by Weber as the sharing of a common market position and those occupying a similar position might share skills and knowledge (for example, professions) or a lack of these capacities. For Weber, those occupying a class experienced shared life chances and a common wish to protect their interests where appropriate. As such, he indicated that class conflict and struggle was likely and would occur when the power interests of classes clashed, but these conflicts were not always economically focused and rather could revolve around power and prestige.

Social class has been a key area of research in youth studies, particularly in the UK and North America, with scholars employing it as a means to understand the patterning of inequalities and social **divisions**. Surveys show significant differences in the experiences of young people because of their different socio-economic backgrounds. Those from lower-class backgrounds will do less well in education, enter poorer quality employment, have poorer health and have shorter lives than their richer peers in the higher classes. In the UK, for example, over 80 per cent of children from professional backgrounds will achieve five good GCSE qualifications by eighteen years of age, whereas for those whose parents have routine, less skilled occupational backgrounds the figure is just 44 per cent (ONS, 2011: 10). Such initial class-based educational inequalities will then influence the subsequent educational careers and employment transitions of young people. Thus in the UK 46 per cent of those from professional backgrounds go on to higher education at eighteen years of age but only 17 per cent of those who are from routine occupational backgrounds enter university (ONS, 2011: 25).

Those living in the richer parts of England will on average live six to seven years longer than those residing in poor boroughs (Marmot Review, 2012). Those developing class theories therefore have been concerned with understanding how we might explain these links between socio-economic conditions (social background, for example) and experiences in education, or patterns of health, or transitions into employment. One way of theorising these links is by using the Marxist conception of class and social structure, and these 'reproduction theories' emerged in youth studies from the 1970s onwards (Roberts, 2009: 14). Roberts identifies several authors adopting a Marxist perspective as they attempted to explain how young people tend to inherit and 'stick close to' their parents' class positions. This early work emphasised a correspondence between the organisation of education and the organisation of work in capitalist societies (Bowles and Gintis, 1976). Others focused upon resistance demonstrated by working-class youths to middle-class values as they rejected school knowledge as useless and instead were 'learning to labour' ahead of future shop-floor **employment** in factories (Willis, 1977). This focus on youth **subcultures** also revealed the so-called, 'resistance through rituals' and how this too led to socio-economic reproduction as cultural responses only offered 'magical solutions' to the economic marginality of working-class youth.

More recently the French social theorist Pierre Bourdieu 'adopted an economic concept – capital – and applied it to social and cultural resources, indicating how these resources could also be accumulated and invested in the expectation of a dividend' (Roberts, 2009: 16). In Bourdieu's formulation different classes of young people possess different levels of economic, cultural and social capital. Social capital (social connections and trust relations) is transformed into cultural capital (knowledge and tastes). But the cultural capital of certain classes is valued more highly and brings far better rewards – with working-class culture and disposition ('habitus') being disparaged. Working-class youths are therefore at a cultural disadvantage when they operate in any 'field' (e.g. education or the labour market) and social mobility is constrained. Bourdieu's use of 'fields', 'habitus' (dispositions) and 'capitals' has been extremely influential in youth studies (Bourdieu and Passeron, 1997) applied in areas as disparate as education (Bloomer and Hodkinson, 2000) and young people and popular music (Thornton, 1995).

Researchers who employ class analytically frame its use within a wider theoretical approach that assumes that social structures and processes of social change are characterised by conflict and inequalities as we see in Marx's original writings. However, social class can also be used more descriptively when studying transitions, for example, indicating socio-economic positions of actors and how these change over time. Here socio-economic category denotes how the social class position of young people divides individuals economically, culturally and socially and generates different class experiences that in turn can result in different youth transitions (Jones, 2002). Both large-scale quantitative surveys and smaller qualitative projects employ these ways of using class categories to explore the relationships between cultural experiences of young people and subsequent transition routes (Banks et al., 1992). Often this more descriptive use of social class in British studies reflects Weber's influence and is derived from the Register General's six-point scale of socio-economic classes based on occupation (labour market position) that was used in the UK from 1911 until 1998. This scale of occupations ranged from Classes I and II (professional and managerial) and Class IIIa (technical and supervisory) through to Class IIIb (skilled manual workers), Class IV (semi-skilled manual) and Class V (unskilled). In 1998 the schema was updated to include a larger number of categories in what is now called the National Statistics Socio-Economic Classification (NS-SEC) and reflects the complex patterns of employment in the UK (Roberts, 2011: 21).

Recently economic and social processes of de-industrialisation mean that the experiences of young people growing up in Western societies are quite different from those encountered by earlier generations (Furlong and Cartmel, 2007). The 'risk society thesis' (Beck, 1992) suggests that young people have greater opportunities to make choices about their lives that are no longer rooted in class processes. So-called 'choice biographies' suggest instead that young people reflexively monitor their lives and take action and negotiate the routes they pursue through different life transitions. These arguments then raise question about the continued relevance of social class to youth research (Savage et al., 2001: 876; Threadgold, 2010).

However, many researchers continue to suggest that social class processes are still significant to an understanding of young people's cultural lives and transition experiences (Skeggs et al., 2008). For example, in her research on young people, social class and schooling, Weis (2009: 49) has called for 'an examination of the deeply woven connections between "official knowledge" and its global distribution, parental capital and the uneven demands of schools, and the contested nature of class, race and gender to identity formation and class production'. Some others have used social class in connection with the characteristics of **place** and shown how the latter influences life chances and opportunities (Roberts and Parsell, 1992). Some suggest the study of youth provides an ideal opportunity to examine the relevance of new social theories about class. This is because if the social order and patterns of divisions have changed and if social structures based on class have weakened, one would expect to find evidence of these changes among young people who are at the crossroads of social reproduction (Furlong and Cartmel, 2007). In this regard, evidence from a great many empirical youth studies continues to demonstrate the significance of social class in conditioning both youth transitions (Gayle et al., 2009) and youth cultures (Hollingworth and Williams, 2009). For class-based economic and cultural processes greatly influence the local structures of opportunities (schools, training, employment) in the areas in which the young grow up, which in turn fashions distinctive classed transitions into adulthood (MacDonald and Marsh, 2005; Roberts, 2011).

Some research in youth studies has drawn on a 'new class analysis' involving a move away from a focus on economic position and class consciousness to more of a focus upon class as an individualised process that works through cultural and moral 'hierarchies of distinction' (Bottero, 2004: 991; Reay, 2005). Such conceptual developments are attempting to show how social class, though having its roots in economic processes, is implicated in individual identity formation as well as young people's positioning in the moral economy. Such work contributes to an understanding of class and demonstrates that it is still a key way of analysing the collective, conflictual, cultural and individual features of young people's lives (Furlong et al., 2003; Shildrick et al., 2009).

REFERENCES

Banks, M., Bates, I., Breakwell, G., Bynner, J., Emler, N., Jamieson, L. and Roberts, K. (1992) *Careers and Identities*. Milton Keynes: Open University Press.

Beck, U. (1992) *Risk Society: Towards a New Modernity*. London: Sage.

Bloomer, M. and Hodkinson, P. (2000) 'Learning careers: continuity and change in young people's dispositions to learning', *British Educational Research Journal*, 26 (5): 583–97.

Bottero, W. (2004) 'Class identities and the identity of class', *Sociology*, 38 (5): 985–1004.

Bourdieu, P. and Passeron, J.D. (1997) *Reproduction in Education, Society and Culture*. London: Sage.

Bowles, S. and Gintis, H. (1976) *Schooling in Capitalist America*. London: Routledge.

Ford, J., Rugg, J. and Burrows, R. (2002) 'Conceptualising the contemporary role of housing in the transition to adult life in England', *Urban Studies*, 39 (13), 2455–67.

Furlong, A. and Cartmel, F. (2007) *Young People and Social Change: New Perspectives*. 2nd edn. Maidenhead: Open University Press.

Furlong, A., Cartmel, F., Biggart, A., Sweeting, H. and West, P. (2003) *Youth Transitions: Patterns of Vulnerability and Processes of Social Inclusion*. Edinburgh: Scottish Executive.

Gayle V., Lambert, P. and Murray, S. (2009) 'School-to-work in the 1990s: modelling transitions with large-scale datasets', in R. Brooks (ed.), *Transitions from Education to Work: New Perspectives from Europe and Beyond*. London: Palgrave Macmillan, pp. 17–41.

Hollingworth, S. and Williams, K. (2009) 'Constructions of the working class "others" among urban, white middle-class youth: "chavs", sub-culture and the valuing of education', *Journal of Youth Studies*, 12 (5): 467–82.

Jones, G. (2002) *The Youth Divide: Diverging Paths to Adulthood*. York: Joseph Rowntree Foundation.

MacDonald, R. and Marsh, J. (2005) *Disconnected Youth? Growing Up in Britain's Poor Neighbourhoods*. London: Palgrave MacMillan.

Marmot Review (2012) *Fair Society, Healthy Lives*. London: London Health Observatory, London University.

Marx, K. (1986). *Das Capital, Vol. 1*. London: Lawrence and Wishart.

ONS (2011) *Youth Cohort Study*. London: DfE, ONS.

Reay, D. (2005) 'Beyond consciousness? The psychic landscape of social class', *Sociology*, 39 (5): 911–98.

Roberts, K. (2009) 'Socio-economic reproduction', in A. Furlong (ed.), *Youth and Young Adulthood: New Perspectives and Agendas*. London: Routledge, pp. 14–21.

Roberts, K. (2011) *Class in Contemporary Britain*. 2nd edn. London: Palgrave.

Roberts, K. and Parsell, G. (1992) 'Entering the labour market in Britain. The survival of traditional opportunity structures', *Sociological Review*, 30: 727–53.

Savage, M., Bagnell, G. and Longhurst, B. (2001) 'Ordinary, ambivalent and defensive: class identities in the North West of England', *Sociology*, 35 (4): 535–41.

Shildrick, T., Blackman, S. and MacDonald, R. (2009) 'Young people, class and place', *Journal of Youth Studies*, 12 (5): 457–65.

Skeggs, B., Thumim, N. and Wood, H. (2008) 'Oh goodness, I'm watching reality TV: how methods makes class in audience research', *European Journal of Cultural Studies*, 11 (5): 1–21.

Thornton, S. (1995) *Club Cultures: Music, Media and Subcultural Capital*. London: Sage.

Threadgold, S. (2010) '"Should I pitch my tent in the middle ground?" On "middling tendency", Beck and inequality in youth sociology', *Journal of Youth Studies*, 14 (4): 381–93.

Weber, M. (1978) *Economy and Society: An Outline of Interpretive Sociology*. Berkeley: University of California Press.

youth and social class

Weis, L. (2009) 'Social class, youth and young adulthood in the context of a shifting global economy', in A. Furlong (ed.), *Handbook of Youth and Young Adulthood: New Perspectives and Agendas*. London: Routledge, pp. 49–57.

Willis, P. (1977) *Learning to Labour: How Working Class Kids Get Working Class Jobs*. Farnborough: Saxon House.

27
Young People, Politics, Protest and Social Movements

The concept of politics has a long history and derives from the Greek word *politika*. The Greek philosopher Aristotle created works in several areas including politics and he defined the concept as 'the affairs of the city'. In the centuries following Aristotle, politics has come to mean the science or art of political government and it is strongly associated with the process through which groups of people make decisions and implement policy. In particular, politics has come to be strongly associated with institutions of government which with **globalisation** operate at several levels and can include the supranational (such as the European Union), national (nation state) and local (such as county or state council). A significant feature of the process of politics and the regulating of affairs within these institutions of government has been the contribution of political parties.

However, in recent years concern has been expressed about what is perceived as young people's lack of interest in 'conventional politics' including constitutional politics, membership of political parties and participation in elections. For example, 'in most countries, even when voting is compulsory and failure to cast a ballot incurs penalties, young people are less likely than their elders to bother voting' (Furlong, 2009: 291).

There has been much speculation among the popular press and politicians about whether this apparent lack of interest is related to apathy or alienation (Marsh et al., 2006a). In the UK some suggest that a lack of participation is down to apathy among young people that results in low turnouts in general elections. They also point to the ageing and shrinking membership of political parties. The argument about alienation appears more benign by suggesting young people's lack of engagement is a product of political institutions that fail to engage young people. However, those pointing to both the apathy and alienation from politics of young people often characterise them as 'free-riders, taking the benefits of citizenship without voting' because they lack or have low 'political literacy'. In this context, a lack of engagement is seen 'as resolvable through technocratic reforms of voting procedures' (Marsh et al., 2006a: 1).

As Hackett (1997: 81) therefore observes, a 'common assumption' of many observers of youth politics is that many young people are indifferent about or disengaged from politics. From this assumption comes the argument that to increase young people's involvement in politics one has to develop more accessible or appealing political systems. Hence several governments across the world have set out 'youth participation' policies connected to political and government organisations (Collin, 2008: 527). In the UK this has involved the encouraging of participation by introducing compulsory citizenship lessons in schools, introducing youth parliaments and elections in local authorities and improving voting registration (Marsh et al., 2006a). Though such policies have made some advances in participation some suggest these initiatives are limited as there is a need for further research into the causes of low participation in traditional political systems (White et al., 2000). Many policies and initiatives to promote young people's involvement in politics appeared to be built around a 'superficial argument' which misunderstands the non-participation of young people in conventional politics (Hackett, 1997: 82). Marsh et al. (2006b) argue that 'young people are not apathetic but feel their interests and concerns are not addressed by politicians. Indeed, they are highly sensitive towards the limited nature of their political citizenship and this plays a key role in their disinclination to participate in mainstream politics.' Several other youth scholars support this conclusion, Harris (2009) highlights how traditional political institutions are the product of adults and serve their purposes – they are always therefore likely to find it difficult to engage young people. This does not mean young people do not share the concerns that many have about the major political issues of the day such as the quality of education, health care and crime. In fact the National Centre for Social Research (White et al., 2000: 1) 'explored in detail the nature of young people's political interests and behaviour' among young people, aged between fourteen and twenty-four, from a range of backgrounds and circumstances in Britain and found the issues that concerned them 'covered the broad political agenda'.

Rather, the picture emerging from recent youth research depicts young people turning away from conventional politics and political institutions rather than politics per se. It also shows that while young people 'may not be enthused by party politics, they do display high levels of involvement in single issue politics' and they are engaged in less conventional forms of politics (Sloam, 2007: 548). This involves political protest, which can take the form of street demonstrations, civic disruption and direct action (Furlong, 2009: 292). Indeed, the French philosopher Michel Foucault's focus on the use of power and its relation to knowledge directs attention to how politics features in eveyday interactions and practices where there can be protest, struggle and resistance to dominant power holders – so between the governing and the governed (Foucault, 1969). This distributed form of power can also be seen in institutional settings such as schools. Stephen Ball (1987) documented the struggles between teachers and pupils in secondary schools in England and how a 'micro-politics' existed where students and staff were often in conflict over the control of the classroom. White et al. (2000: 1) found young people 'consistently referred to their feelings of powerlessness and limited opportunity for them to engage in [conventional] politics'. In this context, Foucault's conceptualisation of power and politics offers a way of understanding forms of political protest in which young people resist and subvert authority and economic and cultural constraints while pursuing their interests and expressing their identities.

Certainly there is a long history of youth involvement in social or what have been labelled 'urban disorders' that are an expression of young people's political powerlessness (Akram, 2009). Flanagan (2009) regards such protest as stemming from the conjunction of historically specific events that galvanise young people to become politically engaged. These include the civil rights movement in the USA in the 1960s, the student protests of 1968 against the Vietnam War and the on-going Campaign for Nuclear Disarmament (CND) from 1957 onwards. The prominent place of young people in the struggle against Apartheid in South Africa is also an example of youth involvement in political protest as resistance.

Within the UK more recent demonstrations against the Iraq war, increases in student fees and changes to the Educational Maintenance Allowance all provide further examples. Unrest and looting of shops across several English cities in the summer of 2011 also generated much discussion about the political significance of this disorder. Some members of the media and the Coalition government described the unrest as 'riots' which were criminally motivated. However, others have explored the social characteristics of the people involved suggesting a link with the powerlessness and disadvantage of many young people in the urban areas in the UK (*The Guardian*, 2011). Caution though has been advised in seeking out simple causal explanations of disorder. Akram recommends 'collecting the accounts of those involved in urban disorders' by way of 'understanding the meaning they attach to events' (2009: 319).

There has also been a focus upon the combined effects of wider social and technological changes on protest among the young and on their level of involvement in civic and political engagement. For example, Flanagan (2009: 299) claims that through wider changes in the structure of work and the decline in trade union membership a 'class divide' in civic engagement and 'an institutional lacuna for working class youth' have emerged. This is an interesting point in the context of a new cyber age where there is a suggestion that information and communication technologies (ICT) may be playing a part not only in the spread of ideas and social movements within national boundaries but also across them internationally. Most young people are ICT literate and because of this there is great interest in using new technologies as 'a mechanism for governments and organisations to extend their reach to otherwise disengaged youth' (Collin, 2008: 527). But Collin has noted how new technologies may also be significant in shaping new types of youth engagement in politics. The Internet is a unique and autonomous platform for the realisation of project-based political identities and it is a legitimising space for new political practices of young people (Collin, 2008: 527). Thus we have seen the role of social media in social movements emerging across several countries of North Africa and the Middle East in 2011 as part of the 'Arab Spring'. Though these movements have local characteristics they also have several similar and shared characteristics. They all include 'young people angry and frustrated at the lack of freedoms, opportunities and jobs, unaccountable and corrupt governments, cronyism and, in a few places, grinding poverty' (Black, 2011). The first social movement for change started in Tunisia after a young man named Mohammed Bouazizi set fire to himself in protest over a lack of freedoms in his country. Since then social movements and protests have moved from Libya to Syria and other Middle East states. Social movements such as those involved in the Arab Spring may be ephemeral and at the time of writing there are doubts about where these protests will take their countries. What is becoming clear is the facilitating role played by the Internet and social media (such as Twitter, Facebook and YouTube) and their use by young people. The importance of the Internet was revealed by governments' response to social unrest by restricting the operations of these social media organisations in their countries. During 2011 and 2012 the Egyptian government blocked access to several social networking websites and the Syrian government went further and attempted to block access to the whole of the Internet. As we write young people are at the forefront of social protest around the world with the hope that they can lead their countries towards better futures for their citizens.

REFERENCES

Akram, S. (2009) '"Riots" or "urban disorders"? The case for re-politicizing urban disorders', in A. Furlong. (ed.), *Handbook of Youth and Young Adulthood: New Perspectives and Agendas.* London: Routledge, pp. 313–20.

Ball, S. (1987) *The Micro-politics of the School: Towards a Theory of School Organisation.* London: Methuen.

Black, I. (2011) 'Where the Arab Spring will end is anyone's guess', *The Guardian*, 17 June, 26. www.guardian.co.uk/world/2011/jun/17/arab-spring-end-anyone-guess (accessed 10 November 2011).

Collin, P. (2008) 'The internet, youth participation policies, and the development of young people's political identities in Australia', *Journal of Youth Studies*, 11 (5): 527–42.

Flanagan, C. (2009) 'Young people's civic engagement and political development', in A. Furlong (ed.), *Handbook of Youth and Young Adulthood: New Perspectives and Agendas.* London: Routledge, pp. 293–300.

Foucault, M. (1969) *The Archaeology of Knowledge.* London: Tavistock.

Furlong, A. (ed.) (2009) *Handbook of Youth and Young Adulthood: New Perspectives and Agendas.* London: Routledge.

The Guardian (2011) 'Reading the riots: investigating England's summer of disorder. www.guardian.co.uk/uk/series/reading-the-riots (accessed 10 January 2012).

Hackett, C. (1997) 'Young people and political participation', in J. Roche and S. Tucker (eds), *Youth in Society.* London: Sage, pp. 81–8.

Harris, A. (2009) 'Young people, politics and citizenship', in A. Furlong (ed.), *Handbook of Youth and Young Adulthood: New Perspectives and Agendas.* London: Routledge, pp. 301–6.

Marsh, D., O'Toole, T. and Jones, S. (2006a) *Young People and Politics in the UK: Apathy or Alienation?* Houndsmill: Palgrave Macmillan.

Marsh, D., O'Toole, T. and Jones, S. (2006b) *Young People and Politics in the UK: Apathy or Alienation?* Book description found at: www.palgrave.com/products/title.aspx?pid=275596 (accessed 20 July 2012).

Sloam, J. (2007) 'Rebooting democracy: youth participation in politics in the UK', *Parliamentary Affairs*, 60 (4): 548–67.

White, C., Bruce, S. and Ritchie, J. (2000) *Young People's Politics: Political Interest and Engagement Amongst 14–24 Year Olds*. York: Joseph Rowntree Foundation. www.jrf.org.uk/sites/files/jrf/520.pdf (accessed 28 June 2011).

28
Young People, Work and Employment

The concept of employment features prominently within youth studies. Indeed, achieving employment as part of the school-to-work **transition** remains one of the core 'problems and priorities in the sociology of youth'. The modern organisation of employment 'creates the modern young person', results in 'differences' and **divisions** between young people and has serious implications for the development of youth identities, wellbeing and futures (Roberts, 2003: 13–17). Employment is usually associated with and sometimes inter-changed with the concept of work. However, the two concepts have differing meanings. A precise definition of employment would highlight the supply of labour by young people in the process of producing goods and services for sale on the market, for their supply by government or for the consumption by the young people that are employed in their production (non-market production). Employment as a concept therefore is connected to activity within the economy and the definition above makes the concept applicable for young people who are situated within several types of economies – market, command, mixed and subsistence. Young people are also paid for employment within what is known as the 'hidden economy'. The hidden economy is usually taken to mean employment as undeclared economic activity. This form of employment can range from casual moonlighting and work paid cash in-hand ('fiddle jobs'). But some young people will 'never establish themselves in jobs which will support an adult lifestyle' (Roberts, 2003: 17) and this can result in alienation and anomic disengagement of youth, especially at a time when 'the kind of occupational security and stability once associated with adult "destinations" has now largely disappeared' (Jones, 2009: 119).

Economic activity as formal employment is only one form of work. Work for young people also involves them supplying physical, cognitive or emotional labour/effort to produce goods/services for consumption by others or themselves such as studying, unpaid domestic labour and/ or voluntary or community work. The latter is sometimes referred to as work in the 'informal economy'. The distinction between these types of work can sometimes be blurred. For example, young people can be involved in care work that is paid and unpaid. But the paid care work is classed as employment whereas the unpaid care work could fall into the categories of unpaid domestic labour or even community work.

Youth researchers tend to focus attention more on young people's employment in the formal and hidden economy than that undertaken in the informal economy. The issue of exploitation or domination of young people at work is a key area of interest hence researchers are interested in the legal protection offered to young people. There are a number of employment rights which are designed to protect young people from exploitation while employed within the formal economy. These rights vary across different countries. Young people in England and Wales under the school leaving age of sixteen years can only be employed in 'light work'. But there are only certain times when this work can be undertaken – for example, not in school time or between 7 p.m. and 7 a.m. Children under fourteen can work in sport, advertising, modelling, plays, films, television or other entertainment but those employing them must obtain a licence from a local authority. They can also be employed to take part in babysitting and odd jobs for parents, friends and neighbours. However, there is some variation across local authorities, with some operating different bylaws allowing certain other types of employment for young people aged thirteen and above. Nobody under sixteen can work in a factory, construction, mining or merchant shipping.

Young people in the UK over the minimum school leaving age of sixteen and under eighteen are known as 'young workers' and they have certain rights in the work place. Employers have a responsibility to ensure that these rights for young workers are enforced. Employers of under eighteen year olds must undertake a risk assessment in regard to young workers' health and safety. There are restrictions which mean young workers should not be given work, first, which they are not capable physically or mentally of doing; second, which brings them into contact with chemical agents, toxic material or radiation; and third, which involves a health risk because of extreme cold, heat or vibration. They can only complete the above work where it is essential **training**, is properly supervised and where it is demonstrated by the employer that any risk is reduced to the lowest level that is reasonable. Young workers aged sixteen or seventeen who have not yet achieved a certain standard of **education** or training are entitled to reasonable time off work for study or training. The time off should be paid at their normal hourly rate. Within the UK those employed and aged above the minimum school leaving age are entitled to receive the National Minimum Wage. At the time of writing, for young workers aged sixteen to seventeen this is £3.64 an hour. For young people in employment aged between eighteen and twenty this rate is £4.98 an hour and for those aged twenty-one and above it is £6.08 an hour.

Securing employment and income is regarded as the key transition into independent adulthood and it is therefore of key interest to youth researchers across European countries. There was a dramatic change in prospects for young people in the UK labour market from the 1970s onwards and this was connected to wider economic and **social change** and processes of **globalisation** (Hickman, 1997). Writing about the changing position of young people in the UK labour market in 1997, Hickman noted how in common with most other industrialised nations, the UK economy had 'seen a major restructuring of industries over the last 20 years or so' producing persistently high levels of youth unemployment. Hickman highlighted 'the rise of the service sector' and the decline in the manufacturing sector – a trend sometimes referred to as 'de-industrialisation', which continued into the first decade of the twenty-first century.

Accompanying this restructuring, 'a large number of countries experienced a collapse in the youth labour market' although at differing rates (Brooks, 2009). Within the UK this collapse resulted in a dramatic decrease in the number of young people in the workforce as the demand for young workers declined and the employment of new recruits slowed down during several recessions including the one currently being experienced as this book is written. The number of jobs in the service sector has increased relative to the manufacturing sector. But in comparison to previous jobs in the traditional industries, the new jobs in the service sector are often part-time and flexible with short-term tenure. Youth researchers have been critical about this 'poor work' (Webster et al., 2004) and the way in which it can result in young people experiencing labour market 'churn', moving from one insecure job to another and in and out of unemployment – so-called 'cyclical employment careers' (Furlong and Cartmel, 2004). Not surprisingly, given these changes, with fewer jobs available for school leavers, education and training opportunities came to be perceived as increasingly attractive, as an alternative was unemployment.

This historical expansion of education and training in the absence of quality employment for young people has led some to talk of the emergence of the 'training state' (Mizen, 2004). Hickman notes how these policy developments can be seen as 'making a virtue out of declining youth employment, enabling young people to build up their level of skills and qualifications in order to meet the demands for up-skilling in many occupations' (Hickman, 1997: 129). However, he points to critics who note new education and training opportunities only serve to 'warehouse' young people until jobs become available (Mizen, 2004).

Within the above context of youth labour market collapse, stagnation and 'warehousing', several researchers have demonstrated how **youth transitions** from education into employment became less linear and extend over a longer time period (Furlong and Kelly, 2005; Roberts and Parsell, 1992; Wyn and White, 1997). Chisholm (2006) also notes how these transitions became more complex as young people increasingly 'blend' periods of education and work. Despite these changes in the nature of young people's transitions from education to employment there are also important elements of continuity with earlier decades. Youth studies research has demonstrated how **social class** continued to be important in shaping transition from education to work – 'with young people from working class backgrounds overrepresented among early labour market entrants' (Brooks, 2009: 4). Also, researchers have noted the tendency for economically marginalised working-class youths to become involved in 'fiddly jobs' (MacDonald and Marsh, 2005), namely work that is unregistered and part of the 'hidden economy'. The nature and type of work-based training taken up by young people also continued to be highly stratified by socio-economic status (Brooks, 2009).

Youth studies has also identified how other factors such as **gender** continue to be important to an understanding of employment training as, for example, women are much more likely to work and be training in the area of child care (Iannelli and Smythe, 2008). Gender had also been identified as a key factor shaping work in the informal economy, with women continuing to be the main providers of domestic labour including the care of children when a young parent (Himmelweit, 2002). Young people from **ethnic** minority backgrounds also tend to be concentrated in certain poor quality work-based training programmes as they are connected with low rates of post-training employment (Furlong and Cartmel, 2007). Burchardt (2005) found that at age twenty-six, young people with a **disability** were nearly four times as likely to be unemployed or involuntarily out of work than non-disabled people. In addition among those who were in employment, earnings were 11 per cent lower than for their non-disabled counterparts with the same level of educational qualification.

The global recession has led to increasing rates of youth unemployment around the world. Indeed, growing youth unemployment is regarded as a significant concern even in countries that are perceived to be weathering the current global economic storm better than others – for example, youth unemployment has risen at a much faster rate than general unemployment over the last few years in Australia (Organization for Economic Co-ordination and Development, 2009). Youth unemployment has risen significantly across Europe. The German Statistical Office figures (Federal Statistical Office, 2012) reveal how in total, the overall unemployment rate among young people aged between fifteen and twenty-four was 20.5 per cent across the twenty-seven nation states making up the European Union by August 2011. This was a rise from 15.7 per cent in the summer of 2008. But there were notable differences between nations – for example, by the summer of 2011 the youth unemployment rate was 46 per cent in Spain, 27 per cent in Ireland and 20 per cent in the UK. These developments have resulted in talk of a potentially 'lost generation' (*The Guardian*, 2009). Concerns have arisen about the potential exploitation of some young people as they desperately try to secure employment in an increasingly competitive labour market. The UK Coalition government's work experience programme exempts young people from national minimum wage laws for up to eight weeks and they are being offered placements by several big companies and it is claimed some are being 'used' as a source of 'free labour' or 'slave labour'. Indeed, the work experience scheme has revealed an element of under-employment – with graduates possessing a high level of education and skills completing unskilled work (*The Guardian*, 2011).

In this gloomy context the UK's Coalition government has faced criticism for acting slowly in addressing rising youth unemployment (Williams, 2011: 34) and for withdrawing spending which supported **policy** directed at trying to help the young unemployed – for example, investment in New Deal and the **training** programme Future Jobs Fund. The Coalition government has retained the apprenticeship initiative but the Institute for Public Policy Research (2011) has called for a 'rethinking' on apprenticeships having identified how less than a quarter of apprenticeship schemes created in 2010 went to young people aged under twenty-five. A Youth Contract was announced in November 2011 in the UK and includes several initiatives designed to support young people into employment. Recognising the youth divide, these include funding to support the 'most disadvantaged' sixteen to seventeen year olds, wage incentives to private sector employers to make it easier for them to employ young people, incentive payments for small firms if they employ young people and careers interviews for those on Job Seekers Allowance for three months with the National Careers Service.

This contribution began by observing how the youth transition into employment is regarded as one of the 'core problems and priorities' in the sociology of youth as it conditions and influences young people's experiences in other domains. It is a problem which is prioritised by sociologists themselves as they identify their own youth questions. Roberts (2003: 15) identifies how youth scholars need to adhere to their own questions 'rather than absorbing or simply responding to the wider society's forever changing youth problems'. In the current climate the prioritising of youth employment as a problem by youth scholars and among wider sections of society such as the media, policy-makers and the general public appears to tally. As such, employment is very likely to remain a key concept in youth studies for the foreseeable future. But as Roberts also notes, youth sociologists 'cannot be content to allow the wider society to define its problem' (Roberts, 2003: 15).

REFERENCES

Brooks, R. (ed.) (2009) *Transitions from Education to Work: New Perspectives from Europe and Beyond.* Basingstoke: Palgrave MacMillan.

Burchardt T. (2005) *The Education and Employment of Disabled Young People: Frustrated Ambition.* Bristol: Policy Press.

Chisholm, L. (2006) 'European youth research: developments, debates, demands', *New Directions for Child and Adolescent Development*, 113: 11–22.

Federal Statistical Office (2012) 'Youth unemployment in Germany one of the lowest in the EU', press release. www.destatis.de/jetspeed/portal/cms/Sites/destatis/Internet/EN/press/pr/2011/08/PE11__293__132.psml (accessed 12 January 2012).

Furlong, A. and Cartmel, F. (2004) *Vulnerable Young Men in Fragile Labour Markets*. York: York Publishing.

Furlong, A. and Cartmel, F. (2007) *Young People and Social Change: New Perspectives*. 2nd edn. Maidenhead: Open University Press.

Furlong, A. and Kelly, P. (2005) 'The Brazilizanisation of youth transitions in Australia and the UK?' *Australian Journal of Social Issues*, 40: 207–25.

The Guardian (2009) 'The lost generation: surge in joblessness hits young', 13 August. www.guardian.co.uk/business/2009/aug/13/surge-in-joblessness-hits-young (accessed 3 January 2010).

The Guardian (2011) 'Young jobseekers told to work without pay or lose unemployment benefits', 16 November. www.guardian.co.uk/society/2011/nov/16/young-jobseekers-work-pay-unemployment (accessed 12 December 2011).

Hickman, P. (1997) 'Is it working? The hanging position of young people in the UK labour market', in J. Roche and S. Tucker (eds), *Youth and Society*. London: Sage, pp. 124–32.

Himmelweit, S. (2002) 'Making visible the hidden economy: the case for gender impact analysis of economic policy', *Feminist Economics*, 8 (1): 49–70.

Iannelli, C. and Smythe, E.E. (2008) 'Mapping gender and social background differences in education and youth transitions across Europe', *Journal of Youth Studies*, 11 (2): 213–32.

Institute for Public Policy Research (IPPR) (2011) *Rethinking Apprenticeships*. London: IPPR.

Jones, G. (2009) *Youth*. Cambridge: Polity Press.

MacDonald, R. and Marsh, J. (2005) *Disconnected Youth? Growing Up in Britain's Poor Neighbourhoods*. London: Palgrave Macmillan.

Mizen, P. (2004) *The Changing State of Youth*. Basingstoke: Palgrave.

Organisation for Economic Co-ordination and Development (OECD) (2009) *Jobs for Youth/Des Emplois pour les Jeunes*. Australia/Paris: OECD.

Roberts, K. (2003) 'Problems and priorities for the sociology of youth', in A. Bennett, M. Cieslik and S. Miles (eds), *Researching Youth*. Basingstoke: Palgrave Macmillan, pp. 13–28.

Roberts, K. and Parsell, G. (1992) 'Entering the labour market in Britain. The survival of traditional opportunity structures', *Sociological Review*, 30: 727–53.

Webster, C., Simpson, D., MacDonald, R., Abbas, A., Cieslik, M., Shildrick, T. and Simpson, M. (2004) *Poor Transitions: Social Exclusion and Young Adults*. Bristol: Policy Press.

Williams, Z. (2011) 'Don't blame the young – it's the jobs that have vanished', *The Guardian*, 3 November. www.guardian.co.uk/commentisfree/2011/nov/02/recession-young-people-unemployment (accessed 12 December 2011).

Wyn, J. and White, R. (1997) *Rethinking Youth*. Sydney: Allen and Unwin.

There is much debate about what one might mean by globalisation though most agree that it is a long-term historical process that has political, economic, cultural and societal dimensions and that we are all in some way being shaped by it. As Robertson notes, globalisation refers to the, 'compression of the world and the intensification of the consciousness of the world as a whole' (1992: 8). Giddens suggests globalisation involves, 'the intensification of worldwide social relations which link distant localities in such a way that local happenings are shaped by events occurring many miles away and vice versa' (1990: 64). Different writers have explored what these processes mean in practice, some have spoken of the increasing mobility or 'global flows' of ideas, capital, technology, information, people and commodities (Urry, 2000) so that people today are increasingly enmeshed in spatially diverse social networks. Technological developments such as the worldwide web, mobile telephony, the mass media and the expansion of trade and transnational companies and organisations have been central to these processes of globalisation.

Youth researchers explore globalisation in several ways. Many suggest that young people are at the forefront of globalisation in that they are early adopters of new technologies, are the first to experience new forms of employment and cultural practices and make up the majority of migrants around the world. This research is interested to explore how these social transformations are impacting on the life course experiences of young people and the nature of **transitions** they are making towards adulthood. In particular, research has focused on the structuring of young people's life chances and how globalisation may contribute to new patterns of opportunity, inequality and social divisions around **class, gender, sexuality, 'race' and ethnicity**. There are also questions about how globalisation is creating differences in life chances between young people living in different societies, between East and West, North and South, developed and developing societies (Blossfield et al., 2005). Researchers have also been unpacking the ways that globalising processes have implications for the identities and cultural lives of young people (Nilan and Feixa, 2006). For example, how do young people use new ideas and information gleaned from global networks and technology to (re)fashion their **cultures** and social identities? One of the key debates in this cultural domain is the extent to which young people from different societies may be experiencing the increasing convergence of youth cultural practices or whether globalisation is providing new tools to explore and promote distinctive local cultures and social identities (Pilkington and Johnson, 2003)?

The more pessimistic commentators suggest that globalisation leads to the exploitation of young people and their continuing poverty in many countries around the world. Transnational companies, abetted by the structural adjustment programmes of the World Bank and International Monetary Fund, are able to generate huge profits in developing societies from the exploitation of young people's labour. Studies estimate that there are over 200 million child labourers (aged five to seventeen) in the world (International Labour Organization, 2006) and some 300 million living in poverty defined as subsisting on one dollar a day or less (Nugent, 2006). Child labour is often dangerous and leads to injury and long-term health problems, so many young people in developing societies suffer from preventable illness (such as HIV/AIDS) and can expect to live shorter lives than those in affluent societies (World Health Organization, 2009). Furthermore, many industries in emerging economies despoil the natural habitat, destroying the local communities that have been home to these young people and their families for generations thus adding to a complex cycle of disadvantage and social inequality. Globalisation therefore leads to uneven economic development with rapid urbanisation creating megacities and sprawling shantytowns around the world. In Brazil, India and China we see millions of young people flooding in from the countryside seeking work and a better life among the city dwellers. Yet though metropolitan areas offer greater economic opportunities than work on the land the benefits are often outweighed by the cost of city living, the need to send remittances home to families and the arduous nature of the work (Pun, 2006). Children and young people in developing societies are also vulnerable to trafficking, forced and bonded labour – the poverty of their families setting up transitions into sexual exploitation or years of work for little or no pay (Bales, 2004). Often young people are unable to break free from a cycle of poor work on the land interspersed with periods of employment as migrant workers in nearby cities – migration to cities tends not to be a long-term route towards a better, more prosperous life for young people in developing societies (De Haan and Rogaly, 2002).

In affluent societies we see also economic restructuring as part of global capitalism transforming the lives of young people – often for the worse. Just as in developing societies, we witness the collapse of traditional local forms of employment leaving young people with the choice of migrating to metropolitan areas for work or seeking out those local jobs that remain which are relatively low skill, poorly paid and insecure (Webster et al., 2004). One response to these uncertain times has been for young people to invest more of their time and money in education and training. Transitions to adulthood in affluent societies have consequently become extended as some young people increasingly participate in further and higher education as they seek to attain some advantage in increasingly competitive labour markets (Brown et al., 2011). Thus **social divisions** have emerged in developed societies as there are pronounced differences between those more affluent young people who have extended educational careers and graduate employment and those from more disadvantaged backgrounds with shorter educational careers and more marginal patterns of **employment** (Bynner et al., 1997).

Youth researchers have documented the deleterious effects of global social change on youth cultures and social identities. Though technological innovations offer new opportunities many studies point to how the Internet and mobile phone use can promote new inward looking, individualistic and narcissistic cultures and lifestyles (Rogers, 2009). Though new technologies promise new innovative ways for young people to interact and to seek out new experiences and resources for identity work, commentators note the superficiality of such interaction and the isolating nature of much online activity (Rosen, 2007). Studies have also shown how the supposed anonymity and security of online interaction can promote the disclosure of personal information and involvement in risky behaviours that lead to vulnerability and exploitation (Dombrowski et al., 2007).

In a similar vein researchers document how the growth in internal and international migration creates tensions between youth groups, as host and immigrant youth clash over what are sometimes struggles for space but are also struggles over cultural recognition and distribution of political and economic resources and opportunities. These conflicts have been a feature of several Australian cities in recent years as often violent strife between Lebanese and the host Australian youth has erupted in beachfront areas (White, 2006). Such tensions between ethnically and sometimes economically distinct youth groups have a long history as we have seen in the street gangs of Californian cities and the barrios of Brazil (Shelden et al., 1997). Though increasing numbers and diversity of young migrants in recent decades raises questions about how these mobilities generate patterns of wider social conflict and the emergence of nationalism, racism and violence in many societies around the world.

Despite the fact that social scientists often document the problems and dysfunctions of modernity, much youth research acknowledges the positive contribution of global processes to young people's lives. The growth of the middle classes in China, India and Brazil suggests new patterns of employment, prosperity and consumption for recent generations of young people in these countries (Ritty, 2005). Studies point to new lifestyle choices and youth cultural formations that are familiar to Western researchers – the popularity of Punk, Rockers, Hip Hop, Skinheads and Bhangra in these societies. These developments, though emerging from newly affluent consumerist youth, have also been aided by the transformation of information technology – the Internet and online interaction providing huge resources for young people to fashion their lives. Mobile phones and online systems such as Twitter, Blogs, Facebook and Second Life all provide the cultural means and virtual spaces for young people to create their multi-faceted selves. Part of the appeal of these mediated selves and spaces, just as the real street corner had in the 1950s and 1960s, is that they seem inexplicable and alien to older people – they offer a distinctive language and space for the young (Holden, 2006).

As some young people in developing societies freely participate in consumer-driven cultures and online activities others find their identities and cultural lives emerging out of the dilemmas and contradictions of globalisation. The social and economic liberalisation in China, for example, though promoting a growing affluence and Western style consumerism among young people, retains vestiges of the state control associated with earlier Communist regimes. Young people in China often have to secure government permission to travel, marry and when choosing higher education programmes and employment. Many young people play out their resistance to this state control through involvement in youth cultural activities drawing on rebellious music, fashion and bodily styles to provide a cultural buffer to a political and social system that is difficult to challenge politically (Cherrington, 2001; Farrar, 2002). But it would be too crude to suggest that such cultural activities offer a convenient way to co-opt and neuter young people's political challenges to state authority. Indeed many young people in China just as young people in other places around the world (see Iran after the Presidential elections in June 2009) use the Internet to highlight and challenge the abuses of state power. In this way blogs and hand-held videos that have documented human rights abuses around the world have been key to young people's struggle for a voice and recognition. As the Internet has circulated ideas around the world about freedom, self-determination and individual rights so the Internet has allowed young people to document the struggles they face achieving their aspirations. We can see how elements of transnational culture and technology are combined with local resources and influences to frame the hybrid cultures and transitions of young people – so called 'glocalization' (Robertson, 1992) or 'reflexive habitus' (Sweetman, 2003).

REFERENCES

Bales, K. (2004) *Disposable People: New Slavery in the Global Economy*. London: Palgrave.

Blossfield, H.P., Klijzing, E., Mills, M. and Kurz, K. (eds) (2005) *Globalization, Uncertainty and Youth in Society*. London: Routledge.

Brown, P., Lauder, H. and Ashton, D. (2011) *The Global Auction: The Broken Promises of Education, Jobs and Incomes*. Oxford: Oxford University Press.

Bynner, J., Ferri, E. and Sheppard, P. (1997) *Twenty Something in the 1990s: Getting On, Getting By and Getting Nowhere*. Aldershot: Ashgate Press.

Cherrington, R. (2001) 'Between east and west: Chinese youth in the era of economic reform', paper presented at the Economic and Social Research Council Interdisciplinary Youth Research Seminar, 26 October, University of Sheffield.

De Haan, A. and Rogaly, B. (2002) 'Introduction: migrant workers and their role on rural change', *Journal of Development Studies*, 38 (5): 1–14.

Dombrowski, S., Gischlar, K. and Durst, T. (2007) 'Safeguarding young people from cyber pornography and cyber sexual predation: a major dilemma of the Internet', *Child Abuse Review*, 16 (3): 153–70.

Farrar, J. (2002) *Opening Up: Youth Sex Culture and Market Reform in Shanghai*. Chicago: University of Chicago Press.

Giddens, A. (1990) *The Consequences of Modernity*. Cambridge: Polity.

Holden, T. (2006) 'The social life of Japan's adolechnic', in P. Nilan and C. Feixa (eds), *Global Youth*. London: Routledge.

International Labour Organization (2006) *The End of Child Labour: Within Reach, Global Report Under the Follow Up to the ILO Declaration on Fundamental Principles and Rights at Work 2006*. Geneva: ILO.

Nilan, P. and Feixa, C. (eds) (2006) *Global Youth*. London: Routledge.

Nugent, R. (2006) 'Youth in a global world', in R. Nugent, *Growing Up Global: The Changing Transition to Adulthood in Developing Countries*. Washington, DC: Population Reference Bureau.

Pilkington, H. and Johnson, R. (2003) 'Peripheral youth: relations of identity and power in global/local context', *European Journal of Cultural Studies*, 6 (3): 259–83.

Pun, N. (2006) *Made in China: Women Factory Workers in a Global Workplace*. Durham, NC: Duke University Press.

Ritty, L. (2005) 'Consuming globalization: youth and gender in Kerala, India', *Journal of Social History*, 38 (4): 915–35.

Robertson, R. (1992) *Globalisation: Social Theory and Global Culture*. London: Theory, Culture and Society/Sage.

Rogers, D. (2009) 'I poke dead people: the paradox of Facebook', *Times Higher Education*, 18 June, pp. 40–2.

Rosen, C. (2007) 'Virtual friendship and the new narcissism', *The New Atlantis*, Summer. www.thenewatlantis.com/publications/virtual_friendship_and_the_new_narcissism (accessed 7 July 2012).

Shelden R., Tracy, S. and Brown, W. (1997) *Youth Gangs in American Society*. Belmont, CA: Wadsworth Press.

Sweetman, P (2003) 'Twenty-first century dis-ease? Habitual reflexivity or the reflexive habitus?' *Sociological Review*, 51 (4): 528–49.

Urry, J. (2000) 'Mobile sociology', *British Journal of Sociology*, 51 (1): 185–203.

Webster, C., Simpson, D., MacDonald, R., Abbas, A., Cieslik, M., Shildrick, T. and Simpson, M. (2004) *Poor Transitions: Social Exclusion and Young Adults*. Bristol: Policy Press.

White, R. (2006) 'Youth gang research in Australia', in J. Short and L. Hughes (eds), *Studying Youth Gangs*. Lanham: Altamira Press, pp. 161–79.

World Health Organization (2009) *Child and Adolescent Health and Development 2008: Progress Report*. Geneva: WHO.

30
Young People and Disability

There is some difficulty in establishing the figure for the number of young people living with disabilities as 'world-wide, estimates vary widely' (Groce, 2004: 14). The United Nations (UN) claims that 'globally, there are over 650 million persons with disabilities, and around a third of these are youth' (United Nations, 2007) so one might estimate that there are almost 217 million young disabled people in the world. Though in contrast Groce (2004: 13) suggests that globally 'almost 180 million young people between the ages of 10–24 live with a physical, sensory, intellectual or mental health disability significant to make a difference in their daily lives'. It is not surprising there is a lack of clarity over the numbers of disabled youth given the different definitions of youth and of disability used in these surveys. 'Frequently, disabled young people are grouped together with children or adults, frustrating attempts to estimate their numbers as a distinct group' (Groce, 2004: 13–14). Different countries have different definitions of disability and so 'disability rates are higher in wealthier countries' and this is felt to be because screening programmes in such countries are 'more accessible' and allow for the identification of more young people with 'moderate and mild disabilities' (Groce, 2004: 14).

The concept of disability is complex and a 'traditional medical model' can include reference to mild, moderate and more chronic impairments. But this model has been criticised for viewing disabled people as medical problems because it emphasises physical, sensory, intellectual and mental impairments. Hence there has been growing awareness of the inadequacy of these traditional categories and how sometimes young people do not fall neatly within them (Morris, 1999: 1). Since the 1970s there has been the development of what is termed 'the social model of disability' (Oliver, 1990) where disability can emerge out of a failure on the part of society (either purposively or inadvertently) to provide appropriate services and facilities that meet the needs of those with particular impairments.

The social model separates disability from impairment by employing a more process-based approach that is sensitive to the ways that disability is socially constructed. It attempts to look beyond a person's impairment(s) and to focus on relevant barriers in the social milieu where they are situated that are affecting/inhibiting a person's ability to fully participate in society. This social model has grown in popularity especially among the disabled themselves (Oliver, 1990). The World Health Organization's (WHO) definition of disability reflects the influence of the traditional medical but also the more recent social model of disability. As such, WHO define disability as, 'an umbrella term, covering impairments, activity limitations, and participation restrictions'. Within this definition impairment refers to 'a problem in body function or structure; an activity limitation is a difficulty encountered by an individual in executing a task or action; while a participation restriction is a problem experienced by an individual in involvement in life situations'. This definition recognises how disability 'reflects an interaction between features of a person's body and features of the society in which he or she lives' (World Health Organization, 2001). As we discuss below, some youth scholars have been interested in exploring such interactions but such research is relatively sparse. The UN describes the disabled as 'the world's largest minority' (United Nations, 2007). But despite the introduction from 2006 of the UN's *Convention on the Rights of Persons with Disabilities* and the passing of legislation across many nation states, the UN claims globally that, 'persons with disabilities are largely ignored'. Indeed, the UN contends that 'youth with disabilities are among the most marginalised and poorest of the world's youth'. This is because disabled young people 'face the same challenges as their non-disabled peers attempting to make successful transitions to adulthood but also face the additional prejudices, barriers, and ignorance associated with their disability'. Significantly almost '80% of youth with disabilities live in developing countries', and although the actual figures are uncertain, young people with disabilities 'form a significant proportion of the adolescent population in every developing society'. Moreover, disabled people tend not to be evenly distributed across the general population, rather 'experts generally agree that disability disproportionately affects the poor' (Groce, 2004: 16).

The welfare policies of developed countries (including the UK) define disability in terms of administrative categories devised by social security services in order to determine access to benefits and services. These categories are strongly influenced by the traditional medical model of disability because it is helpful in identifying impairments 'understood to be legitimate reasons for not working' (Riddell, 2009: 81). For example, in the UK the Disability Discrimination Act 1995 and the amended Disability Discrimination Act 2005, 'operates on the assumption that a distinction may be drawn between disabled and non-disabled people' (Riddell, 2009: 82). Both Acts define a disabled person as someone who has a physical or mental impairment which results in that person enduring substantial and long-term adverse effects on their ability to undertake everyday activities such as eating, washing, walking, going shopping, etc. Disability and impairment continue to be tightly connected within legislation, social security provision and welfare programmes for the disabled. For example, the recently formed Conservative and Liberal

Democrat Coalition government in the UK has announced that it will introduce new assessments based on the medical model of disability from 2013 for those in receipt of Disability Living Allowance. It is hoping to reduce the number receiving this allowance as part of a drive to reduce public spending.

Although part of the 'the world's largest minority', the young disabled have remained an under-developed area of **youth research**, 'with limited data on its prevalence and the effects on youth themselves' (United Nations, 2007). In 1999 UNICEF released a call for research on the many issues that influence the lives of young people with disabilities (UNICEF, 1999). But this call 'remains largely unanswered', and 'with several notable exceptions, there has been little research on disabled young people as a distinct group in developing countries and what exists on young people with disability in the developed world focuses on them largely in the context of formal educational systems and **transitions** to **work** programmes' (Groce, 2004: 14). For example, within the UK in the first decade of the new millennium research accompanied 'an increasing recognition of the need to improve transition planning and support for young disabled people moving into adulthood, and to co-ordinate this support across a wide range of agencies, including health and social care, youth services, **leisure**, careers guidance, housing, education, benefits and employment services' (Morris, 2002). Disabled young people often require extra financial and 'joined-up' personal support from various sources to move towards achieving independence associated with adulthood.

Yet despite government policies that support disabled youth in the UK, Morris (2002) identified the numerous barriers that young people face making transitions into adulthood. She highlighted how 'there is often poor liaison between different agencies and professionals, a failure to involve young people and a failure to cover the issues of most importance to them and their families'. Young disabled people and their families also lacked up-to-date information about options available to them and possibilities. Furthermore, the research projects highlighted how 'many young disabled people have no experience of an independent social life and few opportunities to make friends (via social networks): they spend most of their time with family or paid carers and have no independent access to transport, telecommunications, or personal assistance over which they have choice and control'. Other problems included: failures to respond to the values and communication needs of young disabled people, a lack of support for independent living and an overly complex benefit system (Morris, 2002: 3).

More recent research (Cullen et al., 2009) has highlighted how many of these problems with government support for young disabled people still continue today. This research on the role of the Connexions Service in the UK, which supports transition from education to employment, found staff had limited experience of working with young disabled people and services were often ineffective in overcoming the barriers facing the disabled. There was also a lack of consistency in using recognised best practice when assessing, planning, implementing and reviewing support for young people. The authors recommended 'modifications' to be made if the Connexions service was to meet its full potential in providing important support to young people with special educational needs (SENs) making the transition into adulthood. So, despite attempts to improve transition planning and services over the last decade, research highlights how in the UK young people continue to experience disadvantage because of disability. 'Activity limitations' and 'participation restrictions' continue to feature in the lives of young people with disabilities.

Thus researchers in the field of disability studies such as Riddell (2009) argue that the majority of young disabled struggle to make successful transitions to adulthood and hence social inclusion has proved an elusive goal for many young disabled people. Indeed, Riddell (2009: 87) notes how in recent years, 'the situation for some groups may have worsened as transitions have become more protracted and complex, and the distribution of economic and social risks have become more polarised and linked to educational attainment'. However, drawing on her research, Riddell emphasises how 'disabled young people are not a homogenous group and risks are unequally distributed among them'. She notes how young disabled people entering higher education are mostly from 'socially advantaged backgrounds' and benefit from 'policy measures designed to include their social and institutional inclusion' which are 'relatively generously resourced'. In contrast, young disabled people who do not enter higher education 'come from socially disadvantaged backgrounds and attract little respect and social recognition' (Riddell, 2009: 87). Researchers therefore are beginning to highlight and understand how effects of disability interact with the effects of other structural dimensions such as **social class**, **gender** and **ethnicity** (Chahal, 2004) in perpetuating disadvantage for young people with impairments.

REFERENCES

Chahal, K. (2004) *Experiencing Ethnicity: Discrimination and Service Provision*. York: Joseph Rowntree Foundation.

Cullen, M., Lindsay, G. and Dockrell, J. (2009) 'The role of the Connexions service in supporting the transition from school to post-16, education, employment training and work for young people with a history of specific speech and language difficulties or learning difficulties', *Journal of Research in Special Educational Needs*, 9 (2): 100–12.

Groce, N. E. (2004) 'Adolescents and youths with disability: issues and challenges', *Asia Pacific Disability Rehabilitation Journal*, 15 (2): 13–32.

Morris, J. (1999) *Hurtling into the Void: Transition to Adulthood of Young Disabled People with 'Complex Health and Support Needs'*. Brighton: Pavilion Publishing Limited.

Morris, J. (2002) *Young Disabled People Moving into Adulthood*. York: Joseph Rowntree Foundation. www.jrf.org.uk/sites/files/jrf/512.pdf (accessed 3 July 2010).

Oliver, M. (1990) *The Politics of Disablement*. Basingstoke: Macmillan

Riddell, S. (2009) 'Disability, exclusion and transition to adulthood', in Furlong, A. (ed.), *Handbook of Youth and Young Adulthood: New Perspectives and Agendas*. London: Routledge, pp. 81–8.

UNICEF (1999) *An Overview of Young People Living with Disabilities: Their Needs and Their Rights*. New York: UNICEF Inter Divisional Working Group on Young People Programme Division.

United Nations (2007) *Briefing Note on Youth: Youth Living with Disabilities*. New York: United Nations. www.un.org/esa/socdev/unyin/documents/briefingnotedisability.pdf (accessed 3 July 2010).

World Health Organization (WHO) (2001) *International Classification of Functioning, Disability, and Health*. Geneva: WHO. http://www.who.int/topics/disabilities/en/ (accessed 13 september 2012).

31
Young People and Consumption

Consumption has always been important to any understanding of young people in contemporary societies. The purchase of goods and services offers young people a significant way to express their emerging independence so patterns of consumption can signify the shifting boundaries between childhood, youth and adulthood. Furthermore, the distinctive ways in which young people consume and how firms and organisations target and represent young consumers provides us with insights into **youth cultures**, identities and **transitions**. Since the nineteenth century commentators have either seen youth consumption as problematic, disempowering young people or have offered more positive interpretations of consumerism that offer resources for identity work and sociability. More recently researchers have also acknowledged the complexity and contradictory nature of consumption and have suggested a middle way between these pessimistic and optimistic analyses that characterised earlier studies into youth consumption.

There is evidence from the USA and UK from as early as the 1870s of companies designing and marketing products for youth markets such as sweets and trading cards (Kline, 1993). These markets expanded greatly in richer societies during the twentieth century as rising disposable income of the middle classes led to the mass consumerism that now characterises Western societies. From the 1950s onwards we witnessed the growth in teenager or teen markets and the proliferation of goods and services aimed at young people, notably clothes, music, cosmetics, food, sport and leisure activities (Palladino, 1996). The growth in radio, TV, the Internet and increasingly sophisticated forms of media use and marketing have been central technological innovations that enable the creation and marketing of products to young people. Consequently youth markets in most societies are now worth billions of dollars a year and are central to the global activities of consumer corporations such as Sony, Nike and McDonalds. Recent surveys show how the majority of young people in affluent societies like the UK now own computers (80 per cent), games consoles (70 per cent) and DVD players (74 per cent) (Mintel, 2010).

Writers have raised many concerns about the expansion of consumerism and its influence on young people. Consumer capitalism has been amazingly successful in harnessing the ingenuity of designers and producers to create a never-ending stream of new goods and services that emerge as luxuries but which in time become essentials for ordinary life. One only has to think of mobile phones, computers, electronic games and flat screen TVs to see this process whereby goods once possessed only by an affluent Western elite in the 1980s have become an everyday feature of most people on the globe two decades later. One key issue for pessimistic commentators is that despite the falling real price of consumer goods the creation of new consumer needs and desires requires increasing disposable income (that provides profits for capitalist corporations) and so young people unlike earlier generations need significant financial resources (through their own waged work or parental income) just to live a 'normal life' of technological goods and everyday leisure experiences (Deutsch and Theodorou, 2010). The scope for new **divisions** and patterns of exclusion among young people (within and between societies and regions) are greatly increased if identities and transitions become bound up with expensive consumerism. Sueila (2011) illustrates how a consumerist way of life for young people actually exacerbates the existing social divisions and forms of exclusion in places like Brazil. The aesthetic challenges of 'being cool' through owning the latest technology are an additional challenge for low income youth already struggling with economic hardships. Recently in Britain there have also been debates about a digital divide whereby some young people have access to computers and the Internet and the benefits these bring while others on lower incomes are denied such access. Livingstone et al. (2005) document how a quarter of young people in the UK still do not have regular access to the Internet, which raises questions about the popular claim that modern youth are the 'net generation'.

As young people's lives have become increasingly structured by consumer goods and services so it seems impossible to think of how to live a life outside of these things that we buy in our daily lives. How young people come to see themselves and relate to others, the shaping of their social identities and self-worth are all mediated by things that have been bought. The concern is that the values and morals of young people have been corrupted so that a disproportionate worth is attributed to income and consumption rather than those activities beyond consumerist and commodified relationships. As was discussed in the entry on **wellbeing** consumer culture socialises young people into a materialist way of life where notions of success and wellbeing are understood in terms of acquisitive individualism. Yet much research points to the short-term benefits of consumption for wellbeing and how in fact good subjective wellbeing tends to be rooted in quality relationships (Layard, 2005; Layard and Dunn, 2009). This is a view that echoes Marx's critique of capitalism where he argues individuals become distracted by the lure of things and in the process become alienated from the social relationships and one's 'essence' that are the basis of a richer, more enduring wellbeing (Marx, 1984).

A traditional concern of critics of consumerism is that the mass media and advertisers wield an unhealthy power to influence young people, creating anxieties and insecurities at a time when young people are impressionable and vulnerable. Researchers point to the mass media's fixation on appearance and lifestyle and how dominant notions of attractiveness are established in order to market goods and services to young people. Brookes and Kelly (2009) illustrate this argument in their analysis of Australian women's magazines, noting how conventional heterosexual conceptions of femininity are promoted through a relentless focus on makeup, fashion and dating advice to readers. Just as earlier researchers have argued (Frost, 2001), women in these publications are constructed as objects of the gaze, and to be successful and popular one has to monitor and maintain how one looks and feels. Yet the editorial policies of these publications are not crude and patronising for the content is imbued with a patina of empowerment – that to look good and be popular is positive and enabling for readers. Similar arguments have been made for many years about the influence of advertising on consumption patterns and the shaping of problematic youth lifestyles. Over the past thirty years in most affluent societies there have been moral panics over young people and alcohol use, growing sedentary lifestyles and obesity and video gaming and violence (Brown, 2005).

Other writers have suggested that it is perhaps too easy to overstate the power of the media to manufacture a passive youth audience of compliant consumers. Studies of twentieth-century youth cultures described the creative ways that young people used clothes, makeup and music to fashion unique ways of life that often undermined the conventional meanings associated with the commodities they used. Hebdige (1979) and McRobbie (1994) point to this process of cultural innovation that is at the heart of youth consumption. More recently commentators such as Bennett (2004), Miles (2000) and Pysnakova and Miles (2010) have argued that the economic and cultural restructuring of late modernity (so-called individualisation and de-traditionalisation) sets up risks and uncertainties for young people that in part can be managed by their creative engagement with consumption. In the face of precarious career routes and fluid peer and family relationships the creative use of fashion, music and new technology allow young people to establish and maintain successful identities and 'fit in' with others. Other researchers have illustrated how consumerism, the purchase of new technology, for example, then promotes all manner of productive activities – so called 'prosumption' (Toffler, 1981). Online communities – the virtual cultures that are the heart of many young people's lives today – rely on communication technology and a consumerist way of life. Facebook, Twitter and other social networking systems make up an increasing part of the social lives of youth around the world (ONS, 2011). Social networking has also been implicated in a range of political activities in recent years such as anti-globalisation protests, anti-cuts protests in Europe, green movements and democracy demonstrations across Middle East countries. If one looks hard enough we can find a resourceful and creative youth culture behind the popular image of passive, sedentary youth consumers.

REFERENCES

Bennett, A. (2004) 'Virtual subculture: youth, identity and the Internet', in A. Bennet and K. Khan-Harris (eds), *After Subculture: Critical Studies in Contemporary Youth Culture*. London: Palgrave, pp. 162–72.

Brookes, F. and Kelly, P. (2009) 'Dolly girls: tweenies as artefacts of consumption', *Journal of Youth Studies*, 12 (6): 599–613.

Brown, S. (2005) *Understanding Youth and Crime*. Maidenhead: Open University.

Deutsch, N.L. and Theodorou, E. (2010) 'Aspiring, consuming, becoming: youth identity in a culture of consumption', *Youth and Society*, 42 (2): 229–54.

Frost, L. (2001) *Young Women and the Body: A Feminist Sociology*. London: Palgrave.

Hebdige, D. (1979) *Subculture: The Meaning of Style*. London: Routledge.

Kline, S. (1993) *Out of the Garden: Toys, TV and Children's Culture in the Age of Marketing*. London: Verso.

Layard, R. (2005) *Happiness: Lessons from a New Science*. London: Penguin.

Layard, R. and Dunn, J. (2009) *A Good Childhood: Searching for Values in a Competitive Age*. London: Penguin.

Livingstone, S., Bober, M. and Helsper, E. (2005) *Inequalities and the Digital Divide in Children's and Young People's Internet Use*. London: Children Go Online Project. www.children-go-online.net.

Marx, K. (1984) '"Estranged labour", economic and philosophical manuscripts', in K. Marx, *Early Writings*. Harmondsworth: Penguin.

McRobbie, A. (1994) *Postmodernism and Popular Culture*. London: Routledge.

Miles, S. (2000) *Youth Lifestyles in a Changing World*. Buckingham: Open University Press.

Mintel (2010) *Youth Technology UK Report*. London: Mintel, October.

ONS (2011) *Internet Access: Households and Individuals 2011*. London: HMSO.

Palladino, G. (1996) *Teenagers: An American History*. New York: Basic Books.

Pysnakova, M. and Miles, S. (2010) 'The post-revolutionary consumer generation: mainstream youth and the paradox of choice in the Czech Republic', *Journal of Youth Studies*, 13 (5): 533–47.

Sueila, P. (2011) 'To be cool or not to be cool: young people's insights on consumption and social issues in Rio de Janeiro', *Journal of Youth Studies*, 14 (1): 109–23.

Toffler, A. (1981) *The Third Wave*. London: Pan Books.

32

The Youth Underclass

The underclass is a contested concept but there is broad agreement over the meaning of the term as a group of people that is in some way outside of the mainstream of society. This group experience poverty or social exclusion so that with time they come to have a culturally distinctive way of life. There are differences over how one might explain the emergence of an underclass – a perspective which accentuates structural factors and a perspective which emphasises cultural factors as the chief reasons for the exclusion of the underclass from the mainstream. There are also those that view the concept as problematic as it hinders the empirical investigation of poverty or social exclusion.

The notion of an underclass is just the latest in a long line of terms to describe an outsider group. The idea of a marginal group of poor citizens has a long history as we see with the nineteenth-century discussions of 'the undeserving poor' (Mayhew, 1950) and the 'lumpen proletariat' (Marx and Engels, 1971). In the USA the underclass came into popular usage only from the 1970s and early 1980s when journalists – notably Ken Auletta (1982) of *The New Yorker* – began to use it in articles but made little attempt to explain how an underclass outside the mainstream population had emerged. The first sociological explanations came with authors such as William Julius Wilson – at the time the President of the American Sociological Association. Wilson (1987) situated the underclass in the structural inequalities that particular groups in the USA face and implicitly young black youth growing up in poverty in the Rustbelt cities of 1970s America. Focusing particularly on the urban black population, Wilson pointed to economic failure and the inability of the American labour market to meet the demand for secure employment from this group. He talked of 'a vast underclass of black proletarians – that massive population at the very bottom of the social class ladder, plagued by poor education and low paying unstable jobs' (Wilson, 1987: 1). Wilson's work emphasised the link between class position and colour and set the tone for the racialised nature of early underclass theory in the USA. Following Wilson's work there continued to be debates over the role of **class**, **'race'**, **ethnicity** and **gender** in creating the American underclass.

These structural analyses differed from the journalistic accounts of underclass such as by Auletta, which had focused on the behaviour and values of the alleged underclass portraying them in a largely negative light. But these media accounts only implicitly suggested that these values were the reason why the underclass had emerged. This connection was made explicit by academics during the 1980s such as Charles Murray (1984) who emphasised the cultural factors behind the emergence of the underclass. Murray's controversial thesis claims that a culture of welfare dependency has emerged so that the poor choose to live on benefits rather than pursue waged employment as a source of income. Over time this culture has become established and transmitted to the children of the poor, eroding the work ethic and self-reliance of the working classes and thus contributing to the further social exclusion and poverty of the poor in the USA.

In 1989 Murray visited the UK at the invitation of the *Sunday Times* newspaper in search of an underclass. The underclass in the UK context had previously been discussed by Field (1989) and his account emphasised structural 'forces of expulsion' as explanation for its growth – unemployment, growing social class differences and a widening of the range between the rich and the poor. Murray produced an essay entitled *The Emerging British Underclass* which summed up what he claimed to have found in the UK. He suggested 'the difference between the United States and Britain was that the United States reached the future first' (Murray, 1990). Rather than a structural underclass Murray pointed to a 'deplorable' UK cultural underclass. A large part of the controversy surrounding Murray and his thesis can be found in his adoption of pejorative metaphors such as 'plague' and 'disease' to claim that this underclass defined by illegitimacy, violent crime and labour market drop out was growing across the UK. Murray created a pathological image of those making up his alleged underclass in the UK and claimed it would continue to grow as a result of cross-generational transmission of undesirable practices and values (Murray, 1990). In a later publication Murray focused particularly on the breakdown of the family in the UK and its contribution to the emergence of the underclass (Murray, 1994).

There has been much debate around the concept of the youth underclass and this has been politically charged both in the USA and the UK. Indeed, MacDonald (1997a) suggests that within the UK context the 'underclass debate is largely a debate about youth'. This commentary of underclass therefore concerns the notion of welfare dependency and its alleged effects – including degeneracy of the nation's youth. The language used is often demonising, with one sub-group of young people receiving particular attention – teenage single mothers often accused of choosing the 'mothering option' to gain welfare support and – as Murray claimed – 'spawn illegitimate children' (Murray, 1990). Consequently, within the UK several social pathologies and problems – ranging from **crime**, drug abuse and drunkenness to the breakdown of the family and community values – have all been explained in terms of this young underclass (MacDonald, 1997a: 7).

Writers such as MacDonald (1997b) argue that the condemnatory nature of the cultural underclass thesis allows the media and policy-makers to blame young people for their own poverty, which diverts attention away from some of the structural processes behind the marginalisation of young people. This victim blaming provides the legitimacy for a punitive policy agenda of benefit cuts and surveillance. Recent policies in the UK, for example, have included 'the promotion of workfare and "citizenship" strategies to manage and control unemployed under 25s and punitive policies towards young offenders and authoritarian restrictions on young people's cultures and social lives (such as night time curfews and the outlawing of activities associated with the rave/dance culture)' (MacDonald, 1997a: 7).

Several commentators (see MacDonald, 1997b) have pointed out that there is little empirical evidence to support the underclass thesis. However, until recently there was also little longitudinal qualitative research that might offer alternative accounts for the long-term social exclusion of young people in Western societies. Though since 1997 a number of studies have been researching just these sorts of questions about the emergence of long-term social exclusion in the deprived neighbourhoods of the UK.

This research was to cast serious doubt about the empirical scope of the concept of cultural underclass in wider sociology and within youth studies. MacDonald and Marsh (2005) summed up findings from several qualitative research projects in the North East of England in the deprived neighbourhoods most conducive to underclass formation arguing they could not find the underclass. These research projects were undertaken over several years and tracked the same young people as they moved into adulthood. The authors suggest that despite welfare dependency and unemployment these were young people whose experiences did not emerge solely from their own choices and they were not disconnected from mainstream society.

While rejecting outright the emergence of a cultural youth underclass, MacDonald and Marsh offer some support for Wilson's structural underclass thesis seeing this as a more sophisticated analysis of the social context that frames the lives of the urban poor. The authors are critical of cultural theories of deviancy, suggesting instead that a greater focus on the structures of opportunity, in particular localities, offers more of an insight into processes of economic marginalisation (MacDonald and Marsh, 2005). They suggest the structural underclass thesis is to some extent correct in highlighting labour market forces in marginalising young people in poorer neighbourhoods. Roberts has also observed how youth researchers 'prefer not to use the underclass label lest they become mistaken for Murray sympathisers', but despite this he notes how 'they rarely have difficulty in identifying a bottom group that is set apart by its frequent truancy, seriously disturbed family and housing histories, chronic unemployment, early parenthood and/or repeat offending' (Roberts, 2003: 15).

At the time of writing, social **policies** attempting to address structural deficit problems (i.e. the amount government needs to borrow in order to bridge the gap between receipts from taxation and the amount of public spending) in several developed countries have been accompanied by cuts in public expenditure, falling youth **employment**, increased youth unemployment and a notable prominence of the term underclass in the print media and elsewhere (*The Guardian*, 2011: 4). For instance, the Adecco Group's *Unlocking Britain's Potential* survey research conducted in the summer of 2011 with 1000 UK employers and employees found 73 per cent of employers and 84 per cent of employees believe there is a 'permanent underclass' of young people emerging – excluded from employment by their poor education, skills and background. The focus upon and debate around an apparent youth underclass and **subculture** therefore looks likely to continue. But does this fixation on a marginalised minority mean we risk losing sight of how the majority of 'ordinary kids' live their daily lives (Brown, 1987; Jenkins, 1983)? Jones (2002: 44) notes how a focus on the economically and socially marginalised in youth studies neglects another 'large (and largely invisible) group who are trying to survive on scarce resources, including their own resilience'. She suggests that this emphasis of many youth researchers on the most socially excluded 'should be revised to consider the varying circumstances and needs of all young people. There is a danger that the proverbial iceberg will be overlooked if we focus only on the tip.'

REFERENCES

Auletta, K. (1982) *The Underclass*. New York: Random House.

Brown, P. (1987) *Schooling Ordinary Kids: Inequality, Unemployment, and the New Vocationalism*. London: Tavistock Publications.

Field, F. (1989) *Losing Out: The Emergence of Britain's Underclass*. Oxford: Blackwell Publishing.

The Guardian (2011) 'The unemployable: "permanent underclass" emerging', 17 November. www.guardian.co.uk/education/2011/nov/17/permanent-underclass-emerging-businesses-warn (accessed 12 December 2011).

Jenkins, R. (1983) *Lads, Citizens and Ordinary Kids: Working-class Youth Life-Styles in Belfast*. London: Routledge and Kegan Paul

Jones, J. (2002) *The Youth Divide: Diverging Paths to Adulthood*. York: Joseph Rowntree Foundation.

MacDonald, R. (1997a) 'A new youth underclass?' *Criminal Justice Matters*, 28: 7.

MacDonald, R. (ed.) (1997b) *Youth, the 'Underclass' and Social Exclusion*. London: Routledge.

MacDonald, R. and Marsh, J. (2005) *Disconnected Youth? Growing Up in Britain's Poor Neighbourhoods*. London: Palgrave Macmillan.

Marx, K. and Engels, F. (1971) *The Manifesto of the Communist Party*. Moscow: Progress (1st edn 1848).

Mayhew, H. (1950) *London's Underworld*. London: Spring Books (1st edn 1861).

Murray, C. (1984) *Losing Ground: American Social Policy 1950–1980*. New York: Basic Books.

Murray, C. (1990) *The Emerging British Underclass*. London: Institute of Economic Affairs.

Murray, C. (1994) *Underclass: The Crisis Deepens*. London: IEA Health and Welfare Unit/Sunday Times.

Roberts, K. (2003) 'Problems and priorities for the sociology of youth', in A. Bennett, M. Cieslik and S. Miles (eds), *Researching Youth*. Basingstoke: Palgrave Macmillan, pp. 13–28.

Wilson, W.J. (1987). *The Truly Disadvantaged: The Inner City, The Underclass and Public Policy*. Chicago: University of Chicago Press.

33
Young People and Homelessness

When one thinks of youth homelessness images such as those from the critically acclaimed motion picture *Slumdog Millionaire* (2008) may come to mind. But one must resist falling into the trap of thinking about child and youth homelessness as a phenomenon that is found only in faraway developing countries. Unfortunately, homelessness is something young people in the UK and other Western countries also experience (Smith, 2009; Van Der Ploeg and Sholte, 1997). 'Youth homelessness remains a significant issue across the UK. It can be estimated that at least 78–80,000 young people experienced homelessness in 2008/9 across the UK' – this figure 'includes both young people who are formally accepted as homeless under the statutory definition as well as non-statutorily homeless young people using supported housing services' (Quilgars et al., 2011: 6). In the UK the legal definitions of homelessness vary and there has been divergence in regard to **policy** for homelessness (Jones and Pleace, 2010). For England and Wales the legal definition of homelessness is contained within the 1996 Housing Act and focuses on the rights and entitlements to a place of residence or a home. An individual is regarded as homeless if, first, there is no accommodation that they are entitled to occupy or, second, they have accommodation but it is not reasonable for them to continue to occupy this accommodation.

The 1989 Children's Act places several duties and powers on local authorities in England and Wales to accommodate children in need such as those whose wellbeing would be impaired if the authorities failed to support them. Thus local authorities spend considerable sums accommodating vulnerable children and young people who are at risk of homelessness because of problems associated with parental unemployment, family breakdown, abuse and the incidence of disability.

Local authorities can also use discretionary powers under the 1989 Children's Act so they may provide accommodation to safeguard or promote the welfare of children or young people. But despite these legal provisions the housing rights of some sixteen to seventeen year olds remained unclear until very recently. Though the 1989 Children's Act identifies categories of those in need (predominantly children) local authorities did not necessarily have to provide housing for any other young persons, such as those aged sixteen and seventeen. It was not until the 2002 Homelessness (Priority Need for Accommodation) Order that all sixteen to seventeen year olds regardless of their situation were counted as having a priority need.

Nevertheless local authorities can still choose to interpret homelessness legislation in different ways. The recent Coalition government's emphasis on 'localism' suggests further divergence in the interpretation of homelessness policy and the prospect of some vulnerable young people struggling to gain access to appropriate housing and other welfare support (Jones and Pleace, 2010). Some local authorities, for example, offer housing support to the young homeless but have failed to provide a wider range of welfare and counselling services to these young people, services that are usually needed by those experiencing multiple forms of disadvantage and social exclusion. But in 2009 a landmark House of Lords ruling indicated that local authorities have a duty to assess the wider needs of sixteen to seventeen year olds who become homeless and they are required to support them more widely through their children's services rather than just focus on their housing needs.

In youth studies the concepts of statutory homeless and non-statutory homeless have emerged. Individual youths found to be eligible for assistance, unintentionally homeless and falling within a priority need category are deemed to be 'statutory homeless' and are entitled to advice and support in England and Wales under the Homelessness Order 2002 and in Scotland under the Homelessness (Scotland) Act 2003. Those classed as 'non-statutorily homeless' are young people using hostels, sleeping rough or for whatever reason not coming to the attention of local authorities. The distinction between statutory and non-statutory hints at difficulties inherent in estimating the number of homeless youths identified by youth researchers – for example, does one only count those identified as homeless via the legislation and/or those that are known to agencies or does one also count the 'hidden homeless' such as those that have a temporary solution by staying with friends ('sofa surfers') or in squats? Despite these difficulties there is general acceptance across youth studies that by the early 1990s the numbers of homeless young people in the UK had increased dramatically on previous decades.

The *Inquiry into Preventing Youth Homelessness* (Evans, 1996) set up by leading housing and youth charities highlighted the extent of youth homelessness and its significance as a 'social problem' in the UK (Evans, 1996). Since this review, there have been significant policy developments across the UK to address homelessness generally, and within this, youth homelessness (Quilgars et al., 2008). More recently each separate country of the UK has made its own policy but some commonalities have been identified across these policies. There has been the development of national strategies and a tightening of the legal position to identify young people considered as being in 'priority need' in regard to housing. Those in 'priority need' include sixteen to seventeen year olds; young families headed by someone aged sixteen to twenty-four; care leavers aged eighteen to twenty; and other youths considered 'vulnerable' or 'at risk' in some way (e.g. because they may be disabled or have mental health problems).

As the discussion in this book around the concept of **housing** identifies, moving from the home of one's family of origin to a relatively independent domestic arrangement is regarded as one of the key **youth transitions** to adulthood. But for some young people their route to independent living arrangements has become increasingly extended and even 'chaotic'. Many young people stay at home longer and there can often be returns to the parental home after an earlier departure. The housing transition remains connected to other key biographical events such as becoming a student, moving to find **employment** and forming relationships. Also the increase in the numbers of homeless youths is associated with a concurrent increase in the risks associated with trying to achieve independent living. Housing transitions for all young people – like other key youth transitions discussed in this book – are now regarded as more perilous than they were a few decades ago. But research reveals that a greater risk of becoming homeless remains strongly correlated with a young person's **social class** or socio-economic background. Becoming homeless is also strongly associated with those who have experienced disruption or trauma during childhood such as following the loss of parents or being 'thrown out' of the family home (Quilgars et al., 2008).

The seminal study by Ford et al. (2002), which explored the pathways taken by young people when pursuing independent living away from the family of origin categorised five such routes: *chaotic, unplanned, constrained, planned (non-student)* and *student*. This study highlighted the difficulties of moving from a chaotic housing transition and the state of homelessness to a more stable housing position. Some of the reasons why are revealed by further research which has explored the experiences of homeless youths. Becoming homeless can be an effect of poverty and family disruption. For example, there is a strong correlation between children leaving care and eventual drift into homelessness and this is a feature in several countries (Mendes and Moslehuddin, 2004). But being homeless also causes new problems and/or exacerbates existing problems that make it more unlikely that a young person will be able to change the direction of their housing pathway. Consequently, being homeless has a negative effect on a young person's other transitions in **education** and **work** and it can cause or compound physical and mental **health** problems (Van Der Ploeg and Sholte, 1997). Homelessness is also associated with criminal careers and the onset of substance misuse problems among young people including alcohol and, where there is a supply, illicit drug misuse

(McCarthy and Hagan, 1991). Hence research suggests a significant minority of young homeless people have multiple needs because of the interaction of different problematic transition pathways into adulthood (Quilgars et al., 2008).

Therefore the existing research suggests that youth homelessness or 'housing exclusion' should not be viewed in isolation but rather it is intimately connected to wider social change and transition experiences of young people (Blackman, 1998; Stephens et al., 2010). In particular, homelessness appears central to wider experiences of social exclusion and an understanding of the processes involved in **division** and economic and social marginalisation via youth transitions. Indeed, McCarthy et al. (2009: 235) point to research from the USA and Canada (Hagan and McCarthy, 1997; Whitbeck and Hoyt, 1999) which describes this process as it 'consistently finds that once they arrive on the street, most homeless youth spend much of their day searching for food, shelter and money; hanging out in public spaces with other homeless youth; and travelling from one social service agency to another to acquire various resources'. McCarthy et al. (2009: 238) suggest there are ways young people can escape homelessness and these obviously include the provision of stable housing but also 'job training programs and employment, as well as access to supportive adults'. However, they also note 'fundamental structural causes of homelessness' which must be addressed such as 'instability of family life, the loss of employment opportunities, the shortage of affordable housing (in the UK social housing) and the diminishing interest in using taxes to provide assistance to those in need'.

However, there have been criticisms of some of the research into youth homelessness in the UK and in particular its lack of methodological and theoretical rigour (Fitzpatrick, 2005). Some also suggest such research is 'politically motivated' as it has been undertaken by homelessness charities and pressure groups who are promoting their own sectional interests and agenda (Fitzpatrick and Christian, 2006). Thus in 2009 there was the effort to develop a broad-based research programme to develop new insights into the issues of homelessness drawing on a range of stakeholders from government and professional bodies to research organisations and homelessness charities. This research programme understands youth homelessness more holistically in relation to how it 'intersects with other aspects of multiple forms of social exclusion'. It is hoped this research will offer new ways to understand and manage what is one of the most corrosive aspects of social exclusion experienced by young people.

REFERENCES

Blackman, S. (1998) '"Disposable generation?" An ethnographic study of youth homelessness in Kent', *Journal of Youth and Policy*, 59: 38–56.

Evans, A. (1996) *'We Don't Choose to be Homeless' – The Inquiry into Preventing Youth Homelessness*. London: CHAR.

Fitzpatrick, S. (2005) 'Explaining homelessness: a critical realist perspective', *Housing, Theory & Society*, 22 (1): 1–17.

Fitzpatrick, S. and Christian, J. (2006) 'Comparing research on homelessness in the United Kingdom and United States: what lessons can be learnt?' *European Journal of Housing Policy*, 6 (3): 313–33.

Ford, J., Rugg, J. and Burrows, R. (2002) 'Conceptualising the contemporary role of housing in the transition to adult life in England', *Urban Studies*, 39 (13): 2455–67.

Hagan, J. and McCarthy, B. (1997) *Mean Streets: Youth Crime and Homelessness*. New York: Cambridge University Press.

Jones, A. and Pleace, N. (2010) *A Review of Single Homelessness in the UK: 2000–2010*. London: Crisis UK.

McCarthy, B. and Hagan, J. (1991) 'Homelessness: a criminogenic situation?' *British Journal of Criminology*, 31: 393–410.

McCarthy, B., Williams, M. and Hagan, J. (2009) 'Homeless youth and the transition to adulthood', in A. Furlong (ed.), *Handbook of Youth and Young Adulthood: New Perspectives and Agendas*. London: Routledge, pp. 232–39

Mendes, P. and Moslehuddin, B. (2004) 'Graduating from the child welfare system: a comparison of the UK and Australian leaving care debates', *International Journal of Social Welfare*, 13 (4): 332–39.

Quilgars, D., Fitzpatrick, S. and Pleace, N. (2011) *Ending Youth Homelessness: Possibilities, Challenges and Practical Solutions*. York: University of York.

Quilgars, D., Johnsen, S. and Pleace, N. (2008) *Youth Homelessness in the UK: A Decade of Progress?* York: Joseph Rowntree Foundation.

Smith, J. (2009) *A Comparative Report on Youth Homelessness and Social Exclusion in the Czech Republic, the Netherlands, Portugal and the UK* (Deliverable under European Union 7th Framework Programme under the Social-economic Sciences and Humanities theme). www.movisie.nl/118836/eng/ (accessed 14 July 2009).

Stephens, M., Fitzpatrick, S. and Elsinga, M. (2010) *Study on Housing Exclusion: Welfare Policies, Housing Provision and Labour Markets*. Brussels: European Commission.

Whitbeck, L.B. and Hoyt, D.R. (1999) *Nowhere to Grow: Homelessness and Runaway Adolescents and Their Families*. New York: Aldine de Gruyter.

Van Der Ploeg, J.D. and Sholte, E.M. (1997) *Homeless Youth*. London: Sage.